Medical Screening of Workers

Medical Screening of Workers

Mark A. Rothstein

The Bureau of National Affairs, Inc.   Washington, D.C.

Library of Congress Cataloging in Publication Data

Rothstein, Mark A.
  Medical screening of workers.

    Includes index.
    1. Medical screening—Law and legislation—United States.   2. Industrial hygiene—Law and legislation—United States.   3. Labor and laboring classes—United States—Medical examinations.   I. Title.   [DNLM: 1. Mass screening.   2. Civil rights.   3. Employment.
4. Occupational medicine. WA 245 R847m]
KF3570.R665   1984   344.73′0465   83-25198
ISBN 0-87179-440-3   347.304465

Printed in the United States of America
International Standard Book Number: 0-87179-440-3

To My Parents

CONTENTS

TABLES

FOREWORD

As the use of medical screening in the workplace increases, many practicing physicians are growing increasingly uncomfortable with regard to legal issues that surround their role in screening programs. Despite this discomfort, many physicians continue to evaluate patients in screening programs by employing techniques and a general philosophy derived from the normal office practice of medicine. This transference of skills and approach from office practice to medical screening is inappropriate in view of the significant differences that exist between these types of medical activity.

Workplace monitoring programs typically involve individuals who are basically healthy in contrast to those who seek medical care from a practicing physician out of a concern for some health problem. As discussed extensively in this book, the issue of job security is a central theme underlying medical screening programs and one which has a direct impact on the role of the physician and on the overall success of the screening program. In light of these and other considerations, the role of a physician in a medical screening program must be viewed quite distinctly from that of a physician providing private medical care. A central issue, discussed in Chapter 1 of this book, is whether a doctor-patient relationship exists between a physician and the individual being screened.

There are at least three basic types of medical screening programs which occur with frequency in the workplace. First, screening takes place prior to employment or job placement to identify individuals with health conditions which might render them unable to perform a specific job or task. Second, periodic monitoring programs such as blood pressure monitoring, diabetes screening, and vision or hearing testing are performed in working populations to evaluate factors related to general health status, and such testing is generally justified as being developed to improve productivity within the workplace. Third, specific surveillance programs have been developed to identify work-related illnesses in people exposed to specific hazards. Such screening programs are often mandated by specific standards promulgated by the Occupational Safety and Health Administration.

In considering a medical screening program, the basic assumptions underlying such programs should be first considered. First, the program assumes that detection of disease in the population being tested is desirable. However, in some situations, particularly those in which job security is not assured, disease detection may have important negative consequences for the persons being tested. Furthermore, many individuals prefer not to be informed that they have a health problem. In situations where participation in screening programs is voluntary, such factors may act to reduce the participation rate. An additional assumption is that detection of disease will improve the individual's prognosis or reduce the progression of a diagnosed condition. Within the context of the workplace, the intervention necessary to effect this improvement is often a change of job. Seldom do specific drug therapies exist for occupation-related illnesses. Additional issues which must be addressed in considering screening programs are that the tests to be used have appropriate sensitivity and specificity. The tests must also be acceptable to the individuals being tested and, in the context of workplace screening, invasive tests are usually inappropriate. Finally, the prevalence of the condition being screened for should be sufficiently high to justify the performance of medical evaluation. These basic issues related to the design of screening programs are ones which Professor Rothstein discusses in detail in Chapter 3 and which form an important theoretical basis for additional legal discussions.

Within medical screening programs, the physician has several defined responsibilities. In preemployment evaluations and in other health-related medical monitoring, the physician performing the evaluations should identify health conditions which might render an individual unable to perform a specific job or might make the individual a risk to the health of others. Additionally, the physician should be concerned with the identification of health conditions which might be caused or made worse by a specific job-related exposure. Within the context of a medical screening program performed periodically on workers exposed to specific hazards such as lead, asbestos, or other toxic chemicals, the physician is also performing an important role in evaluating the effectiveness of environmental controls designed to reduce workplace exposure. In addition to monitoring for a recognized work-related condition and other health problems of direct relevance to performing a specific job, the physician should also be alert for the detection of previously unrecognized job-related health problems. Clearly, in the past, alert clinicians have, through early recognition of job-related illnesses, been able to alert other professionals and initiate a process which led ultimately to improved health conditions in the workplace. Within these various roles, the physician has a dual responsibility to the individual patient and to the company. Within this book, Professor Rothstein explores this area of potential conflict of interest with respect to the historical evidence, guidelines of relevant professional organizations, and legal precedent.

For practicing professionals concerned about occupational safety and health, this book offers a unique resource of factual and historical information as well as a lucid discussion of the ethical and political issues underlying these realities and finally presents options for public policy debate and subsequent improved legislation. Specifically, Professor Rothstein provides a detailed review of the medical and epidemiologic issues which form the scientific basis for various medical screening programs in current existence. He also provides a lucid legal history of relevant federal and state laws which bear on this subject as well as important decisions of federal and state courts. He describes with clarity the important interrelationships of legal and scientific issues with regard to developing appropriate public policy. It was particularly interesting for me to note that the epidemiologic concepts of sensitivity, specificity, and predictive value have clear relevance to the legality of screening programs apart from their utility in public health analysis. Professor Rothstein clearly identifies the need for improved legislation and offers specific options which will require careful consideration. Finally, in the last chapter of the book, he recounts an episode which serves as a sobering reminder of the inextricable relationship of societal issues to the performance of medical screening programs in the workplace.

In my view, this important book will serve as a useful reference for all professionals associated with the field of occupational safety and health and will also be used extensively in teaching programs as an authoritative text. In providing this far-ranging discussion, Professor Rothstein has provided a scholarly, thorough treatment of a wide range of issues and has developed a progressive agenda for change of public policy in this area. As such, his work is an important contribution to the health of workers throughout this country.

Edward L. Baker, M.D., M.P.H.
Associate Professor of Occupational
Medicine
Harvard School of Public Health

PREFACE

Issues related to the medical screening of workers cut across a wide variety of disciplines. They not only involve medical and scientific concerns, but entail legal, political, economic, and ethical matters as well. Accordingly, this book attempts to explore medical screening from an interdisciplinary perspective. Two separate glossaries, one containing medical and scientific terms and the other containing legal terms, are included to assist the reader with some of the technical aspects of medical screening.

I am greatly indebted to the following experts in the fields of economics, epidemiology, ethics, law, and medicine who graciously read a draft of the book and offered many valuable suggestions or who contributed other important information: Dr. Ronald Bayer; Dr. Alan Engelberg; Dr. John Finklea; Dr. Vilma Hunt; James Kaplan, Esq.; Dr. John Mendeloff; Dr. Kenneth Miller; Dr. Cecile Rose; Dr. Marvin Schneiderman; Dr. Eileen Storey; and Dr. Lloyd Tepper. The opinions expressed in the book, however, are solely those of the author.

Permission to reprint copyrighted material was given by: Academic Press; *American Journal of Epidemiology; American Journal of Law and Medicine*; American Occupational Medical Association; Ballinger Publishing Co.; *British Journal of Industrial Medicine*; John Wiley & Sons, Inc.; and Lea & Febinger, Publishers.

Some of the research contained in this book was originally published in the article "Employee Selection Based on Susceptibility to Occupational Illness," published in 81 *Michigan Law Review* 1379 (1983). Scientific research assistance on the article was provided by Walter C. Brogan, III, Ph.D.; Kathleen Kennedy, M.P.H.; and Thomas Lambert, M.D., M.O.H., M.S. Legal research assistance on the article was provided by Michael Aloi, Robert D. Boyd, Tara Campbell, William Flanigan, Robert A. Goldberg, R. Scott Long,

Pamela S. Parascandola, Kim Lee White, and Debby Woodburn. Additional scientific research assistance on the book was provided by Cathy Davidson, M.S., and additional legal research assistance was provided by Jacquelyn Custer and Susana Morton.

Special thanks to word processors Joyce Hawkins and Terry Rhodes for a job well done.

                                                        Mark A. Rothstein

February 1984
Morgantown, West Virginia

INTRODUCTION

Workers on offshore oil drilling rigs in the Gulf of Mexico traditionally have been hardy, young males. Recently, an attractive, athletic, 22-year-old woman applied for a job with a drilling company. During her preemployment physical examination she was given a low-back x-ray. This is a common, if inaccurate, technique used to predict whether otherwise healthy persons with no prior back problems might be at increased risk of back injuries caused by heavy lifting and other physical exertion. The x-ray indicated a slight, clinically insignificant curvature of the spine, or scoliosis. Based simply on this x-ray, the woman was told she was physically unfit for the job. Off the record, however, she was informed that a young woman with her good looks might be disruptive and cause a serious morale problem at sea.

The preceding incident, reported to me by the young woman's father, illustrates three of the main themes addressed in this book. First, occupational medical departments too often are vulnerable and susceptible to influence. Structurally, medical departments frequently are a part of the personnel, administration, or some other larger department. This hierarchical system may lead to pressure for medical assessments of individual applicants and employees to be used as a means of justifying personnel decisions unrelated to medical considerations. An employer-provided occupational medical service, even in the most ethical and professional setting, is simply not the same as the traditional mode of patient-retained medical examination and treatment. The result is a pervasive conflict-of-interest problem, with a concomitant assortment of medical, legal, and ethical dilemmas.

A second theme developed in the book is the use, misuse, and abuse of diagnostic and predictive medical screening procedures. With new advances in physiology, toxicology, genetics, cytology, epidemiology, and other disciplines, it is becoming possible to identify high-risk populations. Unfortunately, in some instances expectations have developed at a much faster rate than the medical technology. Thus, "high tech" medical screening, to the largely unknown extent it is currently used, sometimes is based on unproven assumptions and supported by tests with low predictive values.

Congressman Albert Gore, Jr., referring to genetic screening, has observed that "it has potential to serve as a marvelous tool to protect the health of workers or as a terrible vehicle for invidious discrimination."[1] The debate about the effects of genetic and other screening techniques already has begun. Critics have charged that the screening of workers is being used instead of concentrating on reducing or eliminating unsafe and unhealthful conditions.[2] On the other hand, supporters of detailed medical screening emphasize the need to protect susceptible workers and to prevent the economic consequences of job-related injuries and illnesses.[3]

Finally, the book discusses the legal rights and remedies associated with the medical screening of workers. It is ironic that this part of the book is the longest, because there are few direct legal protections for applicants or employees from adverse treatment based on medical screening practices. Precisely because of this, however, it is necessary to analyze the many state and federal laws that may have an indirect bearing on medical screening. The book concludes with a discussion of the economic, ethical, and societal consequences of medical screening and suggests possible reform measures.

In researching medical screening of workers, one of the main problems is the lack of reliable and attributable information on current employer practices. The scant available data are often incomplete or outdated. While there are numerous case and anecdotal reports, it is venturesome to generalize about industry-wide practices on the basis of such information.

Although better data would certainly help to clarify many of the concerns raised in the book, the lack of this information does not necessarily undermine the premises of the book. First, the need for more and better data is one of the book's specific findings. Second, there is no attempt to generalize about whether practices of specific employers are widespread or whether they have continued to the same extent or at all after the reported case, incident, or study. The information is used to demonstrate that a problem existed to some extent in the past, might still exist to some extent in the present, and may continue to exist or may recur in the future. Finally, for many of the theoretical bases of predictive identification of high-risk workers, there have not been any reports of their use in industry. Nevertheless, they are mentioned because it is possible that they *could* be used in the future and they demonstrate the outermost reaches of the problem.

Chapter 1

THE ROLE OF OCCUPATIONAL MEDICINE

1.1 Overview

Modern occupational medicine in the United States began around the turn of the century. Expanding industrial production, the growth of the chemical industry, the advent of workers' compensation laws, and the pioneering work of Dr. Alice Hamilton are some of the factors providing much of the early impetus for the development of the profession.[1] Although it is difficult to document when particular companies began their occupational medical departments, by 1916 when the American Association of Industrial Physicians and Surgeons was formed (now the American Occupational Medical Association—AOMA), its founding members were associated with leading companies such as Du Pont, Ford, and Kodak.[2]

The further expansion and diversification of American industry, increased unionization, protective legislation, wartime production demands, and medical discoveries linking workplace exposures to illness fostered the growth of occupational medical departments and the profession itself. In 1955 the American Board of Preventive Medicine recognized occupational medicine as one of its four disciplines, the other three being general preventive medicine, public health, and aerospace medicine. The importance of occupational medicine was firmly established in 1970 when Congress passed the Occupational Safety and Health Act.

Today's modern occupational medical departments bear little resemblance to their modest predecessors. As Dr. Jean Spencer Felton, now of the University of California, Irvine College of Medicine, puts it, "The occupational medical world has moved from trauma to toxicology to a composite of behavior/chemicals/laws."[3] Nevertheless, the well-equipped, well-staffed, state-of-the-art medical department is the exception rather than the rule. In fact, most employer medical programs are not directed and staffed by trained occupational physicians. A government survey revealed the figures shown in Table 1–1.

The large industrial companies employ the majority of occupational physicians, while smaller businesses (which employ the majority of American workers) either hire part-time consultants, use nurses or clinics, or have no occupational medical program at all.

Even for the companies maintaining professionally staffed medical departments, the nature and functions of these units vary widely. The Gillette Company's facility in Boston has an in-house primary care center staffed with salaried, community physicians that is open to all employees.[4] On the other hand, some companies offer few services beyond first aid. Most companies with their own medical departments appear to offer services in between these extremes, with varying activity in the fields of employee assistance (*e.g.*, alcohol and drug abuse), health promotion (*e.g.*, fitness), dental care, and nonoccupational health maintenance.

Regardless of the specifics, employer medical departments have five main missions, as listed in Table 1–2.

The training that occupational physicians receive is also a cause for concern. Most American medical schools teach little or no occupational health, and even when they do, it constitutes usually only a few hours of a course in preventive medicine or community health.[5] In 1983 only 97 physicians completed specialized graduate training in occupational health.[6] The AOMA estimates that in 1983 there were about 2,000 physicians in the United States practicing occupational medicine full time, although the AOMA has 4,800 members.[7] While there may be as many as 10,000 to 15,000 physicians practicing occupational medicine full time or part-time,[8] as of 1983, only

Table 1–1.   In-Plant Medical Services

Finding	Plants (%)	Employees Covered (%)
Have a formally established health unit	4.0	31.5
Have a health unit with a physician in charge	1.2	15.0
Employ a physician full time	0.7	11.4

Source: Adapted from U.S. Department of Health, Education and Welfare, National Occupational Hazard Survey, vol. III (Survey Analysis and Supplemental Tables), at 30 (table VIII A) (1977).

Table 1–2. Possible Missions and Strategies for Corporate Health

Mission	Related Strategies
Containing workers' compensation and liability costs	Emergency treatment for occupational incidents Accident prevention Workplace monitoring for toxic substance levels Workplace monitoring for stressors Ergonomics Research into occupational disease (toxicology, epidemiology) Stewardship of product safety Control of environmental pollution and toxic waste disposal Preemployment and preplacement examinations Periodic examinations of exposed workers
Compliance with regulatory requirements	Toxicological testing of new substances Workplace monitoring of toxic substance levels Accident prevention Periodic examinations of exposed workers
Improving employee relations	Periodic examinations (nonoccupational conditions) Workplace monitoring for stressors Health promotion and fitness programs Counseling and employee assistance
Improving employee productivity	Any or all of above plus primary care
Containing health benefit costs	Administering/monitoring health benefits Periodic examinations (nonoccupational conditions) Health promotion/employee assistance Accident prevention/workplace monitoring Primary care Activities in outside health care system (alternative delivery systems, coalitions, utilization review)

Source: From Egdahl and Walsh's Industry and Health Care, Volume I: Corporate Medical Departments: A Changing Agenda?, Copyright © 1983, Ballinger Publishing Company. Reprinted by permission.

921 were certified as occupational medicine specialists by the American Board of Preventive Medicine.[9]

The lack of adequate training may be one of the reasons why questionable occupational medical procedures have sometimes been used. For example, during the rulemaking proceedings of the Occupational Safety and Health Administration (OSHA) dealing with the lead standard, "extensive testimony was presented which did demonstrate that prophylactic chelation has occurred and is occurring in workplaces throughout the country...."[10] (Prophylactic chelation is the routine use of chelating drugs to prevent elevated blood-lead levels or to reduce elevated blood-lead levels in workers occupationally exposed to lead.) These practices continued despite over 20 years of general agreement in the medical community that prophylactic chelation is unsound and causes harmful side effects to patients and despite the 1976 AOMA resolution that prophylactic chelation is considered to be an unethical medical practice subjecting the physician to censure. The OSHA lead standard now specifically prohibits prophylactic chelation.[11]

Some members of the occupational medical profession have been accused of conduct even more serious than mere incompetence. They have been accused of engaging in attempts to suppress medical information about asbestos and other hazardous substances; of trying to prevent any effective enforcement of the Occupational Safety and Health Act; of refusing to publish medical information solely to protect their employers against lawsuits, increased insurance premiums, and worker discontent; and of falsely attributing many occupational diseases to nonoccupational sources.[12] These allegations raise important and fundamental questions about the role of occupational medicine and the occupational physician. Indeed, in 1974 Dr. Clifford H. Keene of Kaiser Industries wrote that

> the profession of occupational medicine is in a crisis of strong challenge. The crisis results from our own actions or inactions. To become completely creditable will be difficult— extremely difficult. There is no acceptable alternative.[13]

Unfortunately, there has been little indication of the major structural changes necessary to renew public and professional confidence.

The foregoing charges are not new, and the mention of them is not for the purpose of making one more assault on the integrity of occupational health professionals. Instead, the problems are mentioned so that when the subject of controversial medical screening procedures (such as genetic screening) is discussed, this pervasive skepticism on the part of employees and the general public is kept in mind. No matter how pure the motive of companies or their medical departments, new or debatable medical screening practices are likely to be widely viewed with suspicion.

1.2   Conflicts of Interest

Regardless of their competence or integrity, occupational physicians often find themselves in dilemmas caused by conflicting loyalties and responsibilities to their patients and their employers.

The problem arises when a physician is employed by a company and given the task of protecting the company's workers. There are built-in conflicts between what is needed to protect the workers and what is important to the company for profits.[14]

The preceding characterization of the conflict-of-interest problem has been criticized as being merely an "entrenched stereotype."[15] Nevertheless, "[i]t is fair to say ... that controversy remains over whether the physician may play a part in what corporations consider safe job placement and what workers may consider discrimination based on physical condition."[16] In all, four types of potential conflict-of-interest problems have been identified:

- Whether the physician's obligation to his employer relieves him of the responsibility to report negative clinical findings to the individual;
- Whether the physician's obligation to the patient prohibits him from reporting to the company that a worker's physical condition or substance abuse constitutes a danger to himself and others;
- Whether the physician's obligation to the patient prohibits him from reporting to the company that an individual's physical condition renders him more than usually vulnerable to a work-related hazard;
- Whether the physician should represent the company in disputed workers' compensation claims and in verifying disability/sick leave claims.[17]

The AOMA Code of Ethical Conduct for Physicians Providing Occupational Medical Services provides, in part, that physicians should "avoid allowing their medical judgment to be influenced by any conflict of interest." While this sentiment is commendable, it avoids the question of whether the physician's *first* loyalty is to the employee or employer. The answer to this question, however, is certainly implied in the Code of Ethical Conduct itself. Nowhere in the Code does the word "patient" appear. The recipients of the occupational medical services are referred to as "individuals." This strongly suggests an attempt to define the relationship of the occupational physician and the employee beyond the traditional physician-patient relationship with all of its attendant medical, ethical, and legal implications.

From a legal standpoint, it is important to determine whether a physician-patient relationship exists between an employee and an employer-provided doctor. If there is no such relationship, the doctor owes no duty to the employee except to use ordinary care not to injure the employee during the course of the examination.[18] If there *is* a physician-patient relationship, then the physician must render medical care with the skill and learning commonly possessed by members of the profession in good standing. (An unresolved issue is whether the standard of care required would be that of physicians generally or of occupational physicians, the latter being a higher standard.) If a physician-patient relationship exists, the physician also has a legal duty to discover the presence of disease, to inform the patient of the results of the examination and any tests performed, to advise the employee of risks associated with continued exposures, and to preserve the confidentiality of communications and records.

The traditional view is that there is no physician-patient relationship between an employee and an employer-provided doctor.[19] There is some evidence, however, that this view is changing, and the current state of the law is unclear.[20] Courts that adhere to the dichotomy between employer-provided and traditional patient-obtained medical care look to whether the physician is treating or merely examining the individual[21] or for whose benefit the physician is performing the service.[22] If the physician is merely examining the individual or performing services for the benefit of the employer, no physician-patient relationship will be found.

These distinctions between employer-provided and patient-obtained medical care are simplistic and artificial. Occupational physicians examine *and* treat; the benefit of their services goes to *both* employer and employee. Therefore, to determine if there is a physician-patient relationship other factors also need to be considered, including whether there is an ongoing medical relationship between the parties or merely a single examination, what the reasonable expectations of the physician and patient are regarding the nature of the examination, whether any diagnosis or treatment is contemplated by the examination, and the nature of the employee's consent to the examination.

In those situations where no physician-patient relationship exists it is incumbent on the physician to disclose this fact. Individuals being examined may not be aware that they will not be given a report of the examination and may erroneously assume that "no news is good news"; they may not realize that the traditional rules of medical confidentiality do not apply; and they may not know that the physician may write a report or give testimony adverse to their interest.

Similarly, if only a limited health assessment is being performed, this should be disclosed. The new AOMA Guidelines for Employee Health Services in Hospitals, Clinics and Medical Research Institutions recognize this. "New employees should be advised that the pre-placement health evaluation is not intended to take the place of private medical attention, and they should not be given the impression that they had undergone a complete health assessment."[23]

It is also important to assess whether the conflict-of-interest problem has adverse effects on the quality of occupational medicine being practiced. In theory, management has the authority to determine medical policy, and the physicians simply counsel employers about health matters generally or the medical fitness of particular employees in relation to work. Even this theoretical division of responsibilities, however, has created problems. According to Dr. Norbert J. Roberts, former corporate medical director of Exxon Corporation: "Too often occupational health physicians resign themselves to unpalatable or bad policies of their managements without any genuine efforts to fulfill their own responsibilities for helping change or shape those policies."[24]

Not only do some occupational physicians acquiesce in questionable corporate policy, but in other instances they actually concur in or contribute to the formulation of these policies. Dr. William E. Morton of the University of Oregon Medical School suggests that the problem may be caused by physicians too closely identifying with management.

> Most industrial physicians identify strongly with management for sociological and financial reasons, and some may forget that the ethical guidelines for the medical profession are more restrictive than for businessmen. Failure to recognize and adhere to medical ethical standards can only downgrade those who so stray, and that may be part of the non-recognition problem that the occupational medicine specialty experiences today.[25]

The conflict-of-interest problem interferes with effective occupational medical practice from the employee side as well. The degree of confidence and trust in occupational physicians by employees varies widely. On a continuum, the employees range from the most trusting to the most suspicious. The most trusting employee will freely disclose health-related information, perhaps not realizing that the confidentiality strictures of the traditional physician-patient relationship may not be applied, that an adverse employment decision may result from such disclosures, or that the physician may even testify against the employee in a subsequent workers' compensation hearing. The most suspicious employee may provide incomplete or inaccurate information, thereby limiting the ability of the physician to perform his or her job effectively.

Dr. Dean Belk, corporate medical director of Alcoa, suggests that occupational medical practice should be similar to the private practice of medicine.

> We in occupational medicine have an identity problem because we have not yet really decided what our mission is, to whom we are responsible. I believe that our responsibility is to the health and well-being of the individual employee with whom we're dealing at any point in time. We are *not* part of management in the true sense; we are the personal physicians of the employees. We have not always had the chance to function truly as physicians in a one-to-one relationship with the individual employee, but that is the only way, in my opinion.[26]

In recognition of the conflict-of-interest and identity problems, a number of recommendations have been made to change occupational medical practice. They range from modest proposals for physicians to maintain clear channels of communication to top management and better relations with employees[27] to more sweeping proposals to make the occupational medical operation an independent contractor within the same plant facility.[28] Other proposals are discussed in Chapter 13.

1.3   Medical Screening

OSHA requires that medical personnel be available for advice and consultation on "plant health"; that first aid be available if the workplace is not in "near proximity" to an infirmary, clinic, or hospital; and that for certain enumerated health hazards specific medical procedures be performed.[29] Aside from these requirements, however, employers are under no legal duty to provide employees with medical services.[30]

According to the AOMA statement, "Purposes and Objectives of the American Occupational Medical Association," individual physicians engaged in the practice of occupational medicine and surgery are encouraged to develop skills and competence to carry out the following characteristic functions:

1.   To aid in the placement of job applicants by ascertaining their physical, mental, and emotional capabilities for work which they can perform with an acceptable degree of efficiency without hazard to themselves or others.
2.   To guide and assist all employees in achieving and maintaining optimal health so that they may perform effectively and with satisfaction until retirement.

3. To reduce the incidence, and thereby the cost to both employee and employer, of illnesses and accidents through the development of effective health programs.
4. To provide for the diagnosis and treatment of occupational injuries and illnesses and, where indicated or necessary, of nonoccupational disorders.
5. To promote maximal rehabilitation of all sick and injured employees.
6. To aid in the effective administration of employee benefits concerned with health and disability.
7. To cooperate with those charged with establishing product safety and consumer protection.
8. To cooperate with the health professions and with voluntary and governmental agencies concerned with community health and welfare.
9. To explore, with health planning organizations and the private sector of medical practice, means of integrating occupational medicine into the delivery of total health care.
10. To aid in the assessment of the work and community environment and the control of hazards to health.[31]

The first factor, dealing as it does with "placement of workers," raises the issue of medical screening.

"Medical screening" may be defined as the process by which a work force is selected and maintained by application of medical criteria. Although medical screening is not new, there is increasing concern that it is becoming both more extensive and intensive. According to Congressman Albert Gore, Jr., "The increasing costs of making improvements in the work place environment and the financial burdens of workers' compensation and similar statutes have provided many industries with a strong economic incentive to engage in preemployment screening."[32]

Where management believes that cost savings will result from having the "right" work force, it is foreseeable that occupational physicians will be under increasing pressure from management to develop more detailed medical screening techniques and then to supply personnel departments with the medical data to be used in employment decisionmaking. Indeed, Dr. Max P. Rogers of Southern Railway has testified that medical departments should "provide the railroad industry with applicants who are as near perfect physical specimens as is possible for us to find."[33] Even if such a goal were achievable from a medical standpoint, it certainly raises profound legal and societal questions.

Perhaps more than any other aspect of occupational medicine, medical screening of applicants and employees epitomizes the fundamental difference between patient-obtained and employer-provided medical services. With patient-obtained medical services the physician advises the patient of medical facts and the likely consequences of each of the patient's options. Thus, in the area of preemployment examinations, the physician would advise the patient of his or her medical status and the risks of working in a particular environment. The choice of whether to accept these risks would belong to the patient. By contrast, with employer-provided medical services there may or may not be disclosure to the "patient" of his or her medical condition and environmental risk factors, but invariably the ultimate decision on medical fitness and employability is made by management with the advice of the medical department.

Where the applicant or employee is unable to perform essential activities of the job or where his or her employment would pose serious risks to co-workers, the public, or the employer's property, it is justifiable for the employer to "screen out" the individual. Where the only risks are to the individual, the problem is much more complicated.

Leaving aside for a moment the vast ethical considerations, there is the question of money. Under workers' compensation and similar laws (*e.g.*, Federal Employers' Liability Act covering railroad workers), employers may not defend themselves in court against the claim of an injured employee by asserting the defense of assumption of risk. Moreover, a "high-risk" employee could allege that the failure to use medical screening techniques to discover a predisposition constituted negligence. On the other hand, certain medical screening procedures may be attacked as inaccurate or in violation of antidiscrimination laws. This problem has been characterized as one of "damned if you do, damned if you don't."[34] Before making any attempt to resolve this dilemma, however, it is necessary to develop more information about specific screening procedures, "host" factors, environmental hazards, and the legal framework.

1.4 Medical Surveillance and Research

Preemployment or preplacement medical examinations are only the first step in what may be a continuing process of medical surveillance. For example, OSHA's asbestos standard requires an annual medical examination for each employee exposed to airborne concentrations of asbestos fibers.[35] The examination must include a chest x-ray, a medical history to elicit symptoms of respiratory disease, and pulmonary function tests. The same examination also is required within 30 days before or after the termination of employment of any exposed employee.[36] Medical surveillance also is required by OSHA for several other toxic substances and harmful physical agents.[37]

Periodic medical examinations are given to numerous other employees exposed to a variety of substances, even in the absence of a specific OSHA requirement. In general, the answer to the question of whether and the extent to which these services are provided is most influenced by the nature of the industry and the size of the employer. For example, 80.2% of employees working in primary metal industries and 80.4% of employees working in petroleum and coal products are given periodic medical examinations. For agricultural services, forestry, and fisheries this figure is only 4.6%, and in contract construction it is only 5.0%.[38] Only 12.2% of employees working in small plants (8 to 249 workers) receive periodic medical examinations, but 29.3% of employees working in medium-sized plants (250 to 500 workers) and 65.4% of employees working in large plants receive periodic medical examinations.[39]

Even where medical surveillance is not required by OSHA or a collective bargaining agreement, employee participation in the surveillance program can be made a valid condition of employment. Consequently, employees who refuse to have a periodic medical examination may be discharged.[40] In addition, employees found to be unfit for continued employment on the basis of a periodic medical examination may be discharged, with their only protection being the right to workers' compensation if they can demonstrate that their medical condition is work-related.

Many of the same principles governing medical surveillance also apply to medical procedures that are solely related to the employer's research on the effects of workplace exposures. Employee consent to participation in the experiment may be considered a valid condition of employment. This is not to say that corporate medical departments have been or may use employees as guinea pigs for fiendish experiments. (The discharge of an employee for refusing to participate in such an experiment would probably be held to violate public policy.)[41] Nevertheless, some employers have used employees for research on the effects of workplace exposures. For example, Dow Chemical performed cytogenetic testing on workers exposed to epichlorohydrin to determine whether they had a higher incidence of chromosomal aberrations.[42] When this type of research is performed, employees need not even be informed of the purpose, nature, and results of the testing.

The absence of legal rights on the part of the human subjects of medical research in the private sector differs sharply from the rights of subjects when the research is publicly funded. Under the National Research Act,[43] any recipient of a federal grant or federal contract from the Department of Health and Human Services (HHS) for biomedical or behavioral research involving human subjects must establish an Institutional Review Board to review the research in order to protect the rights of the human subjects. The Department of HHS has promulgated detailed regulations implementing this law[44] and has established high standards for demonstrating that the consent of the subject was truly informed.[45]

Despite these potential problems stemming from a lack of protection for employees in employer medical research, the larger problem is that there is *not enough* occupational medical research being performed. This research is not so much research on human subjects as the compilation of available data (such as mortality and morbidity rates of exposed workers) already available. According to leading epidemiologists, such as Dr. Philip Enterline of the University of Pittsburgh, an unknown amount of epidemiological data is not being analyzed and some important information may be unavailable to the scientific community, exposed workers, and the public.[46] Dr. Samuel Milham of the Washington State Public Health Department has observed that this problem is not limited to employers. National and international unions also have denied access to their worker mortality and morbidity data to epidemiologists seeking to study occupational illness.[47]

The reason most often given is that if studies linking exposures to disease were made available (or even merely compiled and ordered disclosed by a court during the discovery phase of a lawsuit), plaintiffs in personal injury cases would attempt to use this information to prove fraudulent concealment, willful misconduct, and other matters related to litigation.[48] Thus, the fear of civil liability, as well as increased workers' compensation rates and employee discontent, operates as a disincentive for the employer to engage in essential research and data gathering or to disclose existing information.[49]

It is important to address the problem of how to eliminate the disincentives for employers to compile information on employee exposures. There are several alternatives. First, evidentiary rules could be adopted in all jurisdictions prohibiting the introduction of an employer's voluntarily generated medical research as evidence in a lawsuit. Even if this were possible to do, however, there is no assurance that significant numbers of employers would collect or compile the data. Second, OSHA could require that all data collected by employers be compiled and disclosed. But it is questionable whether OSHA's legislative mandate includes requiring employers to engage in epidemiological research, and few employers have the necessary personnel or resources. Moreover, again one of the reactions of employers might simply be to refuse to collect this information.

The best solution would appear to be a requirement that all employers collect specific raw data and either retain the information for possible future use or transmit the information to a central agency for compilation. The National Institute for Occupational Safety and Health (NIOSH), the National Center for Health Statistics (NCHS), or some other agency could be selected. Then, once meaningful associations between exposure and illness are found, appropriate regulatory action could be taken. As long as the companies themselves are not analyzing the data, the likelihood of civil liability would be lessened. The accurate collection of records by employers also would be facilitated by provisions prohibiting enforcement activity based on this data.

The promulgation of a generic occupational exposure and illness recording standard (such requirements are currently limited to OSHA's 21 health standards), along with the elimination of the current disincentives to record maintenance resulting from the fear of civil liability or enforcement action, would certainly facilitate epidemiological study. But other measures also are needed. For example, requiring that (1) birth certificates include parental occupation, (2) death certificates include occupation and cause of death, and (3) workers' compensation recording forms be standardized are other measures which would expand the capability of finding associations between workplace exposure and illness.[50]

Chapter 2

MEDICAL ASSESSMENT OF CURRENT HEALTH STATUS

2.1 Impairment and Disability

The assessment of current health status involves the medical examination of applicants or employees to detect the presence of impairments. At this point, it is important to define impairment and to differentiate impairment from disability. According to the American Lung Association Ad Hoc Advisory Committee on Impairment/Disability:

> Impairment is purely a medical condition. It reflects an anatomic or functional abnormality, which persists after appropriate therapy and with no reasonable prospect of improvement. It may or may not be stable at the time the evaluation is made. If severe, it frequently precludes gainful employment. It is always a basic consideration in the evaluation of disability.... [Disability is] a general term which indicates the total effect of impairment upon a patient's life. It is affected by such diverse factors as age, sex, education, economic and social environment, and energy requirements of the occupation. Two people with an identical impairment may be differently affected in their life situations.[1]

The determination of whether a particular impairment constitutes a disability with respect to a specific job is sometimes made by the medical department and sometimes made by the personnel department. Regardless of which corporate entity makes the final decision on employability, the decisionmaking process often involves three steps. The first step is the assessment of the job's requirements. This "job analysis," which includes a review of the job description, the essential tasks performed, and the working environment in order to develop the job-related critical medical requirements, is usually provided to the physician by someone in the personnel department

14

or elsewhere in management.[2] Second, there is a focus on the individual applicant or employee. This usually involves the physician taking a complete medical and work history, performing a physical examination, and ordering any necessary laboratory or testing procedures. Third, there is a comparison of the individual's medical profile with the job requirements. The physician's determination, it is widely suggested, should be that the individual is either fit for employment, fit for certain limited employment, or unfit for employment.[3] Some employers use more detailed work restriction codes which indicate specific employee restrictions.[4]

2.2   Medical Questionnaires

Most employers regularly record health information about new employees. In small plants (8 to 249 workers), 60.6% of employees have health information recorded; in medium-sized plants (250 to 500 workers), 82.0% of employees have health information recorded; and in large plants (over 500 workers), 97.9% of employees have health information recorded. In certain industries, such as primary metal (99.0%), electrical equipment and supplies (98.2%), and transportation equipment (98.1%), virtually all new employees have health information recorded by their employers.[5]

Detailed medical information is rarely requested on the employment application, but applicants often are informed that a physical examination is a condition of employment.[6] Some application forms specifically ask the applicant for consent to a physical examination.[7] Although some companies inform applicants and employees about the possible use of information supplied on the medical questionnaire, most employers do not.[8] Some employers merely have the applicant or employee sign a general waiver for the employer to use the information as it deems necessary.[9]

Medical questionnaires are filled out by an applicant at the time of, or in lieu of, a preemployment physical examination. Some of the questionnaires are quite detailed. For example, Exxon Corporation has a 25-page, 185-item questionnaire that applicants and employees are required to complete before submitting to a compulsory physical examination.[10] The General Foods questionnaire asks detailed questions about hearing and vision; military service; allergies; prescription and nonprescription medications taken; exercise program; sports participation; sleeping habits; alcohol, beer, and wine consumption; coffee, tea, and soft drink consumption (including whether soft drinks were dietetic and coffee decaffeinated); recent weight changes; cigarette, cigar, pipe, snuff, and chewing tobacco usage; diet description; place of birth and travel to foreign countries; surgery (including urogenital); diseases of parents, grandparents, and siblings; prior workplace exposures; and prior accidents or injuries.[11] All of this information is computerized—a common practice with large companies.[12]

Some employee medical questionnaires are far less detailed, but even the most routine questionnaires often inquire about personal matters, such as the medical history of family members, medication taken, hobbies, sleeping habits, workers' compensation claims filed, insurance records, and military records.[13] If a "community and home environmental profile" is prepared, there may be questions about plumbing, rodents, and home repairs.[14] There are also reports of employers asking about homosexuality, venereal disease, and fertility.

Employers undertaking to screen out high-risk individuals may be tempted to expand the scope of their medical questionnaires. These employers might theorize that, to get a complete picture of an individual's nonoccupational environmental influences, detailed information is needed about an individual's diet, hobbies, sexual activity, smoking and drinking, and life-style. From a scientific standpoint, this information may be of limited usefulness. Nevertheless, there are presently few restrictions on what information may be sought, obtained, used, disseminated, or retained.

Extensive inquiries of this sort raise concerns about whether there is needless intrusion into the privacy of employees. Nevertheless, employees have little recourse. If they refuse to complete the questionnaires they will probably not be hired or will be discharged.[15] If they falsify the questionnaires they will not be hired or will be discharged when the falsification is discovered. These discharges have been upheld by the National Labor Relations Board[16] and by arbitrators.[17]

2.3   Medical Examinations

In Great Britain, a statutory medical service provided for part-time "factory surgeons" as early as 1800.[18] Preemployment medical examinations of young persons were established by law pursuant to the Factory Act of 1855. Periodic examinations of all workers in certain dangerous trades were required by the end of the nineteenth century.[19]

In the United States, preemployment examinations became common during the early 1900s, when the first workers' compensation laws were passed.[20] The first physical examination program may have been instituted by Sears, Roebuck in 1909.[21] Since that time the preemployment medical examination has been a virtual institution in American industry. The purpose of the examination "apparently was to select only physical and mental paragons"[22] and to exclude individuals with medical, psychological, or "other" problems (such as troublemakers and union sympathizers).[23]

Today, these examinations are referred to as preplacement examinations, ostensibly because employers would not refuse to hire anyone but the most seriously disabled person and the purpose of the examination is to correlate the employee with the most suitable job.[24] Individuals who refuse to undergo or cooperate with the examination are rejected.[25]

Preplacement medical examinations are still widely used. Although only 19.2% of employees in small plants (8 to 249 workers) are required to undergo a preplacement examination, 48.9% of employees in medium-sized plants (250 to 500 workers) and 83.3% of employees in large plants (over 500 workers) are required to undergo examination.[26] Furthermore, preplacement medical examinations are even more prevalent in several industries, such as petroleum and coal products (93.5%), primary metal industries (92.4%), and transportation equipment (90.8%).[27]

The avowed purposes of the examinations are (1) to protect the employee from assignment to a job which might be harmful; (2) to protect the employer from having an unfit work force; and (3) to bring about correction of remediable physical defects.[28] The examination also serves an essential function in health surveillance by providing a historical record of previous exposures, a composite of the employee's state of health before work, and a baseline for comparison with later health observations.[29]

Most preemployment medical examinations are quite similar to the "annual checkup" given by a family physician. Although the examinations often are tailored to specific health hazards, it is common for an examination to include a general evaluation and an evaluation of the following bodily parts or systems: skin and hair; eye, ear, nose, and throat; chest (pulmonary and cardiovascular); abdomen; genitourinary; musculoskeletal; neuropsychiatric; and hematologic.[30]

Dr. Bruce Karrh of Du Pont has explained the role of medical examinations in the company's overall occupational health program.

In overview, the key elements of Du Pont's system include thorough high-quality physical examination and medical surveillance programs: a highly reputable toxicology testing program; pioneering efforts in the area of epidemiology as an occupational medical tool; and a commitment to candor and openness so that those who need to know about potential health problems, particularly Du Pont employees, are well informed.

Our formal occupational medical program goes back to 1915, and the concept of preventive medicine forms its backbone. We strive to protect employee health by reducing exposures to known and potential health hazards in the workplace, and by carefully monitoring employee health. Just as we work with the concept that all injuries are preventable on the job—we firmly believe that all identified risks are controllable.

The keystone of this program is a baseline health inventory, which includes a preemployment medical history and a physical examination for each new employee. Data gathered from these early evaluations tell us whether any preexisting medical condition exists which may be aggravated by exposure to certain substances on the job, and would make that individual an increased risk.

Today, we give comprehensive medical examinations annually to all employees over 40 years of age, and every 2 years to all employees 40 and under. The basic content of these exams is an interval history and physical examination which includes a chest X-ray, vision test, hearing, pulmonary functions tests, urinalysis, and a series of blood tests, blood chemistry and hematology tests and electrocardiograms at periodic intervals.[31]

2.4   Laboratory Procedures

Many employers use laboratory procedures as a part of their medical screening and medical surveillance programs. As with other aspects of employer-provided medical services, the frequency with which laboratory tests are performed depends on the size and nature of the company. Periodic blood tests are performed on 14.7% of all employees, but they are given to 55.4% of employees in the primary metal industries and to 51.4% of employees working in ordnance and accessories industries.[32] Urine tests are performed on 14.4% of all employees, but they are given to 46.7% of employees working with petroleum and coal products.[33] Pulmonary function tests are given to 13.5% of all employees, but they are given to 68.5% of employees in petroleum and coal products industries and to 54.8% of employees in primary metal industries.[34] Chest x-rays are given to 24.9% of all employees, but to 76.3% of employees in petroleum and coal products industries and to 74.7% of employees in primary metal industries.[35] Periodic audiometric examinations are given to 21.1%

of all employees, but to 73.6% of employees in the primary metal industries and to 72.0% of employees working in petroleum and coal products industries.[36] Periodic ophthalmologic examinations are given to 22.3% of all employees, but to 73.9% of employees working in petroleum and coal products industries and to 68.6% of employees in the primary metal industries.[37]

Beyond these routine procedures, most companies are reluctant to divulge what additional tests, if any, are performed and how the results are used. This is particularly true with regard to controversial tests such as biochemical genetic screening.[38] Because occupational health programs often are directed by individuals with limited occupational health training and experience, there is concern that laboratory tests may be used increasingly for medical screening purposes. Some of these physicians might be tempted to overrely on laboratory screening procedures because they are easier and less time-consuming than a thorough history and clinical evaluation and may be believed to select a work force in need of less medical attention. These same physicians, however, may be less able to evaluate the scientific limitations on the utility and predictive value of the latest screening procedures.[39]

2.5   OSHA-Mandated Medical Procedures

OSHA's 21 health standards regulating toxic substances require a variety of medical procedures. In general, employers must conduct preplacement examinations, the physician must furnish employers with a copy of the physician's statement of suitability for employment in the regulated area, the employer must conduct periodic (usually annual) examinations, and in some instances the employer must conduct examinations at termination of employment. The failure to conduct these required medical examinations may lead to the issuance of OSHA citations and the assessment of penalties. Table 2–1 contains a summary of the specific requirements.

Under OSHA's new hearing conservation standard employers are required to give employees a baseline audiogram within four months of their first exposure to noise at or above a time-weighted average of 85 decibels. Thereafter, audiograms must be given at least annually to employees exposed at or above a time-weighted average of 85 decibels.[40]

The Mine Safety and Health Act (MSHA) requires that all miners working in a coal mine be given a chest x-ray within six months

Table 2-1.   Medical Requirements of OSHA Health Standards Regulating Toxic Substances

29 C.F.R. §	Substance	Primary Health Risks	Required Medical Procedures
1910.1001	Asbestos	1. Asbestosis 2. Mesothelioma 3. Lung Disorders	1. Pulmonary function tests 2. Chest x-rays
1910.1003 to .1016	13 carcinogens[a]	1. Bladder cancer 2. Bronchiogenic cancer 3. Lung cancer 4. Stomach cancer 5. Skin cancer 6. Liver cancer 7. Kidney cancer 8. Pulmonary edema 9. Central necrosis	1. Complete medical history, including genetic and environmental factors. 2. Consideration of reduced immunological competence of employees, those undergoing treatment with steroids or cytotoxic agents, pregnant women, and cigarette smokers.
1910.1017	Vinyl chloride	1. Angiosarcoma 2. Lung cancer	1. Complete physical exam 2. Liver studies
1910.1018	Inorganic arsenic	1. Neuritis 2. Paralysis	1. Complete medical history and exam 2. Chest x-ray 3. Sputum cytology
1910.1025	Inorganic lead	1. Central nervous system disorders 2. Kidney damage	1. Complete medical history and exam 2. Detailed blood studies
1910.1029	Coke oven emissions	1. Lung cancer 2. Kidney cancer 3. Skin cancer	1. Complete history 2. Chest x-ray 3. Pulmonary function tests 4. Sputum cytology 5. Urine cytology

Table 2-1 *contd.*

29 C.F.R. §	Substance	Primary Health Risks	Required Medical Procedures
1910.1043	Cotton dust	1. Byssinosis	1. Complete medical history 2. Standardized respiratory questionnaire 3. Pulmonary function tests
1910.1044	DBCP[b]	1. Sterility	1. Complete medical and reproductive history 2. Examination of genitourinary tract 3. Serum specimen for radioimmuno assay
1910.1045	Acrylonitrile	1. Asphyxia 2. Weakness	1. Complete medical history and exam, with particular attention to peripheral and central nervous system, gastrointestinal system, skin, and thyroid 2. Chest x-ray 3. Fecal occult blood screening for all workers over 40 years of age

Source: Adapted from 29 C.F.R. §§1910.1001 to .1045 (1983).

[a] 4-Nitrobiphenyl (§1910.1003); Alpha-Napthylamine (§1910.1004); Methyl chloromethyl ether (§1910.1006); 3,3′-Dichlorobenzidine (and its salts) (§1910.1007); bis-Chloromethyl ether (§1910.1008); beta-Napthylamine (§1910.1009); Benzidine (§1910.1010); 4-Aminodiphenyl (§1910.1011); Ethyleneimine (§1910.1012); beta-Propiolactone (§1910.1013); 2-Acetylaminoflurene (§1910.1014); 4-Dimethylaminoazobenzene (§1910.1015); N-Nitrosodimethylamine (§1910.1016).

[b] 1,2-dibromo-3-chloropropane.

after commencement of employment, a second x-ray three years later, and a third x-ray two years later if the second x-ray showed evidence of pneumoconiosis.[41]

All of the OSHA and MSHA standards require medical examinations to be provided "without cost" or "at no cost" to the employees. In *Phelps Dodge Corp.*,[42] the Occupational Safety and Health Review Commission held that the "without cost" provision in the inorganic arsenic standard required the employer to compensate employees for time spent taking the exam (if outside normal working hours) and for extra transportation expenses incurred by the employees in getting to the off-workplace site of the examination.

Besides the medical procedures detailed in OSHA health standards, specific medical surveillance measures may be mandated by the Occupational Safety and Health Review Commission. In *ITT Grinnell*[43] the employer was cited for having excessive levels of silica dust. The employer filed a petition for modification of abatement (PMA) to extend the abatement date. The Commission granted the petition conditioned on the employer's use of the following additional medical surveillance measures: periodic chest x-rays for employees with seven or more years of exposure, annual pulmonary function tests, and annual physical examinations and medical histories. The Commission stated, "Even absent a separate health standard specifying the particulars of a medical surveillance program, the Commission may impose an appropriate medical surveillance program . . . [as] an alternative measure . . . during the extended abatement period requested."[44]

Chapter 3

MEDICAL ASSESSMENT OF FUTURE HEALTH RISKS

3.1 The Purpose of Predictive Screening

The four main agents or factors causing occupational illness and disease are physical agents (*e.g.*, radiation, noise), chemical agents (*e.g.*, pesticides, mineral dusts), biological agents (*e.g.*, viral diseases, bacterial diseases), and psychosocial factors (*e.g.*, repetitive work, shift work).[1] The assessment of future health risks involves the medical examination of applicants or employees to determine the likelihood of future impairments from one or more of these disease-causing agents or factors.

Unlike the assessment of current health status, in which the focus is on symptomatology or established disease of which the individual is unaware, the assessment of future health risk (or predictive medical screening) tries to calculate which asymptomatic individuals are at an increased risk of future impairment.[2] Although from a medical standpoint the differences between the medical assessment of current and future health often blur, there are important legal distinctions, as will be discussed later.

Predictive screening to determine a predisposition to occupational injury or illness from workplace exposures already is done by employers in various industries. For example, some railroad and mining companies require low-back x-rays to predict which individuals are at increased risk of back injuries, some asbestos manufacturers refuse to hire individuals who smoke cigarettes because of the synergistic effect of breathing in asbestos and smoking, and some companies refuse to hire or assign fertile women to jobs where there is exposure to lead or other teratogenic substances.

These three examples demonstrate some of the many forms that predictive screening may take. (Indeed, a great deal of screening focuses on the likelihood of the individual contracting nonoccupational illnesses.) In the following sections there are discussions of the physiological and behavioral factors affecting an individual's susceptibility to occupational illness. For many of these factors, the increased risk is largely theoretical and unconfirmed; for other factors, there is better scientific evidence but little indication that they influence medical decisions on employability; for still other factors, the increased risk is soundly based and also considered in employee selection, job placement, and medical surveillance.

Although some of the bases of increased risk, like geography and diet, do not presently affect employability, they are still appropriate to consider. New studies and new data may soon suggest host-hazard associations previously unconsidered and which will have a direct bearing on health and employment. In the context of genetic screening (discussed in Chapter 4), Dr. Howard R. Sloan of Ohio State University College of Medicine has stated:

> The day is rapidly approaching when possessing a piece of a subject's skin would provide an unscrupulous individual with far more detailed information about that subject than could be obtained from a fingerprint and a high quality photograph. If we know enough about a person's genetic profile, we could exclude him or her from almost any job.[3]

The same statement also may apply to other physiological and behavioral factors.

3.2   Varied Susceptibility in Human Populations

Every human being has a distinct biochemical individuality. A compilation of about two dozen polymorphisms of blood types, red cell enzymes, blood plasma proteins, and leukocyte histocompatability types demonstrates that any two persons, except for identical twins, will have only one chance in three billion of having the same profile for even this short list of biochemical markers.[4]

In addition to genetic factors, a person's environment plays an important role in the total development of the individual. Genes provide the potential; the ultimate expression can be greatly influenced by the environmental conditions in which they operate.[5] In other words, human individuality is the result of the potentialities of heredity working together with the possibilities of the environment.[6]

Human individuality is an important element in the etiology of disease. At one time, controversy existed about whether genetics or environment—"nature or nurture"—was more important.[7] Today, however, it is widely recognized that both factors are essential and that few, if any, diseases are either wholly genetic or wholly environmental in their etiology.[8] The study of the relationship between environmental and host factors is sometimes referred to as "eco-genetics."[9] "Environmental factors" has been given a broad definition that includes everything from intrauterine life to old age. It includes physical and social conditions, food, bacteria and viruses encountered, and medical care—both prophylactic and therapeutic.[10]

It is now well settled that all individuals exposed to a toxic agent do not respond alike, nor are all these differences the result of different levels of exposure.[11] Simply stated, some individuals are more sensitive to particular toxic substances.[12] Sensitivity may be based on a variety of factors, such as preexisting disease, personal habits combined with occupational exposures to create synergistic effects, or inborn errors of metabolism that interfere with detoxification of chemicals or augment their toxic effects.[13]

The term "hypersusceptibility" is defined as an "[i]nordinate response to an infective, chemical, or other agent."[14] Although the term appears frequently in medical and scientific literature, some experts object to the term, fearing that hypersusceptible people will be considered to be ill or defective. Consequently, the term "sensitive" will be used to describe the relationship of a person to a particular environmental agent, and the terms "predisposed," "susceptible," and "high-risk" will be used to refer to the relationship of a person to illness.

Recent studies have shown that the diversity among individuals is much greater than previously believed.[15] There are many degrees of toxin-specific sensitivity due to the enormous amount of genetic variability in human populations.[16] Each genotype (an individual's genetic constitution) responds differently to environmental variations.[17] Disease results only under certain genotype-environmental combinations.[18] Moreover, illness in an individual is the result of a multitude of prior, chance circumstances differing from one individual to another, even when the manifestations of their illnesses are indistinguishable.[19] Seemingly minor differences in diet or in physical or chemical environment determine the reaction of a person to a given microbial or genetic stimulus.[20]

As the list of factors known to be capable of inducing human disease has lengthened, it has become clear that a particular disease manifestation may have more than one causal antecedent.[21] Furthermore, the human environment and gene pool is in a constant state of flux, with exposures to physical and chemical substances suspected or known to cause disease increasing astronomically.[22] Therefore, based on studies of genetic variability and pharmacogenetics (the study of the effects of genetic variation on human response to drugs), the dramatic increase in environmental pollutants will continue to increase the number of genetically susceptible targets.[23] Thus, the concept of varied sensitivity is likely to become of even greater significance in the study of disease causation.

The same principle of wide-ranging individual susceptibility to disease applies with equal force to occupational disease. Genetic and environmental factors determine an individual's predisposition to work-related illness.[24] For example, it is recognized that of a group of workers exposed to an occupational carcinogen, some will develop cancer and others will not. The precise reasons for this variable response, however, are almost always unknown.[25] In fact, human sensitivity to a carcinogen may vary by 100-fold or more among individuals, depending on sex, age, hormonal balance, health, general genetic predisposition, or other factors.[26]

The study of cancer provides a good illustration of the interaction between hereditary and environmental factors.[27] Hereditary or congenital factors are solely responsible for about 2% of cancers, but they contribute strongly to an additional 8%.[28] The remaining 90% are thought to be due primarily to environmental factors.[29] In industrialized nations, approximately 35% of fatal cancers are attributed to air pollution (mostly from cigarettes), 5% to 10% are attributed to occupational exposures, 10% to 20% are attributed to ultraviolet and ionizing radiation, and the remaining 40% to 50% are attributed to life-style (mostly diet).[30] The Office of Technology Assessment has estimated that 60% to 90% of cancer is related to occupational and environmental exposure[31] but of that total percentage occupational factors contribute to 5% to 10% of all cancers.[32]

The World Health Organization has identified four separate occupational disease syndromes, with occupational factors having differing roles in the etiology: (1) diseases solely occupational in origin (*e.g.*, pneumoconioses); (2) diseases in which occupation is one of the causal factors (*e.g.*, bronchogenic carcinoma); (3) diseases in which occupation is a contributing factor in complex situations (*e.g.*, chronic bronchitis); and (4) diseases in which occupation may aggravate a preexisting condition (*e.g.*, asthma).[33]

The principle of individual risk of occupational illness may be expressed algebraically as follows: Genetic factors (G) in combination with environmental factors (E) cause disease (D).

$$G + E = D$$

As discussed earlier, there are numerous environmental factors, but they may be divided into nonoccupational (including prior occupational) (N) and occupational (O) factors.

$$G + (N + O) = D$$

Because an individual brings to the workplace a composite set of genetic and environmental predisposing characteristics, the current workplace exposure may be isolated in the equation.

$$(G + N) + O = D$$

In this formulation, $(G + N)$ is equal to an individual's predisposition to occupational disease caused by toxic substances (O) in the workplace. These factors $(G + N)$ determine susceptibility or resistance. The combination of various factors, of course, may result in synergistic rather than mere additive effects.

3.3   Increased Risk Based on Innate Characteristics

An individual may be at an increased risk of developing an occupational illness because of inherited or life-cycle factors unrelated to behavioral or environmental influences. These innate factors include age, race, ethnicity, and familial health history.

A.   Age

The incidence of cancer increases with age.[34] One possible explanation is that from puberty onward the functioning of the body's cell-mediated immunity progressively deteriorates. Therefore, older workers with a degenerative cell-mediated immunologic capacity may be sensitive to industrial carcinogens.[35] Some epidemiological studies have found that workers exposed to carcinogens at a later age are more likely to develop cancer than younger workers who are exposed at the same levels for the same length of time.[36]

Degenerative changes in other organ systems also may predispose older workers to harmful effects of toxic exposures. For example, after the age of 50 renal fluoride clearance decreases, meaning that higher fluoride levels may be retained by the body. Thus, workers over 50 may be at increased risk from fluoride exposure.[37]

B.   Race and Ethnicity

There are two main ways in which race and ethnicity may affect susceptibility to illness. First, there are certain innate racial characteristics possessed by all or substantially all members of the race. Second, certain genetic markers of susceptibility to illness are found with much greater frequency in certain racial or ethnic groups.[38]

The most obvious racial difference is skin color. Although there is not full agreement on the clinical explanation, it is known that dark skin is more effective in preventing penetration of ultraviolet radiation.[39] Several population studies have confirmed that the incidence of malignant melanoma is much higher among Caucasians than non-Caucasians.[40]

Another racial difference involves lung capacity The normal lung volumes (vital capacity and forced expiratory volume) for blacks are lower, relative to body size, than for whites.[41] This is because, generally speaking, blacks have smaller thoraxes relative to total body weight. Among whites, individuals with low vital capacities have been found to have increased rates of cardiovascular disease.[42] Blacks, however, appear to have lower morbidity and mortality rates due to chronic obstructive pulmonary disease, chronic bronchitis, and emphysema than comparable white populations.[43] Thus, there is no evidence from which to base interracial associations between lung volume and health status. Simply to account for the thorax size differential, however, OSHA's cotton dust standard provides that pulmonary function tests "for blacks shall be multiplied by 0.85 to adjust for ethnic differences."[44]

The second main way in which race and ethnicity may influence susceptibility involves genetic markers prevalent to much greater degrees in certain racial and ethnic groups than in others. Many of the biochemical genetic traits discussed in the next chapter have been found with greater frequency in certain populations. Interestingly, virtually all racial and ethnic groups are predisposed to some illness based on one or more genetic traits. A more detailed treatment of the racial and ethnic effects of medical screening is contained in Chapter 6.

C.   Familial Health History

It has long been known that the incidence of cancer and other diseases in certain families is unusually high, even adjusting for other variables.[45] In general, the risk of the same neoplasm developing in a close relative of a cancer patient is about two[46] or three[47] times greater than would be expected in the general population. Some particular cancers, such as breast cancer and colorectal cancer, are even more likely to exhibit this tendency.[48]

A study of Egyptian workers exposed to silica dust revealed another type of familial association, where cancer risk was related to the degree of consanguinity of the individual's parents. In the region studied there was a high frequency of marriages between blood relatives. As shown in Table 3-1, Dr. Madbuli Noweir and his associates found that the silicosis risks were highest in workers whose parents were cousins compared to workers whose parents were more distant relatives or not related at all.[49]

Table 3-1.   Variation in Risk of Silicosis According to Degree of Consanguinity of Parents

Parents' Relationship	Prevalence of Silicosis (%)	Average Duration of Exposure (years)
Cousins	52.9	15.6
Far relatives	36.1	14.7
No relation	40.0	16.6

Source: Noweir, Moselhi, & Amine, *Role of Family Susceptibility, Occupational and Family Histories and Individuals' Blood Groups in the Development of Silicosis*, 37 Brit. J. Indus. Med. 399, 402 (1980). Reprinted by permission.

The Egyptian study also focused on the risks of workers whose fathers had been employed at the same plant. Many of the fathers who had worked there started before they married. The study found that for workers with less than 20 years of service there was no significant variation in risk based on paternal exposure (see Table 3-2). Workers with 20 or more years at the plant, however, had only half the risk of silicosis. The reasons for this are unknown.

Although familial risk is an area with relatively little data, more information obviously looms on the horizon. OSHA's health standards already require family histories. Dr. Jeanne Stellman has recently cautioned, however, about some of the dangers of indiscriminate uses of family histories.

> It does not take a sociologist to know that the parents of coke oven workers were probably not surgeons and corporate executives, but were probably coke oven workers or similar people themselves.
> Family history, which do[es] not take into account the exposures of the family, will lead us down another primrose path of dalliance towards selecting out workers on a prejudicial basis based on their socioeconomic status.[50]

Table 3–2.   Risk of Silicosis According to Fathers'
History of Exposure to Silica Dust at
Same Plant

Duration of Subjects' Exposure (years)	Father of Subject Exposed (%)	Father of Subject Not Exposed (%)
< 20	40.0	43.4
20 +	24.6	55.2

Source: Adapted from Noweir, Moselhi, & Amine,
*Role of Family Susceptibility, Occupational and Family Histories
and Individuals' Blood Groups in the Development of Silicosis*, 37
Brit. J. Indus. Med. 399, 403 (1980). Reprinted by permission.

3.4   Increased Risk Based on Behavioral and Environmental Factors

A.   Geography

Where a person lives has been shown to have a bearing on the
statistical likelihood of contracting disease. Studies of cancer incidence have identified both natural and man-made causes. For example, malignant melanoma, caused by ultraviolet radiation, increases
with decreasing latitude (in North America) and increases with increasing altitude.[51] Urban and industrialized areas, particularly
areas where there are petrochemical, metal mining, smelting, or asbestos plants, have much higher rates of cancer.[52] These findings are
probably caused by air and water pollution and cigarette smoking,
rather than just by occupational exposures.[53]

At least theoretically, a new employee who grew up in New Jersey (the state with the highest cancer rate) would be more likely to
develop bladder cancer than an employee who grew up in a low-can-
cer-rate state such as Kentucky or Utah.[54] Arguably, this individual's prior predisposition would be most aggravated by occupational
exposures. Even if it were not, an employer might fear that such an
employee might assert that any subsequent cancer was occupationally related. Could such a hypothesis lead an employer whose employees were exposed to benzidine (which has an average latency period of 16 years) or some other bladder-cancer-causing substance to
refuse to hire applicants who grew up in New Jersey, Cincinnati,
New Orleans, or other high-cancer-rate areas? Such a prospect,
while concededly remote at this time, is certainly sobering, and with

more sophisticated epidemiological data being generated all the time, similar screening measures are not totally inconceivable.

B. Diet

The relationship between diet and the etiology of various diseases, particularly cancer, has received widespread attention. It has been estimated that altering dietary practices may reduce cancer by as much as 35%.[55] Cancer risk may be reduced by eliminating the consumption of food containing powerful carcinogens like aflatoxins, nitrosamines, and polycyclic aromatic hydrocarbons.[56] Food dyes, chemical fertilizers and pesticides, artificial sweeteners, salt, and other food additives also may increase cancer risk.[57] Although the data are less clear, some studies have found that persons with high fat, high cholesterol, low-fiber diets seem more at risk of certain cancers;[58] persons with diets containing fresh fruits and vegetables, vitamins, and nutrients seem less at risk of certain cancers.[59]

There has been little research on the associations between diet and occupational disease.[60] According to one theory, workers exposed to vinyl chloride can protect themselves by eating onions, garlic, Brussels sprouts, cabbage, broccoli, and turnips.[61] Some effects of diet, however, are better documented. For example, it has been known for some time that G-6-PD deficiency, which some experts believe to be correlated with sensitivity to certain industrial chemicals,[62] induces hemolytic anemia when people with the Mediteranean variant of the trait eat or breathe the pollen of fava beans.[63]

Some research has been undertaken to discover if low levels of dietary nutrients may cause various toxic agents to have an enhanced toxicity, mutagenicity, or carcinogenicity. Table 3–3 lists some of these suspected nutrient-toxin associations.

C. Tobacco

According to the surgeon general, "Cigarette smoking is clearly the largest single preventable cause of illness and premature death in the United States."[64] It is associated with heart and blood vessel diseases; chronic bronchitis and emphysema; cancers of the lung, larynx, pharynx, oral cavity, esophagus, pancreas, and urinary bladder; and with other ailments ranging from minor respiratory infections to stomach ulcers.[65] Smoking during pregnancy also increases the risk of complications of pregnancy and retardation of fetal growth.[66] An estimated 320,000 premature deaths each year are at-

Table 3-3.   Nutrition Levels and the Toxicity, Mutagenicity, and Carcinogenicity of Toxic Substances

Dietary Deficiency	Enhanced Toxicity, Mutagenicity, and/or Carcinogenicity
Calcium	Cadmium
	Lead
Iron	Cadmium
	Lead
	Manganese
	Plutonium
	Dimethylhydrazine
Selenium	Cadmium
	Lead
	Mercury
	Silver
	Benzene
	Ozone
	PCBs
Zinc	Cadmium
	Copper
	Lead
	Mercury
	Ethanol
	Nitrosamines
Protein	Arsenic
	Cobalt
	Radiation
	Ethanol
	Aflatoxin
	DNT
	Pesticides
Amino acids (various)	Cyanide
	Lead
	Cobalt
	Copper
	Chloroform
	Ethanol
	Methyl chloride
	Nicotine
	TNT

Source: Adapted from E. Calabrese, Nutrition and Environmental Health, vol. 2, at 61, 116, 172, 200, 294, 361 (1981).
Copyright ©1981 by John Wiley & Sons, Inc. Reprinted by
permission.

tributable to smoking, and 10 million Americans suffer from debilitating diseases caused by smoking.[67] The number of cigarettes smoked per day, the degree of inhalation, and the age at which the individual began smoking are important factors in the mortality rates of smokers.[68]

Cigarette smoking has been demonstrated to have important effects on the health of workers exposed to toxic substances. The National Institute for Occupational Safety and Health (NIOSH) has identified six mechanisms by which smoking interacts with occupational exposures.[69] First, certain toxic agents in the workplace, such as carbon monoxide and cadmium, are also present in tobacco or smoke, thereby increasing the exposures. Second, workplace chemicals may be pyrolyzed into more harmful agents, because the temperature of a burning cigarette reaches 1,600 degrees Fahrenheit. Third, tobacco products serve as vectors by becoming contaminated with workplace agents like lead and pesticides, which facilitates entry by inhalation, ingestion, or skin absorption. Fourth, there may be additive effects from smoking and exposures to substances such as chlorine, cotton dust, and coal dust. Fifth, the effects may be synergistic between smoking and asbestos, gold mine, and rubber industry exposures. Sixth, smoking increases accident rates through loss of attention, preoccupation of the hand, irritation of the eyes, coughing, and fires.

Risks associated with pipe and cigar smoking, as well as tobacco chewing and snuff, also have been noted but are not nearly as great, nor is their use as prevalent as cigarette smoking.[70] "Involuntary" smoking also creates hazards in the workplace to nonsmokers.[71]

There has been a great deal of study of the effects of cigarette smoking on asbestos workers.[72] According to a recent report, for example, smoking increased the death rate from lung cancer for both "blue-collar" and asbestos workers by 10 times (see Table 3–4). Asbestos workers had a five-fold higher death rate from lung cancer than other "blue-collar" workers. Thus, smoking asbestos workers had a death rate 50 times higher than nonsmoking "blue-collar" workers.[73]

Smoking obviously greatly increases the mortality rate for workers not exposed to asbestos, and only some of the asbestos-associated diseases are influenced by smoking. Asbestos and cancer of the lung, esophagus, larynx, buccal cavity, and pharynx are influenced by smoking. Pleural mesothelioma, peritoneal mesothelioma, and cancer of the stomach, colon-rectum, and kidney are not influenced by smoking.[74]

Table 3-4. Asbestos and Cigarette Smoking: Death Rate
            From Lung Cancer

	No Smoking	Smoking
"Blue-collar" working men	11.3	122.6
Asbestos workers	58.4	601.6

Source: I. Selikoff, Disability Compensation for Asbestos-Related
Disease in the United States 333, 335 (1982) (report to U.S. Department
of Labor).
Note: Figures are per 100,000 man-years, standardized for age.

Smoking also increases the health risks from exposure to other
substances. Table 3-5, based on a British study of cotton textile
workers, indicates that cigarette smoking increased the risk of developing byssinosis.

Although smokers are at an increased risk of byssinosis, the attributable risk is much less than that of asbestos workers who smoke.
Some employers in both industries have begun to refuse to hire
smokers. These tables suggest a sounder scientific basis for such
action in the asbestos industry.

Finally, cigarette smokers are exposed to pathogenic risks similar to individuals with serum alpha$_1$ antitrypsin (SAT) deficiency
(discussed in section 4.2). Cigarette smoke oxidizes the SAT,
thereby deactivating this important protein which protects the lung
from proteolytic enzymes. Therefore, even though smokers usually
have normal levels of SAT, the SAT is not functioning. The result is
often nonspecific airways disease, or emphysema.

Table 3-5. Prevalence Rates of Byssinosis (All
            Grades) by Smoking Status and
            Sex

	Smokers (%)	Non-Smokers and Ex-Smokers (%)
Men	44.9	32.0
Women	29.0	20.2

Source: Berry, Molyneax, & Tombleson, *Relationships Between Dust Levels and Byssinosis and Bronchitis in
Lancashire Cotton Mills*, 31 Brit. J. Indus. Med. 18, 22
(1974). Reprinted by permission.
Note: Rates are standardized for dust concentration and length of exposure. Includes grades ½, I, and
II of byssinosis.

D. Alcohol

The consumption of alcoholic beverages is known to cause cirrhosis and other diseases. It is less clear, however, whether alcohol causes cancer.[75] Most of the research suggests that alcohol increases cancer risk by acting as a co-carcinogen, enhancing the carcinogenic effect of other agents.[76] Cancer of the mouth, throat, esophagus, larynx, and liver have been associated with alcohol consumption.[77] There is also some evidence of increased risk of cancer of the stomach, rectum, prostate, pancreas, large intestine, lung, kidney, bladder, and breast.[78]

There has been little research on the effects of alcohol consumption on persons with exposures to industrial toxins. One *in vitro* study, however, found that alcohol increased the carcinogenic effects of vinyl chloride vapors.[79] Other synergistic effects have been observed with alcohol and dimethylformamide (DMF),[80] ethylene dibromide (EDB),[81] and carbon tetrachloride.[82]

E. Medical Drugs and Radiation

A number of drugs have been associated with cancer and other diseases in humans.[83] The synthetic estrogen diethylstilbestrol (DES), has been found to cause cancer both in the women who took DES and in their offspring about 20 years later.[84] Of the most widely taken drugs, oral contraceptives have been the subjects of some of the most detailed studies. Although the evidence is inconclusive, there are studies associating oral contraceptives with liver and breast cancer.[85] Little information is available on the effects of medical drugs on occupational exposures, but there is every reason to believe that additional information looms on the horizon. For example, the drug phenobarbital may alter the hepatic enzyme balance, thereby altering the metabolism of carcinogenic polycyclic aromatic hydrocarbons.[86] OSHA's carcinogen standards also require that the examining physician inquire into whether the worker is taking steroids or cytotoxic agents, which have been shown to cause bladder and liver cancer.[87]

Workers who are taking various kinds of medication may be at increased risk when they are exposed to topical sensitizing agents in the workplace. Table 3–6 indicates the combinations of therapeutic drugs and workplace substances that may combine to produce an inordinate response in the worker.

Table 3–6.   Topical Sensitizers and Immunochemically Related Drugs That Can Cause an Eruption Upon Systemic Administration

Topical Sensitizers	Immunochemically Related Drugs
Hydrazine hydrobromide	Isoniazid, Apresoline, Nardil
Para-amino compounds	Para-aminobenzoic acid (PABA) and related local anesthetics (Benzocaine, Procaine)
	Azo dyes in foods and drugs
	Dymelor, Orinase, Diabinese, Sulfonamides
	Diuril, Hydrodiuril, Saluron, Renese
	Para-aminosalicylic acid (PAS)
Neomycin sulfate	Streptomycin, Kanamycin
Resorcin	Hexylresorcinal (Crystoids, Caprokol)
Organic and inorganic mercurials	Mercurial diuretics
Metallic mercury	Calomel
Cobalt	Vitamin B_{12}
Thiamine	Coenzyme B (cocarboxylase)
Ethylenediamine hydrochloride	Aminophylline, Antistine, Phenergan, Pyribenzamine, Synopen, Neohetiamine
Formaldehyde	Urotropin, Maldelamine, Urised
Thiram and disulfiram	Antabuse
Halogenated hydroxyquinolines	Vioform, Diodoquin
Chlorobutanol	Chloral Hydrate
Iodine	Iodides, iodinated organic compounds
Benadryl	Dramamine

Source: Shupack, *The Skin as a Target Organ for Systemic Agents*, in Cutaneous Toxicity: Proceedings of the Third Conference on Cutaneous Toxicity, Washington, D.C., May 16–18, 1976, at 43 (V. Drill & P. Lazar eds. 1977), based on Fisher, *Systemic Eczematous Contact-Type Dermatitis*, in Contact Dermatitis 293–305 (1973). Reprinted by permission.

Finally, there is increasing concern about the amount of unnecessary and unproductive medical and dental x-rays used in the United States.[88] Ionizing radiation has been demonstrated to cause leukemia, birth defects, lung cancer, liver cancer, bone cancer, sterility, and other severe health problems.[89] Because radiation exposure is cumulative over one's lifetime, excessive nonoccupational irradiation could predispose individuals working with radiation to illness. A variety of job classifications, including radiation workers, uranium miners, and television tube makers, involve exposure to radiation.[90] Smoking increases the risk factor.[91]

F.   Recreation and Hobbies

An individual may become predisposed to occupational illness as a result of nonoccupational exposures to the same substances during recreation and hobbies. For example, riding a motorcycle or listening to loud music could involve excess levels of noise. Gardening could expose the individual to dangerous pesticides. Solvents containing benzene are sometimes used in furniture refinishing and paint stripping. There is exposure to lead in ceramics, pottery, hunting, and stained glass window making. Other hazards include mercury in some paints, methylene chloride in paint stripping, and metal fumes in welding.[92] Consequently, it is common for physicians to ask about recreation and hobbies during preemployment medical examinations or for this information to be requested on a medical questionnaire.

G.   Life-Style

A variety of miscellaneous "life-style" factors may influence an individual's occupational health risk. For example, contact lens wearers are more sensitive to formaldehyde exposure. Sleeping habits,[93] cosmetics,[94] and food containers[95] are other factors to consider. There is also some evidence that persons in groups already identified as high-risk can further increase their risk of illness through life-style factors. For example, persons with G-6-PD deficiency may be at increased risk by drinking chlorinated water, having copper plumbing,[96] or living in urban areas where there are high levels of ozone.[97]

One life-style factor of current concern involves personal grooming, specifically, facial hair. Many employees work in environments where respirators are required. The effectiveness (or protection factor) of tight-fitting respirators (both negative pressure and positive pressure) is greatly dependent on a proper seal. It is well documented that it is much more difficult to achieve an adequate seal when the wearer has a beard.[98] Unusual facial configuration, scars, complexion problems, and perspiration also can prevent a proper respirator seal. In fact, OSHA's respirator standard provides:

> Respirators shall not be worn when conditions prevent a good face seal. Such conditions may be a growth of beard, sideburns, a skull cap that projects under the facepiece, or temple pieces on glasses. Also, the absence of one or both dentures can seriously affect the fit of a facepiece.[99]

Because of the seal problem, many companies have adopted "no beard" rules. The validity of these rules is discussed in section 11.3. Loose-fitting respirators (canopy-type positive pressure respirators and complete air supply suits) do not depend on a face-respirator seal and therefore are effective for persons with beards; however, they are cumbersome and much more expensive.

H. Psychological Factors

An individual's psychological makeup may play an important part in the individual's ability to function in a particular job. For example, a person with acrophobia would be a poor steeplejack, a person with hydrophobia would be a poor sailor, and a person with claustrophobia would be a poor coal miner. Other examples of individuals being psychologically unsuited for a particular job are less obvious and more difficult to detect, but they might be important in determining an increased risk of occupational illness. Three such examples are given below.

First, there is increasing evidence that an individual's overall mental state of health may be an important factor in the development of diseases like coronary heart disease and cancer.[100] While there are no studies on the precise question of whether psychologically disturbed persons are more prone to occupationally related diseases, such a finding is theoretically possible.

Second, many kinds of stresses are generated by the occupational environment itself. Poor working conditions, shift work, and physical danger are some of the factors leading to occupational stress.[101] Recent studies have focused on personality factors which would predispose individuals to diseases, such as coronary heart disease, when confronted with workplace stress.[102] Personality and behavioral patterns, therefore, might be used to keep high-risk persons out of stressful jobs.[103]

Third, the wearing of a respirator is an essential part of many occupations including mining and fire fighting. Some individuals exposed to stressful conditions in the workplace, including elevated carbon dioxide, heat, and altitude, react in a panic-like manner known as hyperventilation syndrome.[104] The symptoms of hyperventilation syndrome range from breathlessness and trembling to convulsions,[105] and the individual is in danger from the external environment as well as his or her own physiological reaction. There is evidence that hyperventilation syndrome is associated with certain personality types detectable by various tests.[106]

These three examples illustrate some of the ways in which psychological and personality factors may contribute to an increased risk of occupational illness. It is an area in which much research remains to be done.

I. Multiple Factors

A number of individual behavioral and environmental factors may lead to an increased risk of occupational illness. Different factors, however, may be identified as increasing the same risk, either by additive or synergistic effects. Dr. Bernice Cohen of Johns Hopkins University studied the risk factors for chronic obstructive pulmonary disease (COPD). As the measure of airways obstruction (incipient, potential, or actual COPD), she used $FEV_1\%$, the subject's forced expiratory volume in one second (FEV_1) expressed as a percentage of forced vital capacity (FVC). An abbreviated version of her findings appears in Table 3–7.

The data demonstrate that COPD risk increases with age and with classification in the following categories: male, cigarette smoker, low socioeconomic level, SAT deficiency, close relative of someone with lung problems, and coffee drinker. Even more intriguing than these figures, however, is her hypothesis that pulmonary impairment may be a risk factor for a variety of other diseases.

> The stagnation of inhaled substances in the lungs resulting from pulmonary impairment would increase the likelihood that excessive quantities of inhaled deleterious agents from extrinsic sources would enter the circulation. Meanwhile, toxic metabolites and other wastes of intrinsic origin in the blood, that are usually removed or metabolized by the lungs, would not be effectively eliminated from the circulation, in the presence of impaired lung function. This excessive buildup of harmful agents from both external and internal sources could then lead to vascular damage reflected in the coronary, cerebral, or peripheral vessels and in the clinical disorders associated with that damage.
>
> Furthermore, the toxic waste burden of the circulation secondary to pulmonary inadequacy, would be a potential hazard to all the organs and tissues of the body served by the blood and lymph vessels. Neoplasms of the bladder, prostate, uterus, and gastrointestinal tract, as well as of the respiratory tract; lymphomas; ulcers of the stomach and duodenum; and cirrhosis of the liver are but a few of the conditions found to be more frequent in cigarette smokers, thus likely involving impaired pulmonary function. Accordingly, these and other disorders are apt to result from pulmonary dysfunction irrespective of whether the impairment was originally caused by environmental exposures, genetic factors, or combinations thereof.[107]

3.5 Increased Risk Based on Nonoccupational Health Factors

An important factor in determining susceptibility to occupational illness is the individual's present state of health and general

Table 3-7.   Risk Factors and Adjusted FEV$_1$% in Adults Excluding Patients (each adjusted for all other variables)

Category	Mean FEV$_1$%	Rate of FEV Impairment per 100 Subjects[a]
Age		
20–29	82.4	3.7
30–39	79.4	4.3
40–49	75.8	12.0
50–59	73.6	21.4
60 +	71.2	25.9
Sex		
Male	75.4	16.1
Female	77.6	10.6
Cigarette Smoking		
2 + packs/day	74.0	21.8
1–2 packs/day	74.9	19.4
Never	78.9	7.0
Others	76.3	13.0
Socioeconomic Status		
Lowest fifth	75.9	17.3
Highest fifth	78.0	7.5
Other and unclassified	76.4	13.2
SAT (Pi) (Protease inhibitor)		
Homozygotes & heterozygotes		
Alpha Z (Z + Z carriers)	74.7	18.4
Other—variant	76.6	14.5
Alpha M (normal)	76.2	15.5
Non-alpha M	76.8	12.1
Familial		
1° relatives of COPD patients	74.7	19.0
1° relatives of lung cancer patients	74.9	24.1
1° relatives of nonpulmonary patients	76.4	13.0
Other and unclassified	77.0	11.7
Coffee		
3 + cups per day	75.9	15.5
None	77.5	10.8
Other and unknown	76.6	12.8

Source: Adapted from Cohen, *Chronic Obstructive Pulmonary Disease: A Challenge in Genetic Epidemiology*, 112 Am. J. Epidemiology 274, 278–79 (1980). Reprinted by permission. A detailed description of the study methodology is contained in Cohen et al., *A Genetic-Epidemiologic Study of Chronic Obstructive Pulmonary Disease*, 137 Johns Hopkins Med. J. 95 (1975).
   [a] FEV impairment is defined as FEV$_1$ less than 68% of FVC.

physical condition. This may involve inborn (*e.g.*, height, shape of spine) and acquired (*e.g.*, prior nonoccupational illness) conditions. For example, one study found that individuals with Type A blood have a lower risk of silicosis.[108] As with other indices of susceptibility, the predictive value of each of the nonoccupational health considerations varies greatly.

A. *Musculoskeletal*

Analysis of an individual's musculoskeletal system has been used in some industries in attempting to identify those asymptomatic individuals who are predisposed to back injuries from jobs requiring manual lifting and other forms of exertion. There is little scientific basis, however, for some of the commonly used skeletal screening techniques.

Body weight and stature are two anthropometric attributes used to predict an individual's risk of injury during manual materials handling. There have been a number of studies and a number of theories, but they have not been able to support the notion that either fat or thin or tall or short people are at a significantly higher risk of low-back injury.[109] NIOSH has concluded that "[i]n brief, the selection of people for materials-handling jobs based on their anthropometry is not well justified in terms of reducing low-back pain incidence rates."[110]

Radiological screening, specifically the low-back x-ray, is the most prevalent form of skeletal analysis for susceptibility to future back injury. Although there are no precise figures available, it has been estimated that one million preemployment low-back x-rays are given each year.[111] Despite such widespread use, the low-back x-ray has been discredited in the scientific literature as a basis for employment screening.[112] The test is simply inaccurate and screens out too many people who are healthy and will never suffer from back injury[113] while failing to detect those presymptomatic persons who are actually at risk.[114] Moreover, the x-rays themselves are expensive[115] and present hazards from radiation exposure. Gonadal shielding often is neglected for men and is difficult to accomplish for women. There is also the risk of fetal irradiation (which doubles the risk of childhood leukemia) during the early stages of an unsuspected pregnancy.[116]

The low predictive values and potential dangers of low-back x-rays led the AOMA to conclude that "lumbar spine x-ray examinations should not be used as a screening procedure for back problems, but rather as a special diagnosis procedure available to the physician on appropriate indications for study."[117] A more detailed discussion of low-back x-rays appears in section 3.7.

Other forms of musculoskeletal analyses involve strength testing,[118] aerobic capacity testing,[119] and work-motion profiles.[120] Although these tests eventually may be validated, they still are considered experimental.[121]

B. Prior Illness

An individual's prior nonoccupational illness may establish an increased risk of or cause an earlier expression of occupational disease when the individual is exposed to toxic substances or other workplace hazards. Although relatively few studies have been done on the combined effects of prior illness and toxic exposures, medical recommendations are frequently made on the assumption that the two risk factors have an additive effect.[122]

One example of prior illness increasing an individual's sensitivity to workplace toxins involves individuals with a history of ischemic heart disease, such as angina pectoris and myocardial infarction. While the physiological mechanisms of disease causation may vary with the substance, these individuals have an increased risk of serious cardiovascular illness when exposed to dinitrotoluene,[123] carbon dioxide,[124] methylene chloride,[125] nitroglycerine,[126] and carbon disulphide.[127]

Illnesses of other organ systems also may create additional workplace risk factors. The use of ototoxic drugs or a congenital hearing loss makes an individual more susceptible to occupational noise exposure.[128] A history of Raynaud's disease would predispose a worker exposed to segmental vibration, such as a chain saw operator, to "white finger" syndrome.[129] A diabetic with a subclinical peripheral neuropathy would be sensitive to neurotoxic chemicals, such as tricresyl ortho-isomer (TOCP),[130] arsenic,[131] and lead.[132]

C. Clinical Findings

A physical examination often cannot give an etiologic diagnosis of a medical condition, except for gross organ failure or dysfunction, such as yellow jaundice, an abdominal mass, or cyanosis. The exact etiology may require confirmatory biochemical or microscopic analyses.[133] Dermatologic and musculoskeletal examinations, however, are exceptions to the general rule and are quite useful in assessing a medical condition.[134] Thus, individuals who are found to have eczema, psoriasis, or neurodermatitis on physical assessment are known to have lost some of their natural protective skin barrier.[135] When they are exposed to irritant chemicals, such as solvents, acids, and alkalis, their dermatitic response will frequently be more rapid and severe.[136]

3.6   Increased Risk Based on Occupational Health Factors

As discussed in the preceding chapter, an occupational medical history or preemployment medical questionnaire will customarily ask about prior occupational exposures. This information can be used to identify the cause of present symptoms and to predict the risk from future exposures.

A worker's prior occupational exposures may have a significant effect on his or her susceptibility to occupational disease based on further occupational exposures. Many forms of occupational cancer are characterized by long latency periods—as long as 35 years—before the disease is clinically evident.[137] The leading example would be exposure to asbestos. Consequently, an individual with a history of previous toxic exposures may be considered by employers to be a bad risk.

It is also possible that a prior exposure to a carcinogen may combine with a later exposure (even to a different agent) to produce an effect that neither alone would have produced. For example, the incidence of leukemia among radiation-exposed survivors at Hiroshima and Nagasaki has been shown to be increased where there was occupational exposure to benzene years after the radiation exposure.[138]

Exposure to different toxic substances at the same time is common in many industrial settings. The physiological effects of combined exposures may, in some instances, be greater than simply an additive effect of the single agents alone.[139] Synergistic relationships have been observed in several commonly occurring exposures. The relationship between smoking and asbestos already has been discussed. In addition, ethanol combined with trichloroethylene has been found to enhance acute central nervous system effects and to increase the likelihood of chronic liver disease and liver cancer.[140] Sulfur dioxide and sodium chloride aerosol in a high humidity environment may produce increased pulmonary resistance in workers where either component alone will not.[141] In rare cases, an antagonistic reaction may occur in which the effect actually will be less severe than that observed with a single exposure.[142]

Hypersensitivity is a special condition of certain persons whose bodies react often to relatively low levels of a foreign agent in a pathological process induced by immune responses. For an agent to produce a sensitivity reaction an individual must have had a prior sensitizing exposure to the same agent. Therefore, the process of sensitization to industrial chemicals usually is not initiated until after the individual is employed and exposed to the work environment.

An individual who is hypersensitive to a particular substance may suffer adverse reactions at levels of exposures far below those which the average person tolerates without ill effect. A related condition, hyperreactivity, involves a greater reaction than would be expected. Both of these conditions are considered as types of hyperresponsiveness.[143] Frequently, hypersensitive individuals are also hyperreactive. Clinical symptoms resulting from a sensitivity reaction range from mild skin irritations to anaphylactic shock and even death. A number of common industrial agents are potential sensitizers, including formaldehyde, cotton dust, nickel, and epoxy resins.[144]

Skin reactions are a common occupational problem. Dermatitis accounts for one half of all reported cases of occupational disease,[145] and it is estimated that 20% of occupational dermatitis is caused by a hypersensitive reaction to allergenic materials.[146] Hypersensitivity responses of the respiratory system, however, are of particular concern because these may be life-threatening. An example of a potentially serious respiratory sensitizer is toluene diisocyanate (TDI).

TDI is a liquid used in the manufacture of polyurethane. An estimated 50,000 to 100,000 workers in the United States are exposed to TDI, and as many as five percent develop adverse respiratory symptoms.[147] The following four patterns of respiratory response may occur: (1) chemical bronchitis; (2) an asthma-like condition occurring in sensitized workers at low exposure levels; (3) an acute decrease in ventilatory capacity in one work shift; and (4) a chronic decrease in pulmonary function in those with prolonged exposure.[148] In some instances, a worker with minimal or no respiratory symptoms for several weeks at a low level of exposure may suddenly develop an acute asthmatic attack. Once a person is sensitized to TDI, any further exposure may be extremely dangerous, as even an exposure well below the recommended standard can produce a severe asthmatic attack and may cause death. Although the acute effects may be reversible, continued exposure of affected workers can result in chronic broncho-pulmonary problems.[149]

Efforts are being made to develop methods for detecting hypersensitivity to isocyanates before exposure, but the tests are still in the developmental stage.[150] As yet few clear linear correlations have been found between concentrations of the sensitizing agent and the percentage of the population sensitized. Despite considerable controversy over the predictive value of existing tests, some companies already have begun using immunologic screening to detect individuals hypersensitive to isocyanates.[151]

3.7   Biostatistical Limitations on Predictive Medical Screening

Despite their widespread use, preemployment medical examinations have been criticized as being inaccurate in attempting to screen for high-risk workers. "The routine physical examination itself has serious shortcomings even if supplemented to absurd lengths by mass-screening laboratory and x-ray procedures of little value and some potential hazard."[152] Indeed, more than 20 years ago Dr. Thrift G. Hanks, then corporate director of health and safety for Boeing Company, suggested a more practical reason why corporate medical personnel favor the use of physical examinations:

> To be frank, if one were suddenly to remove physical examinations, a considerable number of physicians working in or for industry would have no reason for being. This, I believe, is why some industrial physicians are fearful of any argument against physical examinations. It attacks their security rather than their principles.[153]

Several studies have confirmed that employee selection procedures that did not use preemployment physical examinations were about as accurate in identifying high-risk workers.[154] Nevertheless, it is unlikely that employer practices will be changed in the near future.[155] Some specific OSHA standards mandate preplacement examinations and there is continued pressure from insurers and management to screen out workers who are likely to become ill. Most occupational physicians, however, probably would agree with Dr. Irving Tabershaw that the assessment of risk to a given applicant or employee, even by the most experienced physician, is "no more than an educated guess."[156]

The purpose of medical screening and laboratory testing procedures is to identify persons who are at risk of disease and those who are not. Because the characterization of a person as being at risk may have important consequences, it is essential that the test being used is

accurate. There is considerable evidence that medical testing procedures are not nearly as accurate as they are commonly thought to be.

The starting point for analyzing the accuracy of a test is its sensitivity and specificity. The sensitivity of a test is a measure of the
test's accuracy in correctly identifying persons with the tested-for
condition. It is the percent of persons with the condition who have a
positive test, or:

$$\frac{\text{true positives}}{\text{true positives} + \text{false negatives}} \times 100\%$$

Therefore, if 100 persons have a condition and the test is able to identify 90 of them, the test would be 90% sensitive.

The specificity of a test is a measure of the test's accuracy in
correctly identifying persons free of a condition. It is the percent of
persons free of the condition who have a negative test, or:

$$\frac{\text{true negatives}}{\text{true negatives} + \text{false positives}} \times 100\%$$

Therefore, if 100 persons are free of a condition and the test is able to
identify 90 of them, the test would be 90% specific.

The predictive value (positive) of a test is the value of a positive
test result in predicting the presence of the condition. It is the percent
of those persons with a positive test who really have the condition, or:

$$\frac{\text{true positives}}{\text{true positives} + \text{false positives}} \times 100\%$$

In other words, when a test is positive, the predictive value represents the likelihood that the condition is actually present.

One of the least accurate tests in widespread use is the low-back
x-ray, which is used to predict future low-back problems. Tables
3–8, 3–9, and 3–10, representing the test results of 1,000 hypothetical workers, are taken from a study by Rockey, Fantel, and
Omenn.[157] They are based on the assumptions that low-back x-rays
are 56% sensitive and 78% specific for detecting future low-back
pain and that 60% of all workers will have low-back pain during
their work life.

The predictive value of a positive low-back x-ray in estimating future low-back pain is 336/424 (79%). Even with a reasonable predictive value, of the 424 persons denied jobs, 88 (21%) will never have low-back pain.

Table 3–9 derives from the fact that of all workers who have low-back pain, only half will lose time from work.

The predictive value of a positive low-back x-ray in estimating future lost work time is 168/424 (40%). Of the 424 persons denied jobs, 256 (60%) would not lose time from work.

Table 3–10 derives from the fact that only 5% to 20% of all workers who miss time from work will require disc surgery, resulting in an overall prevalence rate of 1.5% to 6%. Table 3–10 uses the 1.5% estimate.

Assuming the 1.5% rate of surgery, the predictive value of a positive x-ray is 8.4/424 (2%). Of the 424 persons denied employment, 416 (98%) would never require back surgery.

Besides illustrating the inaccuracy of x-ray screening, the preceding tables demonstrate that the predictive value of a test is greatly dependent on the percentage of the entire population with the tested-for condition. This is known as the prevalence of the condition. (By comparison, "incidence" refers to the frequency of a condition occurring within a stated period of time). "Prevalence is probably the most important—but least understood—factor affecting the usefulness of a test result."[158] Even procedures with high degrees of sensitivity and specificity will have relatively low predictive values if the prevalence of the condition is low.

Tables 3–11 and 3–12 assume that a test is both 99% sensitive and 99% specific (higher than virtually any medical tests).

By merely changing the prevalence rate from 10% to 1%, the predictive value decreased from 92% (990/1080) to 50% (99/198).

The preceding tables confirm the lack of scientific credence in mass screening of asymptomatic individuals to detect the presence of a trait or condition with a low prevalence rate. As Galen and Gambino point out, "[i]ndiscriminate use of laboratory tests on subjects selected at random is doomed to failure if the prevalence of the disease is low."[159]

Table 3–13 lists some of the biochemical genetic markers most commonly screened for and the prevalence rates in the highest risk groups.

Even if it were lawful to do so,[160] the selective screening of only the highest risk groups would still be inaccurate because of the low

Table 3-8.   Predictive Value of Low-Back X-Rays in Screening for Future Low-Back Pain

	Will Have Low-Back Pain During Lifetime	Will Not Have Low-Back Pain During Lifetime	Total
Will have positive low-back x-ray exam	336 (true positives)	88 (false positives)	424
Will have negative low-back x-ray exam	264 (false negatives)	312 (true negatives)	576
Total	600	400	1,000

Source: Rockey, Fantel, & Omenn, *Discriminatory Aspects of Pre-Employment Screening: Low-Back X-Ray Examinations in the Railroad Industry,* 5 Am. J.L. & Med. 197, 208 (1980). Reprinted by permission.

Table 3-9.   Predictive Value of Low-Back X-Rays in Screening for Future Low-Back Pain Resulting in Lost Time From Work

	Will Have Low-Back Pain and Lose Time From Work	Will Never Lose Time From Work Because of Low-Back Pain	Total
Will have positive low-back x-ray exam	168 (true positives)	256 (false positives)	424
Will have negative low-back x-ray exam	132 (false negatives)	444 (true negatives)	576
Total	300	700	1,000

Source: Rockey, Fantel, & Omenn, *Discriminatory Aspects of Pre-Employment Screening: Low-Back X-Ray Examinations in the Railroad Industry,* 5 Am. J.L. & Med. 197, 209 (1980). Reprinted by permission.

Table 3-10. Predictive Value of Low-Back X-Rays in Screening for Future Disc Surgery

	Will Have Disc Surgery	Will Not Have Disc Surgery	Total
Will have positive low-back x-ray exam	8.4 (true positives)	416 (false positives)	424
Will have negative low-back x-ray exam	6.6 (false negatives)	569 (true negatives)	576
Total	15.0	985	1,000

Source: Rockey, Fantel, & Omenn, Discriminatory Aspects of Pre-Employment Screening: Low-Back X-Ray Examinations in the Railroad Industry, 5 Am. J.L. & Med. 197, 210 (1980). Reprinted by permission.

Table 3-11. Predictive Value of Testing for a Condition With 10% Prevalence

Subjects	Number With Positive Test	Number With Negative Test
1,000 with condition	990	10
9,000 without condition	90	8,910
Total	1,080	8,920

Table 3-12. Predictive Value of Testing for a Condition With 1% Prevalence

Subjects	Number With Positive Test	Number With Negative Test
100 with condition	99	1
9,900 without condition	99	9,801
Total	198	9,802

prevalence rates. Moreover, the predictive value of a test will vary according to the prevalence rate of the class to which the subject belongs. For example, the predictive values of routine blood pressure measurements in screening for hypertension vary by age, race, and sex.[161] Laboratory testing procedures are merely an extension of the physical diagnosis and are only valuable when a history or physical examination suggests the need for additional information.[162]

Table 3-13.   Prevalence of Biochemical Genetic Markers in Certain Racial and Ethnic Groups

Racial/Ethnic Group in America With Highest Prevalence	Prevalence (%)	Condition
American blacks	7–13	sickle cell trait
American black males	11	G-6-PD deficiency
Persons of northern European ancestry	4–9	alpha$_1$ antitrypsin deficiency (heterozygotes)
Persons of Italian, Greek, and Syrian ancestry, and blacks	0.1–8	thalassemia

Source: Adapted from E. Calabrese, Pollutants and High Risk Groups 187–93 (1978). Copyright ©1978 by John Wiley & Sons, Inc. Reprinted by permission.

Other theoretical and practical problems exist that are closely related to the biostatistical limitations of laboratory and similar procedures. For example, it is often difficult to define what is a "normal" test result.[163] Moreover, some laboratory testing procedures are easily botched with slight contamination or technician error. Thus, not only should laboratory tests be ordered with care, they must also be performed and analyzed with care.

Modern occupational medicine seems to favor the selective use of diagnostic procedures. One example is the more conservative approach to the use of chest x-rays. In 1983 the AOMA approved new guidelines for the use of chest x-rays. The guidelines recommend that preplacement chest x-rays should be taken *selectively*, based on the individual's occupational and medical history, clinical examination, and proposed work assignment. Where there is exposure to substances that affect pulmonary function or cause pulmonary disease, chest x-ray surveillance should be performed at appropriate intervals. Periodic chest x-rays, unrelated to job exposure, should not be performed unless an individual's history, physical examination, or specific diagnostic testing points to the need for a chest x-ray.[164]

Chapter 4

GENETIC SCREENING AND MONITORING

4.1 Overview

More than any other form of medical screening, genetic screening has received widespread publicity recently in technical journals and the mass media. The growing interest in and concern about genetic screening is attributable to new technological advances in genetics, cytogenetics, and related disciplines and the likelihood of further discoveries that will permit more accurate risk assessment and early detection of the cellular changes leading to cancer and other diseases. Undoubtedly, the attention given to genetic screening is also due in no small part to the fact that the term "genetic screening" conjures up visions of Huxley and Orwell, as well as the specter of eugenics.

The terms "genetic testing," "genetic screening," and "genetic monitoring" sometimes have been used loosely, and it is important to define each term. "Genetic testing" is a generic term referring to any assessment of heritable traits or genetic material. "Genetic screening" is the one-time testing of individuals to determine whether they have heritable traits that would predispose them to occupational illness. "Genetic monitoring" is the periodic examination of a group of workers to assess whether genetic damage has occurred in certain cells.

In 1963 Dr. Herbert E. Stokinger and John T. Mountain published the first of several articles advocating the use of genetic screening.[1] Three specific tests were proposed to reduce worker exposures to hemolytic chemicals: glucose-6-phosphate dehydrogenase (G-6-PD) testing, glutathione (GSH) instability testing, and methemoglobin reduction testing. Ten years later, Dr. Stokinger and L.D. Scheel published a "consensus report," which they claimed represented national and international opinion on the subject.[2] They com-

52

plained that despite the scientific evidence only three U.S. chemical companies used the tests and only one used them for screening purposes.[3] The "unbelievably bad response" was blamed on the "ultraconservative American physician" who ignored the scientific evidence to avoid any confrontation with labor unions.[4] On the subject of employment discrimination the authors stated that "the tests do not deny employment; they merely orient job placement to the advantage of both the employer and the employed."[5] Employers were encouraged to screen for even more genetic traits: alpha$_1$ antitrypsin deficiency, G-6-PD deficiency, carbon disulfide sensitivity, reagenic antibodies to allergenic chemicals, and sickle cell trait.

In 1978 an article in the *Journal of Occupational Medicine* by Dr. Charles Reinhardt indicated that Du Pont had conducted sickle cell testing of black employees.[6] A series of articles in the *New York Times* in February 1980 called further attention to the issue, but the question still existed as to how widespread the use of these techniques was.

In 1982 the Congressional Office of Technology Assessment (OTA) conducted an anonymous survey of the "Fortune 500" companies, the 50 largest private utilities, and 11 major labor unions.[7] Of the 366 (65.2%) organizations responding, six (1.6%) were currently using biochemical or cytogenetic tests, 17 (4.6%) used the tests in the past 12 years, and 59 (16.1%) said they would consider using the tests in the next five years. Of the specific tests performed, sickle cell testing was the most prevalent, followed by G-6-PD, alpha$_1$ antitrypsin deficiency, unspecified immune system markers, and cytogenetic testing for chromosomal aberrations.

The number of companies either using or expressing an interest in using genetic screening has been termed "surprising,"[8] but, if anything, the survey may have underreported the extent of industry activity in this area. Because of the highly sensitive nature of the issue and the reported attempt of one trade association to discourage corporate participation in the OTA study,[9] it is possible that genetic screening is even more prevalent now than reported and likely to increase in the future.

As discussed earlier, the large companies generally employ the occupational physicians with the most training, and, as a result, the problem of genetic screening may be more acute in medium-sized companies. These companies are large enough to have a variety of serious workplace hazards, but they often do not have adequate occupational safety and health, industrial hygiene, and medical programs. This may be one reason why medium-sized companies have higher injury and illness rates than small or large companies. Consequently, some of these companies may be the most tempted, but the least able, to use extensive medical and genetic screening.

Genetic monitoring techniques are even newer than the genetic screening procedures. They also differ in two other important respects. First, genetic monitoring is performed on previously exposed workers to detect chromosomal or other genetic damage caused by exposure, rather than as a preemployment screen. Second, genetic monitoring has not been shown to have the racial and ethnic effects of the genetic screening tests.

4.2   Biochemical Genetic Screening

A number of inborn errors of metabolism and organ-specific genetic conditions have been associated with an increased risk of illness when the host is exposed to toxic substances or other environmental hazards in the workplace. Some of the most widely recognized biochemical genetic conditions are discussed below.

A.   Sickle Cell

Sickle cell anemia is an inherited blood disorder in which the red blood cells become crescent shaped. This results in a clogging of the blood vessels and an impeding of the proper flow of oxygen to all parts of the body.[10] Individuals with sickle cell anemia are genetically homozygous, having inherited sickle cell genes from both parents.[11] Sickle cell anemia usually causes cardiovascular abnormalities and extreme fatigue.[12] Consequently, persons suffering from sickle cell anemia are often overtly disabled and may have limited employment opportunities.[13]

The term "sickle cell trait" (or "sickle gene carrier") refers to a heterozygous individual who has inherited one normal hemoglobin gene and one sickle cell gene.[14] The occupational significance of sickle cell trait is subject to much debate in the scientific community, specifically concerning whether individuals with sickle cell trait are more sensitive to certain environmental hazards.

At least 46 clinical conditions have been associated with sickle cell trait.[15] The most relevant to the occupational setting are splenic infarctions in pressurized aircraft and sudden death during vigorous exercise at high altitudes. This fear has led the armed forces to deny persons with sickle cell trait entry into flight and diving occupations where there is an increased risk of deficient oxygenation of the blood.[16] Some scientists have suggested that sickle cell trait should be evaluated if arduous work may be required in places with relatively limited oxygen, such as in aircraft,[17] and where there is a risk of accidental deoxygenation, such as in mine rescue work.[18] Other scientists suggest that individuals with sickle cell trait may be at increased risk from the action of hemolytic agents and recommend avoiding exposure to anemia producers, such as benzene, lead, and cadmium; methemoglobin formers, such as aromatic amino and nitro compounds; and blood enzyme tension reducers, such as carbon monoxide and cyanide.[19] This recommendation was implemented by at least one chemical company.[20]

A substantial number of other scientists consider sickle cell trait a benign condition with minimal risk under normal circumstances.[21] Several studies of athletes and military personnel support this view.[22] Furthermore, while it is theoretically possible that individuals with sickle cell trait may be at increased risk from hemolytic chemicals, there are no studies or data to support this theory.[23] Even the theory itself has been rejected by some experts.[24]

Sickle cell anemia and sickle cell trait are most often found in persons from equatorial Africa, parts of India, countries of the Middle East, and countries around the Mediterranean.[25] In American blacks of African origin, the prevalence of sickle cell trait is estimated at 7% to 13%.[26] It is virtually nonexistent in other racial groups in the United States.[27]

B.   G-6-PD Deficiency

Glucose-6-phosphate dehydrogenase (G-6-PD) deficiency is a biochemical genetic condition involving the red blood cell. G-6-PD is the first enzyme in the energy-generating process, and a deficiency in the enzyme interferes with the process in which glucose is oxidized.[28]

G-6-PD deficiency was recognized as early as 1926 during detailed study of a drug-sensitivity reaction to hemolytic antimalarial drugs.[29] Of primary concern in the occupational setting is the fact that dozens of industrial chemicals have chemical structures and toxicologic properties similar to the therapeutic antimalarial drugs.[30] Therefore, there is a theoretical argument that these chemicals can cause clinically significant hemolytic anemia in G-6-PD deficient workers.

In addition to some common household and prescription drugs, chemicals suspected of presenting risks to G-6-PD deficient workers include several dye intermediates, aromatic nitro and amino compounds, arsine and related metal hydrides, and lead and its compounds.[31] Ozone,[32] copper,[33] and sodium nitrite[34] may also promote hemolytic anemia in G-6-PD deficient individuals.

Despite *in vitro* and case studies, epidemiologic evidence to prove that G-6-PD deficient individuals are more sensitive to industrial chemicals is generally lacking. Moreover, the compilation of this evidence is complicated by several factors. First, it is not known whether individuals will hyperreact following exposures below current OSHA levels or whether higher doses are required.[35] Second, many other factors, such as preexisting organic disease, medications, viral and bacterial infections, and nutritional status, may interact with environmental exposures to produce health effects in G-6-PD deficient individuals.[36] These interactions may be additive or synergistic. Third, over 100 variant forms of G-6-PD deficiency have been identified,[37] and the reactions of these different subgroups to environmental factors vary greatly.[38] For example, in the Mediterranean variant, G-6-PD activity ranges from 1% to 8% of normal, compared to the A-variant of American blacks, which maintains 15% to 25% of normal G-6-PD activity.[39]

G-6-PD deficiency is a sex-linked trait, occurring homozygously only in males.[40] Although present to some degree in virtually all racial groups,[41] G-6-PD deficiency is found primarily in blacks from Central Africa, populations around the Mediterranean, in East Indians, some Orientals, Oceanians, and Filipinos.[42] Over 100 million males worldwide are believed to have the condition.[43] Prevalence rates vary widely from 0.1%[44] in white American males to 60% in Kurdish Jews.[45]

According to one recent study, the prevalence rates for this trait are as shown in Table 4–1.

C.   Thalassemia

Thalassemia is a term used to describe a heterozygous group of red blood cell diseases characterized by an abnormality in the rate of hemoglobin synthesis.[46] There are two main groups of thalassemia, the alpha-thalassemias and the beta-thalassemias (also known as Cooley's anemia), based on a deficiency in either the alpha or beta globin chain.[47] Each of these main groups consists of several genetically distinct disorders which can be recognized by their hematologic and hemoglobin electrophoretic characteristics.[48]

Table 4–1.   Prevalence of G-6-PD Deficiency by Ethnic/
             Racial Group

Group	Subjects Affected (%)
Americans (white)	0.1
Americans (black males)	16
British	0.1
Chinese	2–5
European Jews	1
Filipinos	12–13
Greeks	2–32
Indians (Asian)	0.3
Mediterranean Jews	11
Scandinavians	1–8

Source: Adapted from Office of Technology Assessment, United States Congress, The Role of Genetic Testing in the Prevention of Occupational Disease 90 (1983).

Very few associations have been found between thalassemia and increased susceptibility to the toxic effects of various industrial toxins. There have been some reports, however, that lead and benzene toxicity may be heightened for individuals with thalassemia.[49] Ozone exposure may also be hazardous to some subclasses of thalassemia.[50]

The frequency of thalassemias is especially high among people living in the Mediterranean area, the Middle East, and the Orient.[51] Approximately 7% to 15% of the people living in certain parts of Italy and Sicily have thalassemia.[52] There is probably a high prevalence of beta-thalassemia in India, the Sudan, Turkey, and parts of Israel.[53] All of the various types of thalassemia genes have been found to be very prevalent in Thailand.[54] In the United States, the following population frequencies have been reported: alpha-thalassemia in blacks, 2% to 7%;[55] beta-thalassemia in blacks, 0.8%;[56] alpha-thalassemia in Greek Americans, 2.4%;[57] beta-thalassemia in Greek Americans, 4% to 5%;[58] beta-thalassemia in Italian Americans 4% to 5%.[59]

D.   SAT Deficiency

Alpha$_1$ antitrypsin is a serum protein that protects the lung from proteolytic enzymes.[60] Research has demonstrated that individuals with an inherited deficiency of serum alpha$_1$ antitrypsin (SAT) are predisposed to alveolar destruction, even in the absence of chronic bronchitis, and to the development of pulmonary emphysema.[61]

In homozygotes, SAT activity may be only 10% to 15% of normal.[62] In heterozygotes, SAT activity may be 60% of normal.[63] It has been estimated that 80% of homozygotes develop chronic obstructive pulmonary disease (COPD).[64] Only one individual in 4,000 to 8,000 displays the homozygous trait,[65] but there are an estimated seven million heterozygotes in the United States (about three percent of the population).[66]

The main occupational health concern centers around the hypothesis that heterozygotes who display an intermediate SAT deficiency are at an increased risk of COPD, especially if they smoke or work in dusty environments. Although there are some conflicting studies,[67] it is generally accepted that SAT deficiency increases the risk of COPD for individuals exposed to a variety of respiratory irritants.[68] Despite an "increased risk," however, 90% of SAT heterozygotes will not develop COPD.[69] Other factors are also important to the etiology of COPD.[70]

SAT deficiency is found most frequently in persons of northern European ancestry. Table 4-2 illustrates the ethnic prevalences of this condition.

Table 4-2.   Percentage of Individuals of Different Ethnic Background With an Intermediate SAT Deficiency

Group	Subjects Affected (%)
Irish	9.0
Russian and Central European	7.9
German	7.0
English	6.6
French and Belgian	4.7
Jewish	2.6
American Negro	1.4
Mexican American	1.3
Italian	0
American Indian	0

Source: E. Calabrese, Pollutants and High Risk Groups 57 (1978), citing Mittman & Lieberman, Screening for Alpha₁-Antitrypsin Deficiency, in Genetic Polymorphism and the Diseases in Man 191 (B. Ramot et al. eds. 1973). Reprinted by permission.

E.   Other Biochemical Genetic Conditions

There are a number of other, less common diseases that may establish an individual as being more sensitive to various occupational environments. Acatalasemia and hypocatalasemia are red blood cell deficiencies of the enzyme catalase which can be aggravated by exposure to oxidizing agents.[71] Persons with cystic fibrosis or cystic fibrosis trait may be predisposed to COPD from exposure to respiratory irritants such as ozone, sulfur dioxide, particulate sulfates, and heavy metals.[72] Wilson's disease, characterized by excess copper levels in the liver, brain, cornea, and kidney, is aggravated by additional exposure to copper.[73] Leber's optic atrophy, a rare inherited eye disease, is affected by exposure to several neurotoxic agents in cigarette smoke and cyanide.[74]

The OTA study of biochemical genetic screening focused on some additional genetic traits, including NADH dehydrogenase deficiency, aryl hydrocarbon hydroxylase inducibility, acetylation rate, carbon oxidation, and diseases of DNA repair.[75]

As with the more common genetic traits, many of these less common biochemical genetic conditions have been shown to predominate in certain racial and ethnic groups. For example, NADH dehydrogenase deficiency, a red blood cell disorder, is most common in Alaskan Eskimos and Indians,[76] Navajo Indians,[77] and Puerto Ricans.[78] Tyrosinemia and porphyria, two other blood disorders, have a high degree of prevalence among French Canadians[79] and South Africans,[80] respectively. Wilson's disease is found most often in Eastern European Jews and Sicilians.[81]

4.3   HLA System

The human leukocyte antigen (HLA) system is a complex array of cellular surface proteins found on chromosome number six in every human cell.[82] The HLA system was originally used to match donor and recipient tissue types for transplantation surgery. Recent biomedical studies, however, have revealed that various HLAs display striking statistical associations with many human diseases.[83] Essentially, the HLA system is used by the white blood cells in identifying foreign substances in the body and alerting the body's immune system to destroy these foreign cells.[84]

The HLA system is a cellular biochemical genetic marker, but many of the inborn metabolic errors or biochemical genetic traits identified by HLA typing are identifiable through other procedures. For example, certain HLA factors have been shown to have an association with G-6-PD deficiency.[85]

Although the precise relationship between HLA and disease has yet to be discovered, the 92 known leukocyte antigens have been accepted as genetic markers for 80 to 186 diseases, and tens more are being discovered every year.[86] Some of these diseases, such as hypersensitivity pneumonitis, bladder cancer, asbestosis, farmer's lung, silicosis, pneumoconiosis, and G-6-PD deficiency, may be related to occupational exposures.[87] Consequently, HLA typing may become of increasing importançe in identifying high-risk workers. At the present time, however, HLA screening of worker populations is not indicated. Even the most accurate of the HLA tests, such as HLA-B-27 testing for ankylosing spondylitis, cannot be used for screening asymptomatic populations.[88] The main proven use of HLA is in paternity testing.

4.4　Cytogenetic and Noncytogenetic Monitoring

A.　Cytogenetic

Cytogenetics is the study of numerical and structural chromosome aberrations.[89] These aberrations (*e.g.*, chromosome breaks, sister chromatid exchanges) may occur naturally or may be induced by exposure to environmental agents known as clastogens. In general, clastogenic agents are also mutagenic and carcinogenic. Indeed, certain specific chromosome aberrations have been linked to specific cancers. Thus, the theory has developed that chromosomal aberrations are the cellular precursors of cancer, and cytogenetic monitoring of workers exposed to carcinogens may indicate increased risk or the subclinical effects of disease.[90]

Some recent studies have found associations between occupational exposures to ionizing radiation, arsenic, benzene, epichlorohydrin, cadmium/lead/zinc, organic solvents, ethylene oxide, and vinyl chloride and elevated frequencies of chromosome aberrations.[91] Nevertheless, the literature is often contradictory and the associations, even when found, are indirect. At the present time, cytogenetics can, at best, establish relationships between chromosome aberrations and cancers for populations as a whole; no correlations have been found between high frequencies of chromosome aberrations and individual risk of cancer.[92] These limitations have led most experts to agree that cytogenetic monitoring, at the present time, is an experimental research tool which should not be used in setting exposure levels or in screening workers.[93] Nevertheless, OSHA's proposed standard for ethylene oxide recommends cytogenetic monitoring of exposed workers.[94]

B.   Noncytogenetic

Unlike cytogenetic monitoring, which looks for damage to the gross structure of chromosomes (the cellular structures containing the genetic material DNA), noncytogenetic monitoring looks for damage to the actual molecular structure of DNA. The DNA damage is caused by mutagens, and therefore the noncytogenetic monitoring attempts to detect the presence of mutagens or the DNA damage caused by the mutagens.[95]

There are three main categories of noncytogenetic monitoring techniques: tests to detect mutagens in body fluids, tests to detect somatic cell damage, and tests to detect germ cell damage.[96] In general, noncytogenetic techniques are still in the developmental stage. The detection of mutagens in urine is thought to be the only assay developed thus far with proven reliability.[97] As with the cytogenetic forms of monitoring, there is the prospect that noncytogenetic screening (faster and less expensive than cytogenetic techniques) eventually may be useful in detecting early damage caused by environmental exposures.

CHAPTER 5

GENDER-SPECIFIC AND REPRODUCTIVE HAZARDS

5.1 Nonreproductive Sex Differences

Aside from obvious external sexual characteristics, there are other biological differences between males and females. For example, on the average, men have greater isometric muscle strength, especially upper limb strength[1] and seem to tolerate heat better than women.[2] On the other hand, there is evidence that women are less likely to suffer hearing loss.[3] Epidemiological data collected on older workers show a tendency for female workers to suffer from chronic debilitating diseases while male workers suffer from more life-threatening diseases.[4]

Sex-related sensitivities to toxic substances have been observed in laboratory animals. Some of the substances known to have sex-related effects are chloroform, barbiturates, benzene, nicotine, lead, alcohol, strychnine, and epinephrine.[5] The most likely explanation for sex-related differences in reactions to toxic substances is that the enzymatic biotransformation of the agent is influenced by sex hormones.[6]

There is insufficient evidence, however, of sex-related differences in toxicity in humans.[7] According to Harrington and Schilling, "Excluding childbearing, men and women are more alike than different in terms of biochemical and pathophysiological processes."[8] Nevertheless, sex-related sensitivities in humans are theoretically possible. A number of sex-related differences in pharmacologic responsivity have been observed.[9] In addition, males have been shown to be at an increased risk of liver cancer, regardless of social, racial, occupational, cultural, and geographical factors.[10] Similar findings have been reported for skin cancer and lung cancer.[11] Although the physiological basis for these differences is not clear, it is believed to involve metabolic and enzymatic actions in the detoxification of carcinogenic substances.

5.2   Pre-Conception Hazards

At birth, the female has an estimated 700,000 to 2,000,000 primary oocytes in her ovaries.[12] By the beginning of puberty this number has dropped to about 40,000, and of these only about 400 oocytes will ever undergo development and be expelled during the ovulatory phase of the menstrual cycle.[13] The oocytes reaching maturity later in life have been dormant for 40 years or more. During this dormant period they are exposed either directly or indirectly to various potentially harmful conditions, some of which may have a cumulative or additive effect on the oocyte. Studies have shown a correlation between increased maternal age and the incidence of offspring with chromosomal abnormalities.[14] Radiation exposures, for example, are known to have a cumulative effect, thereby increasing the frequency of germ cell mutation in older women.[15]

By contrast, the male continuously produces germ cells (sperm) from puberty onward, with a new supply of sperm being produced every 74 days.[16] Although this continuous decontamination process eliminates the danger of cumulative exposure to the sperm itself, exposure to mutagens may cause permanent damage to the germinal epithelium, resulting in the perpetual production of genetically damaged sperm (mutagenesis) or other defects (*e.g.*, decreased motility, abnormal shape, reduced number). In addition, the rapid cell division during the process of sperm production (spermatogenesis) increases the risk of mutagenesis.[17] Male germ cells have been shown to be far more sensitive to the mutagenic effects of ionizing radiation.[18]

Exposure of the male or female to germ cell mutagens prior to conception can result in congenital defects, developmental problems, and mutations in the offspring.[19] Genetically abnormal fetuses also are about 100 times more likely to be spontaneously aborted than are normal fetuses.[20] In addition, because the offspring inherits the genetic defect itself, rather than merely the effects of the defect, there is the possibility that the genetic defect may be passed on to future generations.[21] Such effects, however, have been positively reported only in rodents.[22]

Finally, workplace exposure of the male or female to toxic substances can result in diminished reproductive capacity through loss of libido, impotence, infertility, and sterility. Sterility and infertility are particularly well documented. For example, dibromochloropropane (DBCP) has been shown to cause sterility by lowering the sperm count.[23] Male infertility also has been shown to result from exposure to lead,[24] chloroprene,[25] kepone,[26] vinyl chloride,[27] alcohol,[28] marijuana,[29] tobacco,[30] anesthetic gases,[31] chemotherapeutic drugs,[32] and heat.[33] Female infertility may result from exposure to lead, mercury, cadmium, textile dyes, and noise.[34]

5.3   Post-Conception Hazards

While pregnancy represents a significant alteration in the hormonal and chemical profile of a woman, there is inadequate evidence that this altered state enhances her susceptibility to environmental and occupational hazards.[35] Consequently, post-conception hazards should be analyzed in light of their possible effects on the fetus.

During the period of gestation the fetus is exposed to three types of hazards. First, embryofetotoxins are chemicals which manifest an effect upon the conceptus during any of the stages of gestation, from fertilization until birth. They may cause death, structural malformations, metabolic or physiological dysfunction, growth retardation, or psychological and behavioral alteration manifested at birth or in the postnatal period.[36] Second, teratogens are substances which act on the dividing cells of the growing fetus and cause structural or functional defects, such as limb deformities or organic defects.[37] Third, transplacental carcinogens are substances capable of crossing the placenta and causing cancer in the fetus or child.[38]

Prenatal human development can be divided into three stages: (1) predifferentiation stage, from fertilization to the end of the first week; (2) embryonic stage, from the second to the eighth week; and (3) fetal stage, from the ninth week until term.[39] The stage of development is very important in determining the susceptibility of the embryo or fetus to in utero insults.[40]

During the first week following fertilization, even before placental implantation, embryotoxic agents absorbed by the mother can reach the freelying blastocyst very rapidly, and the clearance rate from the blastocyst of maternally transmitted substances is very low.[41]

The embryonic stage is the time of greatest susceptibility to environmental influences.[42] This stage is also known as the time of organogenesis because most of the major organic systems are being formed. Each organ appears to be most susceptible during its early stages of differentation, with different organs being susceptible at different times.[43] One complicating factor is that pregnancy cannot even be detected by conventional methods until well into the period of organogenesis, although new techniques can detect pregnancy as early as the ninth day after conception.[44]

The fetal stage is generally characterized by lower susceptibility than the embryonic stage, but still greater susceptibility than that of adults or children.[45] Those structures which continue to differentiate during the fetal stage, such as the cerebellum, cerebral cortex, and some urogenital structures, are most susceptible.[46]

Three additional points relating to post-conception hazards deserve mention. First, the usual way in which teratogens reach the fetus is by maternal exposure and transmission to the fetus through the placental membrane.[47] It is also theoretically possible, however, that where there is paternal exposure to teratogens, the teratogens can reach the fetus via semen absorbed through the vaginal mucosa during intercourse.[48]

Second, it is important to note that the fetus may be susceptible to embryofetotoxic and teratogenic substances at exposure levels well below those which would be harmful to either parent.[49] For example, the children of women who ate mercury-contaminated fish in Japan were found to exhibit cerebral palsy-like symptoms when most of the mothers showed no adverse effects.[50] Similar effects have been observed for several other substances, including lead.[51]

Third, numerous substances have been identified as having effects on reproduction. Many of them, like arsenic, asbestos, benzene, formaldehyde, lead, mercury, and vinyl chloride, are common to numerous industries, with literally millions of exposed workers.[52] Only a small percentage of the chemicals used in American industry, however, have been tested for their reproductive effects.[53] Moreover, the same substances are frequently mutagenic, teratogenic, and carcinogenic.[54]

5.4 Offspring Risks Based on Parental Exposures

Most of the documented congenital deformities from parental exposures have manifested themselves by the time of birth. Nevertheless, even after birth a child's health may be affected by parental workplace exposure. One way this may occur is through the exposure of a breast-feeding mother. Heavy metals like lead, cadmium, and mercury; many pesticides; polybrominated biphenyls (PBBs); and polychlorinated biphenyls (PCBs) have been shown to pass to the nursing infant via breast milk. The effects on infants from ingestion of contaminated milk, however, are largely unknown.[55]

In addition, prebirth toxic insults may not become manifested until some time after birth. It is possible that subsequent offspring disease may be caused by *in utero* exposure to toxic agents or even by preconception parental exposures to mutagens. In general, however, there is inadequate evidence to sustain a broad hypothesis of such casual relationships.[56]

One way by which prenatal insults could cause postpartum disease is where the fetus has been protected *in utero* by the mother's ability to detoxify certain agents. After birth, the infant may be born with the agent in its tissues, and it could lack the enzymes or other metabolic mechanisms needed for detoxification. Therefore, a substance that does not appear to harm the fetus *in utero* may well be toxic to the infant.[57] Indeed, the effects of some fetotoxins may not be manifested or diagnosed until years after birth. Prenatal exposure to lead, for example, may cause learning disabilities when the child is several years old.[58]

One of the best-documented examples of the delayed effect of an *in utero* insult involves diethylstilbestrol (DES), a synthetic estrogen commonly used in the 1940s and 1950s to prevent spontaneous abortion. In 1971 it was determined that female offspring (16 to 22 years old) exposed to DES *in utero* had an increased incidence of carcinomas of the vagina and cervix,[59] as well as various reproductive dysfunctions.[60] Males exposed to DES *in utero* had an increased incidence of malformations of the testes and abnormal sperm.[61]

Several recent studies have investigated the effect of parental (usually paternal) occupation and early childhood death due to various neoplasms. These studies have focused on hydrocarbon-related occupations,[62] lead-related occupations,[63] and solvents used in the aircraft industry.[64] Despite some apparent correlations, it is widely believed that the studies are inconclusive, at best.[65]

CHAPTER 6

MEDICAL SCREENING AND
EMPLOYMENT DECISIONS

6.1 Employee Selection

In most instances it is extremely difficult to determine the basis upon which an applicant is rejected for employment. The process has been characterized as a "black box" problem. An individual may know what information was presented to the employer and may know the outcome, but the individual usually does not know what decision processes produced the outcome.[1] This veil of secrecy covers refusals to hire based on a single or aggregate set of medical conclusions. Applicants often complete medical questionnaires or submit to physical examinations and are simply not hired or deemed to be physically unsuitable without further elaboration. There is evidence, however, that applicants are denied employment on the basis of such dubious conditions as obesity, color blindness, arthritis, hypertension, allergies, and varicose veins.[2]

In 1974 a group of industrial physicians was polled to assess whether the members of the group would recommend hiring a hypothetical 38-year-old applicant with a history of either myocardial infarction, angina, valvular disease, hypertension, diabetes, proteinuria, tuberculosis, or psychiatric illness.[3] The physicians polled seemed more concerned about possible liability for further injury or illness than about possible increased compensation rates or loss of work time.[4] In addition, the nature of the illness was more important than the degree of exertion required by the job.[5] The study concluded that "even patients with mild illness, which may not increase their morbidity or mortality, are being denied work. The criteria used for determining employability appear, in some cases, to have little relation to modern medical judgment."[6]

Although most medical screening programs consist of several tests and procedures, there are certain medical criteria which will result in the automatic exclusion of the applicant. Employers are extremely reluctant to divulge what these factors are. Nevertheless, some known employer selection practices clearly suggest that, at least in some instances, medical screening of workers is being used instead of reducing hazards in the workplace. For example, one employer reportedly hires only men over the age of 50 for work where there is exposure to a potent carcinogen with a long latency period. By the time the cancer would manifest itself, the men would be dying of old age anyhow.[7] Another employer, a steel producer, hires only deaf individuals to work in areas where there are excessive noise levels.[8]

Perhaps the most graphic illustration of employer insouciance concerning health risks to employees was the reaction of an industry spokesman in 1977 after the discovery that the pesticide DBCP caused sterility to workers. In a letter to then Assistant Secretary of Labor Eula Bingham, Robert K. Phillips, executive secretary of the National Peach Council, wrote that sterilization of workers is not necessarily bad.

> After all, there are many people who are now paying to have themselves sterilized to assure they will no longer be able to become parents. If possible sterility is the main problem, couldn't workers who were old enough that they no longer wanted to have children accept such positions voluntarily? They would know the situation, and some might volunteer for such work posts as an alternative to planned surgery for a vasectomy or tubal ligation, or as a means of getting around religious bans on birth control when they want no more children.[9]

DBCP, of course, is also a known carcinogen.[10]

Even some medical screening procedures with little scientific basis are used by employers. The scientific limitations on the use of low-back x-rays for the screening of applicants have been discussed previously. Why, then, would railroads and some other employers continue to use them? The answer is a simple matter of dollars and cents. According to Dr. Max P. Rogers of Southern Railway, 20% to 25% of the $13.5 million annual cost of employee personal injury claims goes for back injuries.[11] The average cost of settling a case of a ruptured intervertebral disc in 1980 to 1981 was $125,000 to $150,000.[12] Even though the predictive value of low-back x-rays is extremely low and thousands of healthy individuals are screened out, the railroads consider the practice cost-effective because reducing only a few back injury claims could save the railroads thousands of dollars.[13]

The unfairness of an unfavorable employment decision often goes beyond the exclusion from a single job. Railroads often ask applicants whether they have ever been denied employment on the basis of a back x-ray.[14] Thus, once refused employment for this reason, applicants will find it extremely difficult to get a similar job with another employer. Another concern is that employers will simply go too far in applying these techniques. For example, Dr. John E. Meyers of Southern Pacific Railroad has indicated that as recently as 1974 his company even gave back x-rays to applicants for clerical positions.[15]

Long-term consequences of exclusion from a job also attach to employees screened on the basis of genetic traits. By definition, genetic traits are inheritable, and therefore all the children of a person with a certain genetic trait may be denied employment on the same basis. Moreover, substantial portions of a racial or ethnic group could be disqualified.

Economic conditions certainly influence the degree of medical screening performed, but the societal consequences cannot be overlooked. With high unemployment in industrial jobs, some employers may be tempted to conduct extensive medical screening to hire only "low-risk" workers. Such actions, however, are likely to disqualify increasing numbers of medically fit applicants. It is well settled that "the more tests performed on a healthy subject the more likely is the discovery of an abnormal result."[16] Of course, genuinely handicapped workers have even less of a chance of being hired, regardless of their ability to perform job-related tasks. According to one study, seriously handicapped workers are hired mostly by small, nonunion firms in the service industry.[17] This finding calls into question the effectiveness of state and federally mandated affirmative action to hire the handicapped.[18]

6.2   Reassignment and Discharge

As with initial hiring decisions, the basis for other personnel actions, such as reassignment and discharge, are difficult to ascertain. Employees working under a collective bargaining agreement often have "just cause" or "reasonableness" clauses in their contracts, with arbitration as the final step in the grievance process. Therefore, arbitration decisions can provide information about medical reassignment and discharge for a class of employees with the most protection against unreasonable employer action.

The arbitration decisions generally confirm the view that present employees have greater protection than applicants but are still vulnerable to adverse action based on medical judgments. Arbitrators generally have upheld the employer's prerogative to decide whether high-risk employees remain on the job,[19] but personnel decisions based on totally unreliable medical evidence will not be upheld.[20] Where the employee is at risk only in a particular job, discharges are upheld where no ''safe'' positions are available.[21] Where there are safe positions, however, an employee's ability to transfer is a matter of contract.[22]

Another consequence of medical screening is stigmatization. In one plant where workers are exposed to vinyl chloride, when production workers ''flunk'' the required bilirubin test, they are reassigned to lower paying jobs in the warehouse. The transfer is often accompanied by derision from other workers.

A. Marijuana Screening

Adverse personnel actions also may result from medical screening that is unrelated to occupational health concerns. Specifically, urine screening for marijuana usage is becoming increasingly common. In 1982 the Army performed over 600,000 urine tests and the Navy 1.5 million. The city of Detroit, Alcoa, Greyhound Bus Company, the District of Columbia, and other large employers have used or are using the test. Each year thousands of applicants are not hired or employees are discharged because of the test. Members of the armed services, including nine members of the Army White House Guard, have been reassigned or otherwise disciplined as a result of marijuana screening.[23]

The most common urine test for marijuana usage is the EMIT (Enzyme Multiplied Immunoassay Technique) test, made by Syva Company. The test measures the presence of delta-9-tetra hydrocannabinol (THC), the primary active cannabinoid metabolite. Other tests analyze serum by using gas chromatography/mass spectrometry.

Although studies by developers of the EMIT test have shown fewer than 5% false positives,[24] other studies have shown a lower degree of accuracy.[25] Of course, the predictive value of the test will depend on the prevalence of marijuana usage in the screened population.

What is most disturbing about marijuana screening is that the tests are highly sensitive. A subject will have a positive EMIT test with as little as 75 nanograms (billionths of a gram) of THC per milliliter of urine. The tests can detect a casual usage within the last 14 days and chronic usage for much longer periods following discontinuance of usage.[26] In one study, six chronic marijuana users had THC in their urine 14 to 36 days following discontinuance of usage.[27] In addition, there is still widespread disagreement about whether an individual who merely breathed marijuana smoke—passive inhalation—would have a positive test.[28] Because intoxication lasts only one to four hours, even the test's developers caution that the test is useful only as an indicator of the use of marijuana, not as a measure of intoxication.[29]

Drug screens are relatively inexpensive. A urine test for marijuana costs about $4.50.[30] This fact, coupled with increasing problems of drug abuse in our society, suggests that drug screening may become even more common in the employment setting. The Syva Company, manufacturer of the EMIT test, also markets screening tests for amphetamines, barbiturates, benzodiazepines, cocaine metabolite, ethyl alcohol, methadone, methaqualone (Quaaludes), opiates, and phencyclidine (PCP).

Nobody would question an employer's right and duty to ensure that its employees were not working while intoxicated by any substance. But these tests do more than that. They constitute an unwarranted intrusion into the private lives of employees and attempt to detect matters unrelated to the safe and efficient performance of the job.

After studying the efficacy of routine drug screening of applicants, Dr. Robert Lewy, Director of the Employee Health Service at Presbyterian Hospital, New York, recently concluded that such a practice was unjustified.

> [T]he addition of a routine preemployment urine toxicology screen is not an effective means of distinguishing drug use from drug abuse. A more rational, cost-effective approach to screening for potential drug abuse problems would be to perform preemployment urine toxicology examinations selectively based on the results of the preemployment medical examination.[31]

Some legal challenges to the use of these marijuana screens are currently pending.[32] A variety of legal theories have been raised under state and federal law. The 1978 amendments to the Rehabilitation Act certainly recognize that the denial of employment opportunities on the basis of drug use is justified only under limited circumstances.

[The term handicapped individual] does not include any individual who is an alcoholic or drug abuser whose current use of alcohol or drugs prevents such individual from performing the duties of the job in question or whose employment, by reason of such current alcohol or drug abuse, would constitute a direct threat to property or the safety of others.[33]

B. AIDS

From 1981 until December 1983, Acquired Immune Deficiency Syndrome (AIDS) struck over 3,000 Americans, causing at least 1,000 deaths.[34] The cause of AIDS is unknown as is its precise etiology, but it is known to be transmitted predominantly or possibly exclusively by casual homosexual sex and intravenous needles. It is usually manifested in either or both of the following ways. First, AIDS patients may develop Kaposi's sarcoma, a rare dermal malignancy of epithelial origin. Named after Moritz Kaposi, who described the neoplasm in 1892, Kaposi's sarcoma appears most often as multiple small reddish-purple or hyperpigmented brown macules, papules, or nodules located on the extremities, trunk, or mouth.[35] Second, AIDS patients have a reduced number of "helper T cells" and therefore are susceptible to often fatal opportunistic infections. The infections may be protozoan, mycotic, mycobacterial, or fungal. The most common reported infection is a type of pneumonia caused by the organism *Pneumocystis carinii*.[36]

A number of epidemiological studies have been performed on AIDS patients. Homosexual and bisexual men (71%), intravenous drug users (17%), and Haitian immigrants (5%) have the highest incidence of AIDS.[37] Forty-two percent of AIDS cases are in New York City.[38]

Because of the unknown origin of the disease and uncertainty about its mode of transmission as well as the high mortality rate, a veritable panic has set in.[39] Although there is no evidence of AIDS transmission by casual contact or airborne spread, or of AIDS being transmitted to health-care or laboratory personnel,[40] there have been widespread reports of various forms of discrimination against persons in the high-risk groups—particularly gay men and Haitian immigrants.[41]

Much of the discrimination against actual, potential, or presumed AIDS patients is in employment. Because fever, malaise, weight loss, and lymphadenopathy often precede the diagnosis of AIDS, some employers have fired or laid off known homosexual men who have displayed these symptoms. Employment discrimination based on the fear of AIDS contagion has been reported against even asymptomatic homosexual men.

A number of legal challenges have been brought against AIDS-based discrimination, including actions against United Air Lines, Columbia University, and Mount Sinai Hospital of New York. From a legal standpoint, the cases raise several novel issues, such as whether a presumed disease carrier is "handicapped." From a public health and occupational medicine standpoint, the issue is similar to the basic issue in all of medical screening: how best to accommodate individual employment rights in light of legitimate concerns about the consequences of employing actual or suspected high-risk workers. The AIDS epidemic is a public health problem demanding a cautious, rational response, rather than the heedless exclusion from employment of vulnerable minorities.

6.3 Racial and Ethnic Effects of Medical Screening

The prevalence rates of some of the more common biochemical genetic traits by racial and ethnic group were discussed in section 4.2. Many of these traits predominate in one or more racial or ethnic populations. For example, it has been estimated that one out of 625 blacks has sickle cell anemia, but only one out of 6,250,000 whites has sickle cell anemia—a ratio of 10,000 to 1.[42] Can occupational medical screening procedures affecting one racial group but not another be justified?

Recent experience with sickle cell laws cautions against single-race genetic screening. Some early sickle cell laws may have resulted from ignorance on the part of legislatures. Virginia had a law, repealed in 1973, which required screening for sickle cell anemia and sickle cell trait to be conducted on all inmates of state prisons and mental institutions. According to one commentator, this practice equated sickle cell with antisocial, criminal, or retarded behavior.[43] Other laws were influenced by political considerations. In 1971 President Nixon responded to increasing political pressure and supported federal aid in developing voluntary sickle cell screening programs.[44] The National Sickle Cell Anemia Control Act, enacted in 1972, was successful in reversing the movement toward mandatory state laws by limiting the use of federal funds to voluntary screening programs.

During this time, 30 states passed sickle cell screening laws and 21 states still have these laws on the books.[45] Three states still have mandatory screening. Massachusetts[46] and Indiana[47] require sickle cell screening before admission to school and Kentucky[48] mandates sickle cell screening as part of the premarital examination for venereal disease.

A 1975 report by the National Academy of Sciences observed that sickle cell disease and sickle cell trait screening programs "evolved in a rapid, haphazard, often poorly planned fashion, generated in large measure by public clamor and political pressure."[49] In 1983 the President's Commission for the Study of Ethical Problems in Medicine and Biomedical and Behavioral Research identified the following deficiencies with these screening programs:

> First, the objectives of the programs were often not clear. Second, the target populations were often poorly chosen. For example, screening schoolchildren, who would make little use of the information, was found to be counterproductive. Third, a lack of full protection of confidentiality in some programs led to stigmatization and misunderstandings. Most important, inadequate genetic counseling and public education resulted in misconceptions about the difference between being a sickle-cell carrier (who is typically not at any increased health risk) and having sickle-cell disease (which can be very debilitating and even fatal).[50]

Besides raising needless fears among sickle trait carriers and contributing to unfair stigmatization, the sickle cell alarm caused other problems.

> Evidence of stigmatization in the United States is seen in job discrimination, in proposals to limit admission to the armed forces to noncarriers, and in increases in insurance premiums. Nine of twelve insurance companies in one sample charged higher rates for individuals with sickle trait even though mortality curves for such individuals do not differ significantly from blacks without the trait.[51]

Employers in some states even rejected applicants for clerical positions simply on the basis of sickle cell trait. Eventually, Florida,[52] Louisiana,[53] and North Carolina[54] passed laws prohibiting discrimination in employment based on sickle cell trait.

The ironic thing about genetic traits and predisposition to occupational illness is that virtually every racial and ethnic group is likely to have a higher relative prevalence of one or more traits, making those members of the group with the trait (theoretically) at an increased risk. Table 6-1 demonstrates the fact that "[i]n one way or another, we are all genetic lemons."[55] Two caveats about the table: First, some of the associations between the traits and susceptibility to occupational illness have not been proven, but this does not necessarily mean that screening has not or would not take place. Second, the

Table 6-1. Occupationally Related Genetic Traits by Racial and
Ethnic Background

Group	Trait/Susceptibility
1. Arabs	G-6-PD
2. Blacks	sickle cell
	alpha-thalassemia
	G-6-PD
3. Central Europeans	SAT
4. Chinese	G-6-PD
	alpha-thalassemia
5. Danes	SAT
	porphyria
6. East Indians	G-6-PD
	beta-thalassemia
7. English	SAT
8. Eskimos and Alaskan Indians	NADH
9. Filipinos	G-6-PD
10. French and Belgians	SAT
11. French Canadians	tyrosinemia
	porphyria
12. Germans	SAT
13. Greeks	G-6-PD
	alpha-thalassemia
	beta-thalassemia
14. Irish	SAT
15. Italians	beta-thalassemia
	G-6-PD
16. Jews (Eastern European)	Wilson's disease
17. Jews (Kurdish)	G-6-PD
18. Jews (Mediterranean)	G-6-PD
19. Navajo Indians	NADH
20. Norwegians	SAT
21. Portuguese	G-6-PD
22. Puerto Ricans	NADH
23. Russians	SAT
24. Sardinians	G-6-PD
25. Sicilians	Wilson's disease
	G-6-PD
26. South Africans (whites)	tyrosinemia
	porphyria
27. Spaniards	G-6-PD
28. Sudanese	beta-thalassemia
29. Swedes	SAT
	porphyria
30. Syrians	alpha-thalassemia
	beta-thalassemia
31. Thais	alpha-thalassemia
	beta-thalassemia
32. Turks	beta-thalassemia
33. Yugoslavs	G-6-PD

Source: Adapted from E. Calabrese, Pollutants and High Risk Groups
187–93 (1978) and other authorities cited in section 4.2. Copyright © 1978
by John Wiley & Sons, Inc. Reprinted by permission.

selection of traits for each group is based on relative risk and not necessarily on high prevalence within that group.

With this background information, it is possible to address the issue of whether biochemical genetic screening for traits like G-6-PD deficiency and sickle cell trait are discriminatory. Scientific authorities and employers who defend sickle cell trait screening argue that the racial impacts are unfortunate and incidental. They assert that it would be irresponsible to permit employees with sickle trait to work in extreme environments, and therefore exclusionary policies are in the best health interests of employees and the best economic interests of employers.[56] Opponents, like MIT's Dr. Jonathan King, who called sickle trait screening "scientific racism,"[57] contend that the exclusionary policies unfairly attempt to shift the focus from the work environment to the genes of the worker and that the policies have been used to exclude only the groups that have been the traditional victims of discrimination based on race, sex, or national origin.[58]

To view this debate from a slightly different perspective, consider the following hypothetical situation. The XYZ Company is a large, multinational corporation headquartered in the United States. It has an opening for the position of Director of International Operations, a well-paying and glamorous job requiring frequent worldwide travel. Numerous executives in XYZ Company apply for the job. Some of the travel involves going to portions of Africa where malaria is rampant. Persons with sickle cell trait (and G-6-PD deficiency) have been shown to be at a significantly *decreased* risk of contracting malaria.[59] Based on this fact, XYZ Company's medical department recommends that employees without sickle cell trait be disqualified for the position. Such a policy would disqualify several black applicants for the position, but all of the white applicants. What is XYZ Company likely to do?

Finally, it should be noted that besides genetic screening, there are a variety of other neutral employment criteria, designed to screen out poor health risks or adopted for other reasons, that may have a disparate impact on the basis of race, color, religion, or national origin. The criteria may relate to the individual's immutable biological makeup, diet, life-style, or other behavior-based factors.

6.4   One-Sex Exclusionary Policies

Exposure to embryofetotoxins and teratogens poses grave health risks to the fetus throughout the term of the mother's pregnancy, including, and often especially, during the period of organogenesis, which occurs between the second and eighth week of gestation. Because virtually all women do not become aware of their pregnancy until well into this period of fetal development, it may be too late at that point to have the woman removed from exposure—the harm already may have been done. Consequently, many employers have initiated work rules prohibiting women of childbearing capacity from working where there is exposure to embryofetotoxic or teratogenic substances.

The implications of these exclusionary rules are enormous. It has been estimated that as many as 20 million jobs in this country may involve exposure to possible reproductive hazards.[60] A 1980 survey of married mothers indicated that 314,000 women (17% of married mothers who were employed at some time during the year preceding delivery) worked in occupations which could involve exposure to teratogenic agents.[61] As many as 100,000 jobs are closed to women already because they involve working in areas where there are reproductive hazards.[62] Some of the companies known to have such policies are Allied Chemical, American Cyanamid, B.F. Goodrich, Dow Chemical, Du Pont, Firestone, General Motors, Goodyear, Gulf Oil, Monsanto, Olin, St. Joe's Minerals, and Sun Oil.[63]

Quite apart from the complex legal considerations discussed in section 11.4, four main arguments can be raised to challenge the validity of these exclusionary policies from a policy perspective. First, what some employers euphemistically call a "fetal protection program" is, in reality, nothing more than a "liability prevention program." Employers are simply trying to avoid civil liability in the event a child is born deformed as a result of maternal exposures. If employers were genuinely interested in the health of the offspring of their employees, the argument goes, then they would ban pregnant women from smoking at work and would counsel pregnant women on the need to avoid taking drugs, to limit alcohol intake, and to maintain proper diet, rest, and prenatal medical care.[64] Only where there is the possibility of employer liability, however, have any actions been taken.

Second, it has been argued that exclusionary practices are applied selectively to women working in jobs thought to be traditional male jobs. Thus, for example, no employer has yet ordered that all female nurses of childbearing capacity be excluded from working in operating rooms where there is exposure to anesthetic gases, which are teratogenic.[65] Moreover, exclusionary practices have been focused only on exposures to workplace chemicals. Few efforts have been made to remove fertile or pregnant women or to reduce their exposures when they are exposed to high noise levels,[66] infectious agents (*e.g.*, rubella),[67] or ionizing radiation[68]—all of which may retard fetal growth or cause birth defects. In one employment discrimination case settled in September 1983, the plaintiffs asserted that the company hired no women until 1974 and thereafter hired only about 25 women into a work force of 600.[69]

Third, a forceful argument (especially from a legal standpoint) is that prohibiting *all* women of childbearing capacity is overinclusive. Employer practices generally do not consider the woman's age, marital status, sexual activity, use of contraception, or the fertility of the woman's husband or partner. Such an approach may be viewed as a conclusive presumption that a woman biologically capable of conception may, in fact, become pregnant and carry the child to term. Women are considered not responsible enough to act prudently. Moreover, these policies tend to exert economic coercion on fertile women to become sterilized in order to retain their jobs.

Finally, the most compelling argument is that excluding only women of childbearing capacity is underinclusive. The same substances that pose teratogenic hazards often are mutagenic as well and pose serious health threats to the offspring of male workers. Some substances, in fact, pose greater danger to male reproductive systems than to female reproductive systems. Nevertheless, only women are excluded from employment. Even if individual women were at a greater risk than individual men, the fact that the overwhelming number of workers exposed to reproductive hazards are male strongly suggests that offspring are more likely to be affected by reproductive hazards their fathers have been exposed to in the workplace than by reproductive hazards their mothers have been exposed to.

One would be tempted to ask why, in light of all the evidence establishing relationships between paternal exposures and birth defects, employers would choose to implement one-sex exclusionary policies. Aside from the theory that this is merely a blatant form of sex discrimination,[70] at least four possible reasons may be suggested. First, the employer may be unaware of the scientific evidence and is proceeding under the stereotypical notion that birth defects are attributable only to maternal exposures. Second, perhaps the employer or its lawyer believes that only the employee-mother of a deformed child would associate the birth defect with the workplace exposure and would sue the employer or that the child of an exposed mother would be more likely to recover damages than would the child of an exposed father.[71] Third, an employer may reason that it cannot remove all of its employees from hazardous exposures and women are more at risk than men. Fourth, controls to reduce exposure to below spermatogenic effect levels may be considered technologically achievable, whereas controls to reduce exposures to below teratogenic and embryofetotoxic levels may not be achievable.[72]

The goals of fetal protection and equal employment opportunity are, for the most part, not necessarily mutually exclusive. There are some legal approaches to the problem (discussed in section 10.5) which will permit equal employment opportunity while minimizing the risk of birth defects from maternal and paternal exposures. Nevertheless, it should be understood that any approach that results in the returning of fertile women to an embryofetotoxic or teratogenic work environment creates some risks that cannot be eliminated altogether. The facile argument that all workplaces should be made safe from all reproductive hazards ignores the constraints imposed by technological feasibility. As discussed earlier, the fetus may be harmed by exposure levels considerably below the safe level for adults. Moreover, the costs of engineering controls often increase exponentially for slight reductions of very low exposure levels.

While it is extremely unpleasant to couch the issue in such Draconian terms, the question may be whether society is willing to accept some risks of miscarriages, stillbirths, and deformed children from maternal exposure to teratogens as the price for equal employment opportunities for hundreds of thousands of women. Society has been willing to accept the risks of mutagenesis from male exposures, which may be even worse because the effects of mutagenesis may carry beyond a single generation. Society has been willing to accept the risks of teratogenesis from other maternal exposures such as infections, cigarette smoking, alcohol, and drugs. The Reagan administration has even limited eligibility for the government's prenatal nutrition program and cut its budget by one-third. These budget cuts, decreases in health care funding generally, and high unemployment have resulted in sharp increases in birth defects and the infant mortality rate. Society has been willing to accept the reproductive risks to adolescent farm workers exposed to toxic pesticides and to urban children whose mental development may be retarded by air polluted with lead, ozone, and other substances. The U.S. government has even subsidized the tobacco industry, while acknowledging that cigarette smoking causes 320,000 excess deaths a year.[73] Is it logical, then, to have a "no-risk" approach to maternal workplace exposures (with its obvious discriminatory effects) while maternal non-workplace risks and paternal workplace risks are considered acceptable?

Deciding whether risks are acceptable is a very difficult proposition. The societal implications must be carefully considered before any reproductive hazards policy is adopted. Notwithstanding their fear of liability or their economic leverage, employers should not be permitted to abrogate to themselves this decisionmaking authority. Perhaps one-sex exclusionary policies based on reproductive health need to be revised to provide for greater worker autonomy or, at least, informed, noncoercive decisionmaking shared between the employer and the employee.

A discussion of the legal issues related to reproductive hazards is contained in sections 10.5 and 10.6. The economic, ethical, and policy issues are further explored in Chapter 13.

CHAPTER 7

MEDICAL SCREENING AND THE COMMON LAW

7.1 The "At-Will" Doctrine and Its Exceptions

At common law, absent a statutory prohibition, an employer had virtually unfettered control in selecting its employees. The employer could hire or refuse to hire any person for any reason or no reason at all.[1] This right included the right to refuse to hire an individual because of the employer's opinion that the prospective employee was physically incapable of performing the job.[2] Once hired, the employee could be fired "at will" by the employer for any reason or no reason at all,[3] and, again, this included the employer's belief that the employee could no longer perform the job because of his or her physical condition.[4]

In recent years there has been considerable erosion of the at-will doctrine.[5] Some courts have relied on contract theory, holding that employment contracts have implied covenants of fair dealing or impliedly adopt personnel manuals of the company.[6] Most courts rejecting the absolute rule of the at-will doctrine, however, have done so by recognizing the existence of a tort action for wrongful discharge.[7] These cases are grounded on a new "public policy exception" to the at-will doctrine.[8]

The public policy exception has been applied to a variety of situations where employers have retaliated against employees in bad faith or for other reprehensible reasons, such as the following: retaliation for filing a workers' compensation claim,[9] retaliation for serving on jury duty,[10] retaliation because an employee refused to give false testimony at a legislative hearing,[11] retaliation because an employee refused to alter pollution control reports,[12] retaliation for an employee's attempts to obtain his employer's compliance with consumer credit laws,[13] retaliation for an employee's spurning of her supervisor's sexual advances,[14]

81

and retaliation because a doctor refused to violate medical ethics in drug testing.[15]

It is not clear how the courts will construe occupational safety and health matters within the context of the public policy exception. In one case, the Supreme Court of New Hampshire held that the discharge of an employee who was acting to protect his subordinates from dangerous working conditions violated the public policy exception.[16] On the other hand, the Supreme Court of Oregon has held that an employee discharged after complaining to his foreman about a health hazard has no action for wrongful discharge because OSHA's antidiscrimination clause (section 11(c)(1)) already provides adequate protection.[17]

The question of whether a statutory remedy already exists may be important to employees who allege they were discharged for failing to undergo employer-mandated medical examinations or tests. Because employees lack an existing remedy, they might be better able to maintain an action than where suits involve other safety- and health-related issues. Nevertheless, the employee must still prove that the discharge violated public policy. In an analogous case, the Third Circuit held that an employee who was discharged for refusing to take a polygraph test could sue for wrongful discharge because the Pennsylvania antipolygraph statute clearly embodied a public policy against such a requirement and the statute did not create any statutory remedy.[18]

Another important potential application of the tort of wrongful discharge involves dismissals of employees who sought treatment for or who reported occupational illnesses to their employers. Even where employees were still unimpaired and capable of performing the job, some employers have discharged the employees because they feared possible liability if the employees would become ill in the future. Obviously, such discharges have a chilling effect on workers seeking treatment for occupational illness and therefore a strong argument could be made that a dismissal of this sort violates public policy.

The elimination of the at-will doctrine is extremely important to employment rights generally because the vast majority of workers in the United States are nonunion and work in the private sector.[19] For them, the only limits on an employer's decisionmaking are the federal, state, and local employment discrimination laws which proscribe discrimination based on specific class membership, such as age, race, sex, religion, national origin, handicap, union activity, and veteran status.

Removing an employer's ability to terminate an employee at will only offers protection against abusive or groundless discharges. In effect, it puts the employee on the same legal footing as if there were a contract of employment for a fixed term. At common law, an employer may lawfully terminate an employment contract where the employee is physically unable to continue performance. This has been construed to apply not only to a present inability to perform[20] but also to an employee's physical predisposition to injury.[21] Therefore, the issue of "good cause" is still not clear and would require analyses of "job-relatedness," "predictability," and other concepts of employment discrimination cases discussed in later chapters.

In Great Britain, the Employment Protection (Consolidation) Act of 1978, as amended, prohibits employers from unfairly dismissing employees. Unfair dismissals for medical reasons are prohibited. In *Glitz v. Watford Electric Co.*,[22] the plaintiff was employed as a typist, and her duties included operating a duplicating machine. Fumes from the machine gave her headaches, even though the machine was working normally. She was removed from her position, but when there was no other available work she was dismissed. The Industrial Tribunal found the dismissal fair and the Employment Appeals Tribunal affirmed. The case demonstrates that even with "good-cause" requirements, individuals with inordinate responses to workplace conditions may not be protected.

Finally, it should be emphasized that the preceding discussion has only addressed the issue of wrongful discharge. In the absence of a statute, monumental changes in the at-will doctrine will be required before anything even approaching a good-cause standard can be applied to employer hiring decisions or promotion, transfer, work assignment, or other related matters.

7.2 Employer's Common Law Duties

At common law, employers had five main duties for the protection of employees. These included the duty to (1) provide a safe place to work; (2) provide safe appliances, tools, and equipment for the work; (3) give warnings of dangers of which the employee might reasonably be expected to remain in ignorance; (4) provide a sufficient number of suitable fellow employees; and (5) promulgate and enforce rules for the conduct of employees which would make the work safe.[23] These duties are still recognized by the law in all 50 states and the District of Columbia.[24]

At common law, employees who suffered work-related injury or illness had a right of action for damages against their employer. Because these actions were based on common law negligence, the employers were usually able to escape liability by invoking the common law defenses of contributory negligence, assumption of risk, and the fellow servant rule.[25] Thus, if the injury or illness was caused in any part by the negligence of the injured worker or any co-worker, or if the employee expressly or impliedly assumed the risk of working in a hazardous occupation, there was no recovery.[26] The passage of workers' compensation laws in the early part of this century abolished both common law actions and common law defenses, replacing them with an exclusive compensation system under which the fault of either party is irrelevant.[27]

The "exclusive remedy" rule generally applies only to actions for damages and does not apply to actions for injunctive and declaratory relief. In *Shimp v. New Jersey Bell Telephone Co.*,[28] an employee who was allergic to cigarette smoke sought an injunction requiring the employer to prohibit smoking in general working areas. The court held that the action for an injunction was not barred by the New Jersey Workmen's Compensation Act and that the plaintiff had a common law right to a healthful work environment. The employer was ordered to restrict smoking to nonwork areas.

Judicial reaction to *Shimp* has been mixed. Although it has been followed by a Missouri court,[29] a virtually identical case brought by federal government employees was dismissed.[30] The most recent case on this issue is *Gordon v. Raven Systems & Research, Inc.*[31] An employee who was hypersensitive to cigarette smoke was fired when she refused to work in an area where other employees smoked. While acknowledging that an employer has a common law duty to supply a reasonably safe place to work, the District of Columbia Court of Appeals rejected the argument that this duty extended to employees with special sensitivities. "[T]he common law does not impose upon an employer the duty or burden to conform his workplace to the particular needs or sensitivities of an individual employee."[32] *Shimp* was distinguished because the plaintiff in that case presented evidence of the danger that cigarette smoking poses to all employees, not just those of special sensitivity.

Even if *Shimp* were followed in other jurisdictions, it is not likely to open the door for sweeping injunctive relief. *Shimp* involved a hazard, cigarette smoke, that has not been regulated by OSHA. If a specific OSHA standard already had existed, the action might have been preempted by federal law. In addition, the hazard in *Shimp* did not result from a work process and could be remedied rather easily. The courts are not likely to issue broad injunctions for the correction of "traditional" workplace hazards or require the reduction of exposures in the workplace to the level where the most sensitive individual is risk-free.

As discussed earlier, at common law employers had no duty to conduct medical tests of applicants or employees. Except as modified by OSHA requirements, this is still the law. If an applicant or employee is injured as a result of an employer-provided examination (either during the course of the examination or by a failure to diagnose), however, a malpractice action may lie against the physician, the employer, or both. These personal injury actions are discussed in Chapter 12.

Another theory upon which an action might be brought involves an action against a physician for negligence where the wrongful diagnosis of an applicant or employee resulted in the denial of employment. In *Armstrong v. Morgan*,[33] an employee, upon being promoted, was requested to have a physical examination performed by a company-retained physician. The physician's report indicated that the employee was in very poor health, and as a result, the employee lost his job. According to the Texas Court of Civil Appeals, a negligence action against the physician stated a valid claim. "Dr. Morgan owed Appellant Armstrong a duty not to injure him physically or otherwise. If Dr. Morgan negligently performed the examination and as a result gave an inaccurate report of the state of appellant's health, and appellant was injured as a proximate result thereof, actionable negligence would be shown."[34]

Based on this theory a number of other possible actions could be brought, such as actions against laboratories that negligently performed screening tests, actions against the manufacturers of testing equipment, and actions against prior employers or other entities that negligently supplied inaccurate information about the health of the individual.

Actions for failure to hire or dismissal of an employee based on a negligent medical examination, however, may encounter several difficulties. First, the court must recognize a physician-patient relationship giving rise to a duty to report medical findings accurately. Second, the action may be precluded by the terms of a collective bargaining agreement. In *Williams v. St. Joe Minerals Corp.*,[35] an employee who was not reinstated because of the company physician's alleged negligent diagnosis of a nonexistent hernia brought an action against the company and the physician. The Missouri Court of Appeals held that the employee was required to exhaust his remedies through the grievance procedures in the collective bargaining agreement. Finally, the courts may not demand absolute precision in reports by physicians to personnel departments. In *Beadling v. Sirotta*,[36] the Supreme Court of New Jersey held that it was not negligence for a radiologist to diagnose a prospective employee's medical condition as "reinfection pulmonary tuberculosis" instead of "possible tuberculosis."

7.3   Employees' Common Law Rights

As discussed earlier, at common law the process by which employers selected their employees was almost exclusively within the prerogative of the employer. Consequently, employees have few common law rights related to the selection process, including the medical screening aspects. One part of the medical screening process giving rise to increasing activity on the part of legislatures and courts concerns employee privacy rights.

Although constitutional and administrative constraints limit the amount of information that can be demanded of public sector employees,[37] private sector employees have few, if any, rights in this area. In *Cort v. Bristol Myers Co.*,[38] three long-time sales employees of a pharmaceutical company were required to complete a "biographical summary," which sought information about business experience, education, family, home ownership, physical data, activities, and aims. In the medical history section, they were asked about serious illnesses, operations, accidents, nervous disorders, smoking and drinking habits, off-the-job problems, principal worries, medication being taken, age and health of parents, and other matters. The employees considered this information personal and irrelevant and either refused to answer these questions or did so in a flippant manner. The employees were discharged, ostensibly for poor performance.

The employees then brought actions for unlawful invasion of privacy and wrongful discharge. With respect to the invasion-of-privacy claim, the Supreme Judicial Court of Massachusetts ruled that because they did not complete the questionnaires, there was no invasion of privacy. "[T]he short answer is that the plaintiffs declined to provide any information they regarded as confidential or personal. The defendant's attempted invasion of privacy, if it was one, failed."[39] As to the wrongful-discharge claim, the court left open the question of whether the dismissal of an employee for failing to comply with a more intrusive inquiry would violate public policy,[40] but concluded that the dismissals in this case did not violate the public policy exception to the at-will doctrine.

The invasion-of-privacy theory has been rejected in other cases as well. For example, it has been held that a utility's requiring an employee to sign a form consenting to investigations to screen out security risks did not constitute an invasion of privacy[41] and that an employer was justified in asking an applicant if he had ever filed an industrial accident claim.[42] In *Larsen v. Motor Supply Co.*,[43] the Arizona Court of Appeals upheld the discharge of employees who had refused to sign a standardized consent form which was required before employees could take a mandatory "psychological stress evaluation test" designed to detect untruthful answers to various questions.

In one recent case, however, an invasion-of-privacy claim related to a sex discrimination action was partly successful. In *Wroblewski v. Lexington Gardens, Inc.*,[44] a woman applied for a job in a new plant store and was required to complete a medical history form. One section of the questionnaire marked "Women" asked about menstruation, "pap" smears, and the like. The woman chose not to complete this portion of the questionnaire, and her physician, who performed the preemployment physical examination, wrote "healthy female" in the section marked "physician's summary." When she was denied employment for failing to complete the medical questionnaire, the woman brought a legal action under the Connecticut Fair Employment Practice law, alleging sex discrimination. The woman contended that the form contained no questions about the urogenital health of male applicants and therefore was discriminatory.

The Supreme Court of Connecticut held that the plaintiff established a prima facie case of sex discrimination by demonstrating that male applicants were not required to answer similar questions. The court also rejected the employer's defenses that the questions were necessary to detect specific health problems and that some insecticides potentially dangerous to pregnant women might be used in the plant store. The company was ordered to cease using the discriminatory form.

The most troubling part of the invasion-of-privacy issue is that these lawsuits arise only when applicants or employees refuse to supply the requested information. The overwhelming majority of individuals faced with such inquiries probably acquiesce to employer demands and provide the information. The answer, then, is not simply to order the reinstatement of the few who refuse to comply, but to prohibit employers from making these inquiries in the first place.

In 1976 Maryland enacted the first law[45] that limits the permissible scope of employer inquiry in preemployment or postemployment questioning. It provides in pertinent part:

(a) An employer may not require an applicant to answer any questions, written or oral, pertaining to any physical, psychological, or psychiatric illness, disability, handicap or treatment which does not bear a direct, material, and timely relationship to the applicant's fitness or capacity to properly perform the activities or responsibilities of the desired position.

(b) This section does not prohibit a proper medical evaluation by a physician for the purpose of assessing an applicant's ability to perform a job.

In addition to administrative mediation and conciliation, the statute provides for injunctive relief and damages. Because there are no reported cases involving the law, it is not clear how the various provisions will be construed, especially subsection (b) on medical evaluations.

The most intrusive employer medical procedure is the requirement that all applicants or employees submit to a medical examination. Again, there are few legal controls on these procedures except for an occasional state law like a West Virginia law providing that an employer may not require the payment of fees for a medical examination as a condition of employment.[46] With the increasing use of occupational medical screening, examinations, and procedures there is a growing likelihood that an applicant or employee would refuse to take such an examination on religious, ethical, medical, privacy, or other grounds. The question thus arises whether an applicant or employee has a right to refuse to undergo medical tests. The answer seems clear that there is no constitutional or common law right to refuse the examination or test. Unless the test procedure violates a specific statute, regulation, or collective bargaining agreement, the individual must submit to the examination or suffer the consequences.

In *Garguil v. Tompkins*[47] a female school teacher was dismissed for insubordination and incompetency for refusing to take a medical exam after an extended leave of absence. The teacher asserted that being examined by the school board's male physician "violated her sense of privacy and was anathema to her private creed."[48] In upholding her dismissal, the United States District Court for the Northern District of New York held that there was no constitutional right to refuse a medical examination because the physician was male. In similar cases decided under collective bargaining agreements, arbitrators and courts have upheld the discharge of an employee who refused to take a medical examination[49] and an employee who refused to have an annual chest x-ray because of fear of radiation exposure.[50]

OSHA's coke oven emissions standard contains a requirement that the employer must inform any employee who refuses a required medical examination of the possible health consequences and must obtain a signed statement from the employee indicating that the employee understands the risks involved in such a refusal.[51] It is not clear, however, whether this provision would prevent the employer from disciplining an employee who refused a medical examination. An employee's best source of protection for refusing an examination, under certain circumstances, may be Title VII of the Civil Rights Act of 1964.[52]

Another area of importance involves the rights of employees to obtain the results of their medical examinations and to be informed of workplace health hazards. While OSHA requires that employees (but not job applicants) be given access to certain employee medical records if they so request, with the exception of seven health standards,[53] it does not establish an affirmative duty to disclose the results of medical examinations to employees. The OSHA access regulation (further discussed in section 8.5) may be causing companies to reassess their policies, but the prevailing mode still appears to be that employees are not informed of the results of medical examinations and tests. As a result of its hearings on this issue, OSHA concluded "that denial of direct, unrestricted employee access to exposure and medical information is commonplace, if not the universal practice of industry."[54] In one study of Fortune 500 companies, 83% of the companies responding to a survey denied workers access to their medical records.[55]

The main legal limitation on the withholding of medical information is the possibility of civil liability. Thus, a company and the physician may be liable for breaching the duty to inform the applicant or worker of any illness, occupational or nonoccupational, that was detected or should have been detected by medical personnel.[56] In Massachusetts, when an employer requires an employee to have a medical examination the employee must be furnished with a copy of the medical report.[57]

Employers have a common law duty to apprise employees of latent dangers, including the health hazards associated with toxic chemicals. In reality, however, few employees are informed about the identities, properties, and health risks of the chemicals and other toxic materials with which they work.[58] Such company policies, of course, are the responsibility of management generally and not just of the occupational physician.

In November 1983 OSHA published its final Hazard Communication standard.[59] The standard covers an estimated 14 million employees in 300,000 manufacturing establishments. Among other things, it requires chemical manufacturers and importers to assess the hazards of chemicals which they produce or import, and all employers engaged in manufacturing to provide information to their employees concerning hazardous chemicals by means of hazard communication programs including labels, material safety data sheets, training, and access to written records.[60] One of the purposes of the new standard is to preempt the "right-to-know" laws already enacted in 16 states.[61]

Another federal law with recordkeeping requirements is the Toxic Substances Control Act (TOSCA). Section 8(c) of TOSCA requires that "any person who manufactures, processes, or distributes in commerce any chemical substance or mixture" must keep "records of significant adverse reactions to health or the environment. . . ." It further requires that allegations of adverse reactions to the health of employees be kept for 30 years.[62] Although the Environmental Protection Agency (EPA) has the statutory authority to require the submission of these records, under its regulations EPA does not require the automatic reporting of the records. EPA regulations exempt retailers, processors and distributers that are not engaged in manufacture.[63]

7.4   Medical Records

Occupational health records usually contain identification and demographic background, narrative, objective findings and measurements, opinions, judgments, and recommendations.[64] The records may also contain sensitive personal information on topics such as psychiatric problems, drug and alcohol abuse, and reproductive matters. As more medical information is collected about applicants and employees and with technologically expanded capabilities to store, retrieve, and disseminate the information, a variety of legal, ethical, and practical problems have arisen.

Ironically, medical records are not usually accessible to employees, nor are employees informed about occupational health determinations.[65] This is particularly disturbing in the context of employee medical testing. If elaborate screening and monitoring measures have any value, it is the ability to inform high-risk workers so they can make a reasonable judgment about whether to accept such risks and to identify workers in need of additional medical surveillance or personal protective equipment. The avowed reason for nondisclosure is that employees are too unsophisticated to be able to understand their own health measurements and records and that giving such data to an individual could cause stress.[66] It is hard to imagine that such paternalism is justified, and it takes only a little cynicism to theorize more self-serving reasons for such policies.

As of 1980, employees have a right to see their medical records pursuant to OSHA's Access to Employee Exposure and Medical Records Standard.[67] This comprehensive standard, which is further discussed in section 8.5, was promulgated to facilitate (1) worker participation in personal health management; (2) worker discovery of, and efforts to control, occupational health hazards; (3) improved ability to diagnose and treat occupational disease; and (4) employee awareness and improved work practices.[68] Besides OSHA's Access Standard, which only applies to toxic substances, there are few legal requirements that employers give employees a right of access to medical records. Five states give employees the right of access to their medical records, usually as part of a broader right to review their entire personnel record.[69] The only other source of an access right is through a collective bargaining agreement.

While employees have limited legal rights with respect to their own medical records, there are no legal restrictions on the intracompany dissemination of employee medical records. The Code of Ethics for Physicians Providing Occupational Medical Services provides, in part:

> Physicians should treat as confidential whatever is learned about individuals served, releasing information only when required by law or by overriding public health considerations, or to other physicians at the request of the individual according to traditional medical ethical practice; and should recognize that employers are entitled to counsel about the medical fitness of individuals in relation to work, but are not entitled to diagnoses or details of a specific nature.[70]

In practice, however, management access to employee medical records is often much more extensive.[71] Both OSHA and the Privacy Protection Study Commission found that significant abuses of employee medical records occur regularly.

Unfortunately, employees have few legal remedies. First, as a practical matter, it is often difficult, if not impossible, for the employee to know of such disclosures. Second, as a condition of employment, employees often sign blanket waivers authorizing the company to use medical and personnel records as it deems necessary. Third, liability for wrongful disclosure would have to be based on a breach of the physician's duty of confidentiality, and, as discussed earlier, many courts have found that there is no physician-patient relationship where the physician is provided by the company.

It has been asserted that because workers have little genuine expectation of true confidentiality as to employment medical records, there is an implied waiver of confidentiality by the employee's consenting to the examination. Nevertheless, consent to medical examination is often a condition of employment and carries with it none of the usual elements of voluntariness on the patient's part. Moreover, the employees are not usually informed about the lack of the traditional confidentiality that patients expect from members of the medical profession.

Even more disturbing than the intracompany disclosure of medical records is the considerable risk that these same medical records will be widely available to various third parties through one of the vast computerized networks dealing with private medical records.[72] Some employers already have established procedures for exchanging medical surveillance records of workers known to have had prior exposures to hazardous substances.[73] There are even reports that some companies compile lists of workers who have filed work injury lawsuits, which are made available to employers for use in screening employment applications.[74]

Common law actions for company disclosure of medical information to third parties again must overcome the defense that there is no physician-patient relationship between an applicant or employee and the company doctor. Invasion-of-privacy actions have been recognized, however, where the employee's personal physician divulged to her employer that she was pregnant[75] and where a physician was induced to divulge confidential information under false pretenses.[76] Several state and federal statutes also provide a variety of limited protections from disclosure.

At the federal level, the Privacy Act of 1974 controls federal government maintenance of information, affords individuals the right of access and the right to correct their files, and prohibits nonconsensual disclosure to third parties. The Fair Credit Reporting Act provides that if an applicant or employee is rejected on the basis of a credit report the individual has a right to be informed of the report.

At the state level, two-thirds of the states have statutorily created a physician-patient testimonial privilege.[77] Also, state medical licensing statutes mandating confidentiality of information disclosed by patients may provide the basis for a judicially implied cause of action.[78] The most extensive state regulation of medical information, however, is California's Confidentiality of Medical Information Act.[79] It provides, in part:

> Each employer who receives medical information shall establish appropriate procedures to ensure the confidentiality and protection from unauthorized use and disclosure of that information. These procedures may include, but are not limited to, instruction regarding confidentiality of employees and agents handling files containing medical information, and security systems restricting access to files containing medical information.
>   . . . No employer shall use, disclose, or knowingly permit its employees or agents to use or disclose medical information which the employer possesses pertaining to its employees without the patient having first signed an authorization . . . permitting such use or disclosure [except if the disclosure of the records is compelled by legal process, the records are an issue in a pending legal action, the information is used in administering an employee benefits plan, or the information is used in diagnosis or treatment].[80]

Under the law, an individual whose records have been disclosed may recover compensatory damages, punitive damages up to $3,000, attorney fees up to $1,000, and costs of litigation. Violations are also punishable as misdemeanors. This statute is, by far, the most sweeping protection for employee privacy.

Another form of extracompany disclosure is involuntary on the employer's part—the production of employee medical records for the government. Although employers have been permitted to assert the privacy interests of their employees, medical records subpoenas have been enforced. The courts have held that employee privacy interests and the interests of the National Institute for Occupational Safety and Health (NIOSH) are not mutually exclusive, and that, with proper security administration, the records should be accessible with minimal incursions on employee privacy.[81] The Occupational Safety and

Health Review Commission has adopted a similar position with respect to discovery of medical records in the course of an adjudicatory
proceeding.[82] OSHA's Access to Exposure and Medical Records
Standard gives OSHA the right to obtain employee medical records,
but limits the disclosure of this information and provides safeguards to
ensure confidentiality.

CHAPTER 8

THE OCCUPATIONAL SAFETY
AND HEALTH ACT

8.1 OSHA and Occupational Medicine

The Occupational Safety and Health Act of 1970 was enacted "to assure so far as possible every working man and woman in the Nation safe and healthful working conditions...." It is the only comprehensive statute addressed to hazards in the workplace and therefore is the primary vehicle for hazard elimination. Section 5(a) of the Act requires employers to furnish a place of employment free from recognized hazards and to comply with all standards promulgated under the Act. Section 5(b) requires each employee to comply with "all rules, regulations, and orders issued pursuant to this Act which are applicable to his own actions and conduct."

Despite the seeming similarity of these provisions, it is clear that "[f]inal responsibility for compliance with the requirements of this Act remains with the employer."[1] Only the employer may be issued citations, assessed penalities, and ordered to abate violative conditions. In essence, employees are the third-party beneficiaries of a new set of legal duties imposed on the employer by the government. Employees may only petition the Secretary of Labor to enforce the requirements of the Act; the employer is required by law to obtain the compliance of employees, even if this entails the sanctioning of disobedient employees.

Employer duties under OSHA are specific and the legal responsibility is nondelegable. An employer may not rely on a union to provide safety training, it may not contract out safety and health responsibility for its employees to another employer or a political subdivision, and it may not shift the burden of compliance to employees or supervisors. Under OSHA employees may neither assume the risk nor consent to work in conditions that violate the Act's requirements.

The Act's statement of purpose recognizes the role of occupational medicine in the prevention of work-related illness. The goal of safe and healthful working conditions, set out in section 2 of the Act, is to be implemented, among other ways:

> (6) by exploring ways to discover diseases, establishing causal connections between diseases and work in environmental conditions, and conducting other research relating to health problems, in recognition of the fact that occupational health standards present problems often different from those involved in occupational safety;
> (7) by providing medical criteria which will assure insofar as practicable that no employee will suffer diminished health, functional capacity, or life expectancy as a result of his work experience;

Despite this language, OSHA's focus on occupational medical problems has been rather limited. Indeed, occupational safety has generally taken precedence over occupational health matters. As documented in section 2.5, there are few OSHA-mandated medical procedures. Even the 21 health standards with specific medical examination requirements fail to address three crucial issues. First, the Occupational Safety and Health Administration, the Labor Department bureau charged with enforcement of the Act, has not developed any medical criteria to be used by physicians in conducting required examinations. Second, OSHA requires that certain procedures be performed, but with only one exception, it does not prohibit other procedures from being used. Third, there is no indication of how medical information may be used in employment decisionmaking.

In general, OSHA has not become involved in regulating the actual determinations by physicians of the medical fitness of employees. One notable exception concerns the "multiple physician review" procedure. In *Taylor Diving & Salvage Co. v. United States Department of Labor*,[2] the Fifth Circuit struck down the medical examination provision of the commercial diving standard. The standard required medical examination of employees who were to be exposed to hyperbaric conditions. If the employee was found to be unfit by the examining physician selected by the employer, the employee could seek a second opinion. If the first two physicians disagreed, a third physician was to be selected by the first two physicians and that physician's determination would be dispositive. All costs were to be borne by the employer.

The Fifth Circuit, citing its decision in *American Petroleum Institute v. OSHA*,[3] held that the standard was not "reasonably necessary or appropriate to provide safe or healthful workplaces." The court concluded that the standard imposed a mandatory job security provision controlled by the third physician. "[T]he employer has no control over the third doctor's fitness standards, so that the employer is prevented from setting higher health standards for employees than the secondary examining doctors choose to set."[4]

In *United Steelworkers of America v. Marshall*,[5] the D.C. Circuit reached the opposite result and upheld the multiple physician review procedure of the lead standard. According to the court, the provision is authorized by section 6(b)(7)'s broad mandate to require examinations that can "most effectively determine" a threat to worker health. In addition, the provision is reasonable in light of two findings supported by the record. First, lead diseases are often difficult to diagnose and multiple physician review increases the chances of a correct diagnosis. Second, some company physicians have engaged in the unsound and harmful practice of prophylactic chelation to reduce the blood-lead levels of employees. The court distinguished *Taylor*, where employees would seek multiple physician review to obtain a finding of fitness, thus forcing the employer to retain employees considered unfit by its own physician and standards. In the lead standard, the multiple physician review procedure was to prevent excess exposure of "leaded" employees and together with the medical removal protection, the employer is not precluded from imposing more stringent health standards.

Besides the multiple physician review *procedure*, OSHA has not acted to facilitate the analysis of medical data by occupational physicians. OSHA has not published guidelines about what information obtained from a medical history is significant, what clinical symptoms are meaningful, or what test measurements indicate impairment or increased risk. OSHA standards simply require that these medical services be performed. From a purely medical standpoint, the identification of high-risk workers is extremely difficult. The most knowledgeable and experienced occupational physicians will frequently differ on the likely consequences of employee health from toxic exposures in light of prior occupational and nonoccupational medical history; genetic, environmental, and behavioral factors; laboratory results; and the like. Considering that only about 11.4% of employees work in a plant where there is a full-time physician,[6] the need for more concrete medical guidance is essential.

On February 6, 1980, the *New York Times* published an article by Richard Severo, entitled "Federal Mandate for Gene Tests Disturbs U.S. Job Safety Official." The article reported that Dr. Eula Bingham, Assistant Secretary of Labor for OSHA, was "astounded" to learn that an OSHA regulation required genetic factors to be considered during a preemployment physical examination. In actuality, there are 13 OSHA carcinogen standards[7] containing the following provision:

> Before an employee is assigned to enter a regulated area, a preassignment physical examination by a physician shall be provided. The examination shall include the personal history of the employee, family and occupational background, including genetic and environmental factors.[8]

No one has been able to say how this provision got into the OSHA carcinogen standards or what the term "genetic factors" was intended to mean. Nevertheless, on August 22, 1980, OSHA issued a clarifying memo providing that the term "genetic factors" in the carcinogen standards does not require genetic testing of any employee and does not require the exclusion of otherwise qualified employees from jobs on the basis of genetic testing.[9]

The "genetic factors" provision in the carcinogen standards became a *cause célèbre* and OSHA moved promptly to explain that no genetic testing was required. On the other hand, genetic testing by employers was not prohibited. In fact, there is only one OSHA standard that prohibits any type of occupational medical procedure—the ban on prophylactic chelation in the lead standard.[10]

If an employer were to base an adverse personnel action on the results of a dubious medical test, the question is raised whether this adverse treatment is prohibited by OSHA. The Act's antidiscrimination provision is the most likely source of protection. Section 11(c)(1) of the Act provides, in pertinent part: "No person shall discharge or in any manner discriminate against any employee . . . because of the exercise by such employee on behalf of himself or others of any right afforded by this Act." This provision and OSHA's regulations implementing it[11] have been broadly construed by the courts.[12] Moreover, section 11(c)(2) authorizes the Secretary of Labor to bring an action on behalf of any discriminatee in United States district court to restrain violations of section 11(c)(1) and to obtain all appropriate relief, including reinstatement and back pay. Individuals may not proceed on their own, however, even if the Secretary refuses to bring an action on their behalf.[13] Because the antidiscrimination provision of section 11(c) is the only "job security" section of the Act, it should be considered as a possible means of protecting high-risk workers.

OSHA has promulgated a regulation providing that disciplinary measures taken by an employer solely in response to an employee's refusal to comply with safety and health regulations are not considered discrimination in violation of section 11(c).[14] Thus, it could be asserted that section 11(c) would prohibit the discharge of an employee for the professed reason that the employee had violated the Act when, in fact, the employee had not violated the Act. Similarly, this would prohibit the discharge of an employee when the employer erroneously claims that an employee's employment violates the Act. For example, an employee might be discharged because the employer erroneously considers the employee to be at a high risk of manifesting symptoms indicative of unlawfully high exposure levels. The employer action could even be taken after a periodic biological monitoring of the employee, as mandated by the OSHA standard, indicated an "abnormal" reading. Because OSHA regulations define "employee" to include job applicants,[15] it could be argued that it would be a violation of section 11(c) for an employer to refuse to hire a high-risk worker because of an erroneous belief that hiring that individual would violate the Act.

Even if OSHA were inclined to extend the scope of its antidiscrimination protections to the limit of its authority, it is doubtful that such a strategy would be successful. In fiscal year 1980, OSHA received over 3,500 discrimination complaints, which were handled by a staff of only 59. During the same year, the case backlog grew from 1,559 to over 2,100. More importantly, 446 cases found to be meritorious could not be filed in district court because of inadequate resources. Recent budget cuts at OSHA make it even more unlikely that new and complex antidiscrimination protections could or would be enforced.

One final provision of OSHA has a direct bearing on occupational medical practice. Section 20(a)(5) of the Act provides, in part: "Nothing in this or any other provision of this Act shall be deemed to authorize or require medical examination, immunization, or treatment for those who object thereto on religious grounds, except where such is necessary for the protection of the health or safety of others." Although there are no reported cases dealing with this part of section 20(a)(5), OSHA has shown an appreciation for the potential conflict between religion and safety and health. For example, an OSHA requirement that hard hats be worn while working in carpentry trades and construction was ruled by OSHA to be inapplicable to Old Order Amish, whose religion requires members to wear a wide-brimmed black felt hat, even while working. A similar exemption also has been granted to the Sikh Dharma Brotherhood. As further discussed in section 10.2, religious objections to medical procedures also may be protected under Title VII.

8.2   Medical Removal Protection and Rate Retention

OSHA's only attempt to regulate the effects of medical examinations on employment involves medical removal protection (MRP) and rate retention (RR) of previously exposed employees. When a periodic medical examination indicates that the employee is showing symptoms of the adverse effects of exposure to the toxic substance, the employee is removed from further exposure—to a "safe" job if there is an opening—until it is medically advisable for the employee to return. If the new, safe position is at a lower rate of pay, RR would require the maintenance of wage and benefit levels during the period of medical removal. Thus, MRP and RR attempt to protect employee health without a reduction in employee benefits, thereby shifting the economic burden to the employer and ultimately to the consumer.

MRP and RR provisions in OSHA health standards have become increasingly stringent. For example, the vinyl chloride standard provides for MRP, but not RR,[16] and the asbestos standard provides for MRP of employees for whom respirators are ineffective, but RR is required only if there is an available position.[17] The most sweeping MRP and RR provision is in the lead standard.[18] Employees whose blood-lead levels are above the specified limit or who show symptoms of lead disease must be removed until the blood-lead has returned to an acceptable level and their general health is good. The employer may transfer the employee to a nonlead plant or low-lead area of a plant, or may keep the employee in a high-lead area for a shorter work week. When an employee is removed in any way, the employee retains his or her earnings rate, seniority, and benefit levels for up to 18 months and upon return must be restored to his or her original job status.

In *United Steelworkers of America v. Marshall*,[19] the D.C. Circuit upheld the validity of the MRP and RR provision. The lead industry argued that Congress did not intend to have MRP and RR under OSHA because the Act is silent on this subject, while the Coal Mine Health and Safety Act of 1969 (CMHSA), passed the year before OSHA, contained an MRP provision. The court rejected this argument, noting that the CMHSA covered a single industry and was drafted with much greater specificity than OSHA.

The lead industry next argued that the provision violated section 4(b)(4)'s prohibition on OSHA interfering with workers' compensation. Although acknowledging the "seriousness" of this argument, the court noted the limited duration and scope (for example, there is no payment for medical expenses) of RR benefits and indicated that the group of workers to benefit from this provision will become increasingly smaller as the permissible exposure limit (PEL) is lowered. "We conclude that though MRP may indeed have a great practical effect on workmen's compensation claims, it leaves the state schemes wholly intact as a *legal* matter, and so does not violate section 4(b)(4)."[20]

Finally, the court rejected the argument that requiring MRP and RR violates the national labor policy of allowing all substantive provisions of labor-management relations to be left to collective bargaining. Simply because earnings protection is a mandatory subject of bargaining and could be adopted through collective bargaining does not mean OSHA has no authority to mandate such a program.

In *American Textile Manufacturer's Institute, Inc. v. Donovan*,[21] the Supreme Court struck down the MRP and RR provision of the cotton dust standard as promulgated and remanded it to the Secretary for further consideration. Although the Court did not decide the issue of whether OSHA has the statutory authority to promulgate *any* regulation containing MRP and RR, the Court held that OSHA failed to publish a statement of reasons explaining why the MRP and RR provisions were needed to protect worker health and safety.

It would be a mistake to dismiss this aspect of the decision as merely the Court's response to a procedural blunder by the Secretary. According to the Court, "the Act in no way authorizes OSHA to repair general unfairness to employees that is unrelated to achievement of health and safety goals...."[22] Therefore, any wide-ranging attempt by OSHA to improve employment terms and opportunities for high-risk workers would likely be held outside of OSHA's authority, but a standard with a documented need for MRP and RR may be upheld.

As mentioned earlier, under CMHSA, as amended, MRP and RR are provided for in the statute itself. Any miner who shows evidence of the development of pneumoconiosis must be given the *option* of transferring to another position in the mine where the concentration of respirable dust in the mine atmosphere is not more than 1.0 milligrams of dust per cubic meter of air. Any miner transferred on this basis must continue to receive compensation at the rate of pay received immediately prior to transfer.[23]

In two areas MRP and RR may be of particular importance in the future. The temporary removal of male and female employees attempting to parent children may be one way of accommodating the interest of equal employment opportunity with the interest of preventing harmful exposure to reproductive hazards.[24] (Such a provision, of course, would not help where the pregnancy is unplanned.) Appendix C of the lead standard provides that MRP for employees attempting to become parents should be considered as an optional procedure by the physician.

The second area in which MRP and RR may be helpful involves exposure to carcinogens. If genetic monitoring of previously exposed workers indicates mutagen- or clastogen-induced genetic damage, MRP and RR could prevent continued exposure while preserving the employment and economic interests of the employee.[25] There is some concern, however, that employers would be reluctant to undertake any genetic monitoring of employees unless they were required to do so. According to Dr. Marvin Legator of the University of Texas, some employers fear that if genetic monitoring discovered a high-risk worker and the worker later developed cancer, then the employer may be sued. On the other hand, if no tests were performed, there could be no legal action. As Dr. Legator put it, "the good guys get punished, and the bad guys get off scot free."[26]

There is no doubt that Dr. Legator has accurately summarized the view of many industry leaders. As a legal matter, however, this position is not necessarily correct. First, MRP (with or without RR) could eliminate the possibility of occupational disease and therefore of litigation. Second, even without MRP, a worker who was informed of all the risks associated with continued exposure may well be precluded from a subsequent civil recovery.[27] Third, it may be negligence, fraudulent concealment, or some other actionable tort for an employer to *fail* to conduct genetic monitoring of exposed workers when the available technology indicates the utility of such measures.

MRP and RR are very expensive personnel actions and the vast costs should not be taken lightly. Alternative "safe" positions are often unavailable and even where they are, the base pay is often less than that for the job with the hazardous exposure. From a practical standpoint, there are other issues. The lead standard requires MRP and RR for 18 months for blood-lead to come down to acceptable levels. Carcinogen exposure, however, may not be reversible and therefore raises new questions. For how long should the company be required to maintain wage and benefit levels? At how close a location should the employee be required to accept alternative employment? How many reproduction-related medical removals should each employee be entitled to? Finally, as a scientific matter, "rotating in" new employees when previous workers have suffered chromosomal damage from exposures will only increase the worker population at risk.

Any new use for MRP and RR would raise these and other issues. Obviously, considerable thought is needed before implementing any wider MRP and RR program. The experience of the lead standard would be an appropriate place to start. As for the expense, a good argument could be made that the costs of working with reproductive and cancer hazards should be borne by the company and passed along to consumers. Where there is elasticity of demand, market forces will support substitute products made more safely and inexpensively. Where demand is inelastic, the price of the product will rise to its true market cost rather than its previous, artificially deflated cost. The problem of competition from imported products made in countries where the working conditions would not satisfy American standards, of course, remains a complex political problem yet to be addressed.

8.3   Employee Variability and Standards Promulgation

The bedrock of the OSHA scheme is the requirement that employers comply with all duly promulgated standards. Under the Act, there are three bases of standards promulgation. Pursuant to section 6(a), the Secretary of Labor was initially authorized to adopt as the agency's own regulations "established federal standards" and "national consensus standards." "Established federal standard" is defined by section 3(10) as "any operative occupational safety and health standard established by any agency of the United States and presently in effect, or contained in any Act of Congress in force on December 29, 1970" (the date the Act was signed). Essentially, these standards included other federal occupational safety and health measures already "on the books."

The term "national consensus standard" is defined by section 3(9) as any occupational safety and health standard which (1) has been adopted and promulgated by a nationally recognized standards-producing organization under procedures whereby it can be determined by the Secretary of Labor that persons interested and affected by the scope of provisions of the standard have reached substantial agreement on its adoption; (2) was formulated in a manner which afforded an opportunity for diverse views to be considered; and (3) has been designated as a national consensus standard by the Secretary of Labor after consultation with other appropriate federal agencies. Essentially, these standards are professionally developed private standards.

The important thing about section 6(a) standards is that the Secretary could simply *adopt* them without resort to the detailed rule-making provisions required by the Act for other standards. Congress was concerned that without a provision for prompt adoption of standards the Act's implementation would be delayed unnecessarily until standards could be drafted and promulgated. National consensus standards and established federal standards were considered to be sufficiently accepted and acceptable to be adopted summarily by OSHA. Although the special authority to adopt section 6(a) standards was in effect for only two years (and expired in 1973), the standards adopted in this manner are still valid and enforceable and remain the backbone of OSHA's safety and health standards.

Section 6(b) of the Act sets out detailed procedures to be followed in promulgating new OSHA standards or modifying or revoking existing OSHA standards. Standards promulgation or rulemaking under section 6(b) has been a hybrid form of rulemaking. While the statute only requires informal or notice-and-comment rulemaking, OSHA regulations have provided for hearing procedures, such as the right to present oral testimony and to cross-examine adverse witnesses—normally associated with formal rulemaking.[28] Consequently, the rulemaking on new standards often has been quite exhaustive. For example, the hearing record for OSHA's generic carcinogen standard was 250,000 pages.

The third type of OSHA standard is the emergency temporary standard (ETS). Section 6(c) provides that if the Secretary of Labor determines that workers are "exposed to grave danger from exposure to substances or agents determined to be toxic or physically harmful or from new hazards," an ETS may be issued. An ETS is effective immediately upon issuance and no detailed rulemaking is required. An ETS may remain in effect for only six months, however; thereafter, the Secretary must promulgate a permanent standard under section 6(b).

In 1971, pursuant to section 6(a), OSHA adopted 450 threshold limit values (TLVs) developed by the American Conference of Governmental Industrial Hygienists (ACGIH). The standards, adopted as established federal standards (they were adopted as federal standards in 1969 pursuant to the Walsh-Healey Act), set exposure limits for toxic substances in the workplace. They still are the major part of OSHA health standards, with only 21 new health standards having been promulgated under section 6(b).

A threshold limit value represents the maximum time-weighted average concentration to which a healthy worker may be exposed for a normal 40-hour week up to eight hours a day over a working lifetime (40 to 50 years) without becoming ill. As such, the TLVs do not attempt to protect high-risk workers. This fact is recognized in the preface of the 1983–84 ACGIH TLV booklet.

> Threshold limit values refer to airborne concentrations of substances and represent conditions under which it is believed that nearly all workers may be repeatedly exposed day after day without adverse effect. Because of wide variation in individual susceptibility, however, a small percentage of workers may experience discomfort from some substances at concentrations at or below the threshold limit; a smaller percentage may be affected more seriously by aggravation of a pre-existing condition or by development of an occupational illness.[29]

In setting exposure levels under new health standards promulgated under section 6(b), OSHA also has not made special provisions for high-risk workers. Section 6(b)(5) provides that in promulgating standards regulating toxic substances or harmful physical agents the Secretary must set standards to assure, to the extent feasible, that *"no employee"* (emphasis added) will suffer material impairment of health, even if exposed for his or her entire working life. As documented earlier, however, all humans vary in their susceptibility to illness and only zero exposure limits could protect *all* employees from the risk of occupational disease.

An important question is whether, based on the seemingly absolute language of section 6(b)(5), OSHA has the authority to promulgate standards with permissible exposure limits (PELs) low enough to protect sensitive workers. Two recent Supreme Court decisions suggest that such sweeping rulemaking might not survive judicial review.

In *Industrial Union Department v. American Petroleum Institute* (*API* or *"the benzene case"*),[30] the plurality opinion rejected OSHA's policy of setting the PEL for carcinogens at the lowest feasible level and held that the Secretary must determine that a standard is reasonably necessary or appropriate to remedy a significant risk of material health impairment. It is therefore quite possible that a PEL designed to safeguard the health of relatively few sensitive workers would be struck down by the courts.

A second potential stumbling block to an "absolute" standard is the Supreme Court's decision in *American Textile Manufacturers Institute v. Donovan* (*ATMI* or *"the cotton dust case"*).[31] While rejecting the argument that "feasible" in section 6(b)(5) requires or permits cost-

benefit analysis, the Court held that "feasible" includes both technological and economic considerations. A PEL designed to safeguard
the health of relatively few sensitive workers might also be struck
down as being infeasible.

It is not only as a legal matter, but as a practical matter as well,
that inadequate scientific documentation, the lack of available technology, and high costs will, for the foreseeable future, prevent workplaces from becoming safe for sensitive workers. The coke oven
emissions standard certainly recognizes this fact. The preamble to
the standard contains the following:

> Because of the variability of individual response to carcinogens and
> other factors, the concept of a "threshold level" may have little appli-
> cability on the basis of existing knowledge. Cancer may be a process
> which can be initiated by the transformation of only one or a few cells;
> its development may take close to a lifetime to manifest itself; and some
> individuals may be more susceptible than others. Thus, while a
> "threshold" exposure level, below which exposure does not cause can-
> cer, may conceivably exist for an individual, susceptible individuals in
> the working population may have cancer induced by doses so low as to
> be effectively zero.[31a]

Some OSHA health standards, such as those regulating arsenic,
lead, and acrylonitrile, offer protection for sensitive employees by
the requirement of medical surveillance for all employees exposed to
concentrations above the "action level." (An action level is an exposure level below the PEL that initiates an employer's legal requirement to conduct medical surveillance, environmental monitoring, or
other measures.) Then, if harmful effects are detected, personal protective equipment, administrative controls (such as shift rotation),
medical removal, or other measures may be taken. In *API*, the Supreme Court's plurality opinion supported the principle of action
level medical screening, observing that it "could ensure that workers
who were unusually susceptible . . . could be removed from exposure
before they had suffered any permanent damage."[32]

OSHA's efforts at protecting one class of sensitive workers, fertile employees—men and women of procreative capacity—has been
the subject of considerable controversy. In *United Steelworkers of America v. Marshall*,[33] the lead industry argued that no feasible lead standard could protect fertile women and therefore fertile women should
be excluded from the workplace or "counseled out" on a case-by-
case basis. The D.C. Circuit rejected this argument and held: (1)
OSHA has statutory authority to protect the fetuses of lead-exposed
working mothers; (2) lead also poses a severe threat to the reproduc-

tive capacity of male employees; and (3) OSHA proved that blood-lead levels contemplated by the standard are capable of protecting fertile women if supplemented by other provisions of the standard, such as medical removal protection.

8.4   Medical Testing and the General Duty Clause

Section 5(a)(1) of OSHA, the "general duty clause," provides that each employer "shall furnish to each of his employees employment and a place of employment which are free from recognized hazards that are causing or are likely to cause death or serious physical harm to his employees." There are two ways in which section 5(a)(1) could affect medical testing. First, the general duty clause could *require* that certain procedures be used as a means of safeguarding employees. Second, it could *prohibit* certain employer medical practices. In general, however, it is not likely that section 5(a)(1) will be very effective in the area of occupational medical practices.

To analyze whether section 5(a)(1) could be used to regulate medical matters, it is important to note the purpose and requirements of this section. Congress realized that it would be impossible and undesirable to have a specific standard covering every conceivable workplace hazard. Therefore, section 5(a)(1) was included in the Act to require employers to provide workplaces free of serious "recognized hazards." A hazard is considered "recognized" if it is known to be a hazard by the employer or generally recognized as such by the employer's industry.[34]

In the leading case of *National Realty & Construction Co. v. OSHRC*,[35] the D.C. Circuit outlined the Secretary of Labor's burden of proving a section 5(a)(1) violation. The Secretary must prove (1) that the employer failed to render its workplace free of a hazard which was (2) recognized and (3) causing or likely to cause death or serious physical harm, and (4) that the citation has specified the particular steps the cited employer should have taken to avoid citation and that these measures are feasible and have a likely utility. In addition, because the general duty clause was designed to supplement standards, citation is proper under section 5(a)(1) only when there is no applicable standard. "The standards presumably give the employer superior notice of the alleged violation and should be used instead of the general duty clause whenever possible."[36]

In applying these principles to the first possible use of section 5(a)(1), to *require* certain medical practices, it will be helpful to consider a specific question. Could section 5(a)(1) be used to require the use of cytogenetic monitoring of workers exposed to clastogens such as vinyl chloride? The answer is probably not. To begin with, it is extremely unlikely that a hazard detectable only by an experimental and unproven technology could be considered "recognized." Even if it were recognized, the existence of a specific standard regulating vinyl chloride and detailing other medical procedures would preclude citation under section 5(a)(1). The vinyl chloride standard would have to be amended or some new standard promulgated before cytogenetic monitoring could be required.

The second possible use of section 5(a)(1), to *prohibit* certain medical practices, has already been attempted. In *American Cyanamid Co.*,[37] the Occupational Safety and Health Review Commission was faced with the question of whether the employer's policy, which excluded from certain employment women aged 16 to 50 who had not been surgically sterilized, constituted a "hazard" under section 5(a)(1) of OSHA. Five women employed in the lead pigments department submitted to surgical sterilization in order to retain their positions. A majority of the Commission held that "Congress did not intend the Act to apply to every conceivable aspect of employer-employee relations and that due to its unique characteristics this condition of employment is not a hazard within the meaning of the general duty clause." "Hazard" was defined to mean processes and materials which cause injury and disease by operating directly upon employees as they engage in work or work-related activities.

In dissent, Commissioner Cottine charged that the sterilizations resulted from a condition of employment imposed by the employer, and therefore should be considered a hazard subject to the general duty clause. Moreover, he cautioned that "[t]he exclusion of fertile women from certain employment invites employers to exclude other highly susceptible groups from employment when the effect varies among the exposed classes of individuals." The case is presently on appeal in the D.C. Circuit.

Even if an employer's reproductive hazards policy were held to be within the purview of section 5(a)(1), it is not clear that a violation could be found. As discussed earlier, citation under section 5(a)(1) is inappropriate if a specific standard applies. An argument could be made that the "hazard" is not the employer's policy, but exposure to lead. The employer's policy is simply the employer's attempt to deal with the hazard. Therefore, citation under section 5(a)(1) is arguably precluded because of the existence of a standard dealing with lead.

Another question is whether the Secretary would be able to prove all the necessary elements of a general duty clause violation. Specifically, the Secretary must specify the particular steps the cited employer should have taken to avoid citation and to demonstrate the feasibility and likely utility of those measures. Simply ordering the return of the women to the toxic environment will not correct the problem of reproductive hazards. Finally, an order directing the company to end its exclusionary policies would be prospective only and would not help the women already excluded or who had undergone sterilization. Back pay and other traditional employment discrimination remedies are better pursued under section 11(c) of OSHA or Title VII.

8.5 Access to Exposure and Medical Records

Section 8(c)(3) directs the Secretary of Labor to issue regulations requiring employers "to maintain accurate records of employee exposures to potentially toxic materials or harmful physical agents which are required to be monitored or measured under section 6." In 1980 OSHA promulgated its final rule granting employees a right of access to exposure and medical records. The primary purpose of this important standard is "to enable workers to play a meaningful role in their own health management."[38]

The standard applies to all covered general industry, maritime, and construction employers. A separate standard has been proposed for agricultural employers. It is, however, limited to employers having employees exposed to toxic substances or harmful physical agents. Any current or former employee or an employee being assigned or transferred to work where there will be exposure to toxic substances or harmful physical agents has a right of access to four kinds of exposure records: (1) environmental monitoring records; (2) biological monitoring results; (3) material safety data sheets; and (4) any other record disclosing the identity of a toxic substance or harmful physical agent. Any worker who has a right of access to exposure records may designate a representative to exercise access rights. Recognized or certified collective bargaining agents (labor unions) are automatically considered "designated representatives" and have a right of access to employee exposure records without individual employee consent. OSHA also has a right of access to exposure records.

Access to employee medical records is more restricted. Employees have a right of access to their entire medical files regardless of how the information was generated or is maintained. Excluded from the definition of "employee medical record" are certain physical specimens, certain records concerning health insurance claims, and certain records concerning voluntary employee medical assistance programs. A limited discretion is also given physicians to deny access where there is a specific diagnosis of a terminal illness or psychiatric condition. Collective bargaining agents must obtain specific written consent before gaining access to employee medical records. OSHA has a right of access to employee medical records, but those records in a personally identifiable form are subject to detailed procedures and protections.

With a few exceptions, employers must preserve exposure records for at least 30 years and must preserve medical records for the duration of employment plus 30 years. With the exception of x-rays, employers may keep the records in any form, such as microfilm, microfiche, or computer. Upon receipt of a request, access must be provided in a reasonable time, place, and manner within 15 days. In responding to an initial request an employer may provide a copy without cost, provide copying facilities at no cost, or may loan the record for a reasonable time. Administrative costs may be charged for subsequent copying requests.

Although identities of substances, exposure levels, and health status data may not be withheld, the employer may delete any other trade secret data which discloses manufacturing processes or discloses the percentage of a chemical substance in a mixture so long as the employee or designated representative is notified of the deletion. Access to other trade secrets may be conditioned upon a written agreement not to misuse this information.

In *Louisiana Chemical Association v. Bingham*,[39] the Fifth Circuit held that the access rule was a "regulation" promulgated under section 8 to be challenged in district court rather than a "standard" promulgated under section 6 to be challenged in the court of appeals. On remand, the district court held that the access rule was within the Secretary's statutory authority and consistent with the congressional intent of the Act.[40]

> Even a cursory examination of the Act's overarching policy and the means by which it may be achieved make plain the fact that the records access rule bears at least a reasonable relation to that purpose. The rule will serve to establish a primary data base regarding long term exposure to toxic substances and harmful physical agents. Such a pool of information will obviously be of great utility to medical/industrial research. . . .[41]

The court rejected a number of arguments raised by the industry plaintiffs. First, the court held that the rule did not violate the fourth amendment because, even though the rule does not specifically provide for the issuance of warrants to inspect the records, there is every indication that in implementing the regulation the Secretary intends to respect fourth amendment rights. Second, the court held that the rule did not violate the privacy rights of employees because there is ample security for dealing with personally identifiable information and the rule carefully limits the use of such information. Third, the court held that the rule does not violate the Trade Secrets Act because the law only prohibits *unauthorized* disclosure of trade secrets to nongovernmental personnel and the access rule makes these disclosures *authorized*. Fourth, the court rejected the argument that the terms under which this information can be disclosed to unions are governed by the National Labor Relations Act. According to the court, the two statutory schemes are not inconsistent. Finally, the court rejected claims that the rule is overbroad in its definition of "toxic substance" and that its promulgation violated the Administrative Procedure Act.

In 1982 OSHA proposed revisions of the access to exposure and medical records regulation.[42] The following six proposals would "relax" some of the requirements of the regulation: (1) to be covered by the regulation, an employee would have to have direct, rather than incidental, exposure to toxic substances; (2) exposure records would be defined to include only environmental and biological monitoring results and material safety data sheets, but not purchase orders or other records showing the identity of a substance; (3) the regulation would apply only to 3,492 substances in the NIOSH Registry of Toxic Effects of Chemical Substances (RTECS) that meet certain toxicity standards, rather than all 39,000 substances in the RTECS; (4) medical records would have to be retained for the duration of employment plus five years or for 30 years, whichever is longer, rather than duration of employment plus 30 years; (5) x-rays would be allowed to be stored on microfilm; and (6) employers would be permitted to seek monetary damages for breaches of trade secret confidentiality agreements.

Although these proposals would limit the scope of the access regulation and even the present regulation is pending on judicial review, it is possible to speculate how an even more far-reaching medical records rule could be used to protect high-risk workers. Under the present regulation employees have the right to see their medical records. Mere access, however, may be inadequate to help some employees. For example, an employee's medical file may contain the diagnosis of a disease such as epilepsy or heart disease, which diagnosis upon subsequent examination by the employee's own physician proves to be inaccurate. Nevertheless, the initial erroneous diagnosis may be the only one in the employee's medical file. There are presently few legal safeguards on the dissemination of employee medical files both inside and outside a company. Consequently, the employee may, without even being aware, receive adverse treatment in insurance, employment opportunity, credit, and other matters based on the contents of his or her medical file. The obvious solution would be to give employees the right to make additions and corrections to their files.

If employees were given the right to correct their files, the next step would be to prohibit employees from being discriminated against because of erroneous information after it had already been corrected. For example, suppose employee X's medical file mistakenly contains the results of employee Y's pulmonary function test, which indicates a severe respiratory condition warranting medical discharge. Employee X's right to correct his file with the proper test result would be meaningless if the employer could still discharge employee X on the basis of employee Y's pulmonary function test.

Finally, if an employee may not be discriminated against based on erroneous medical data, the next step would be to prohibit discrimination based on unreliable medical data. For example, during a periodic medical examination of employees who load heavy drums of toxic chemicals, the employer's medical personnel give each employee a lumbar spine x-ray. Employee A's x-ray indicates a minor congenital anomaly, such as a slight curvature of the spine. The employer, believing that this physical condition predisposes employee A to low-back problems, discharges or transfers the employee. Because leading medical authorities agree that spine films have little or no predictive value, there is little difference between this situation and that of employee X, who was discharged based on a mistaken test report. If employee A is permitted to challenge the discharge, it would be tantamount to permitting all employees to contest the reasonableness of any medically related company decision. This would raise complex scientific questions of expert opinion, laboratory procedures, and diagnoses. Moreover, a new procedural system would be needed to consider these claims.

The present access to exposure and medical records regulation has been criticized for, among other reasons, encroaching upon employee privacy, trade secrets, and corporate medical practice. When these concerns are added to the other problems already discussed, it becomes clear that new substantive protections for high-risk workers are unlikely to be achieved via the access regulation.

8.6   The Role of NIOSH

The National Institute for Occupational Safety and Health (NIOSH) was established by section 22 of the Act as a part of the Department of Health, Education and Welfare (now the Department of Health and Human Services) to conduct research and to establish training and education programs. As OSHA's "research arm," NIOSH is directed to develop information regarding potentially toxic substances or harmful physical agents. It is specifically authorized by section 20(a)(5) "to establish such programs of medical examinations and tests as may be necessary for determining the incidence of occupational illness and the susceptibility of employees to such illnesses."

Based on its expertise and express statutory authority, NIOSH is the most appropriate agency to conduct extensive research on medical screening. NIOSH could analyze the scientific basis for determining the risk of exposure to individuals, certify approved screening procedures, and develop criteria for evaluating test and examination results. This new allocation of responsibility would be well within NIOSH's statutory mandate. Even now, NIOSH tests and certifies respirators and other personal protective equipment and its parent agency, the Centers for Disease Control, develops proficiency criteria for certifying laboratories authorized to conduct blood-lead analyses.

Although NIOSH has the authority to conduct inspections and to subpoena documents and medical records needed for research, it has no enforcement authority. Therefore, if NIOSH developed guidelines on the use of medical assessments, implementation and enforcement of the guidelines would probably be the responsibility of another agency. Moreover, some statutory amendment invariably would be required for the *other* agency (such as OSHA) to act to prohibit medical-based discrimination. These and other legislative prospects are further explored in Chapter 13.

CHAPTER 9

THE REHABILITATION ACT AND
STATE HANDICAP LAWS

9.1 Background and Procedure

The Rehabilitation Act of 1973 was the first comprehensive federal effort to bring handicapped individuals within the mainstream of American life. Its expressed purpose, as restated in the 1978 Amendments, is "to develop and implement, through research, training, services, and the guarantee of equal opportunity, comprehensive and coordinated programs of vocational rehabilitation and independent living." Most of the earlier handicap laws were postwar acts to aid returning members of the armed services and attempts to aid the needy handicapped by providing jobs considered "suitable" for the handicapped. For example, the Randolph-Sheppard Act of 1936 licensed qualified blind persons to operate vending stands in government buildings.

Of the several provisions of the Rehabilitation Act, sections 501 (which protects federal government employees against discrimination on the basis of handicap), 503, and 504 have a direct bearing on the employment rights of the handicapped. In addition, largely as a result of the federal initiative, 44 states and the District of Columbia have enacted laws prohibiting discrimination in private employment, and three states prohibit discrimination in state employment on the basis of handicap.[1] Unlike the federal law, which has limited coverage, state laws prohibiting employment discrimination against the handicapped actually have a wider coverage and usually only exempt small employers. Therefore, state law is more important in handicap cases than in other kinds of employment discrimination.

Section 503 provides that any contract in excess of $2500 entered into with any federal department or agency shall contain a provision requiring that the contracting party take affirmative action to employ and promote qualified handicapped individuals. The term "handicapped individual" is defined as "any person who (A) has a physical or mental impairment which substantially limits one or more of such person's major life activities, (B) has a record of such an impairment, or (C) is regarded as having such an impairment." Based on this broad statutory definition, and on the definition contained in the implementing regulations, it has been estimated that as many as 40 million to 68 million handicapped persons are covered by the statute.[2]

Responsibility for enforcing section 503 is vested in the Office of Federal Contract Compliance Programs (OFCCP) in the Department of Labor. Any applicant for employment or employee of a covered contractor must file a complaint with the Director of the OFCCP within 180 days of the alleged discrimination. If the OFCCP investigation results in a finding of discrimination, the contractor is given an opportunity to defend its action in a hearing before an administrative law judge (ALJ) of the OFCCP. The ALJ's findings and recommendations are then certified to the Assistant Secretary of Labor, who may accept or modify the recommendation before issuing a final order.

By regulation, the director of the OFCCP may seek to (1) withhold progress payments on the contract; (2) terminate the contract; or (3) bar the contractor from future contracts. The Labor Department also has awarded back pay to individuals who have been denied employment or advances in employment solely because of their handicap.[3] Individuals who believe they have been discriminated against may only pursue their administrative remedies through the OFCCP; all eight circuit courts to consider the issue have held that there is no express or implied private right of action.[4]

Section 504 provides that no otherwise qualified handicapped individual shall, solely by reason of handicap, be (1) excluded from the participation in, (2) denied the benefits of, or (3) subjected to discrimination under, any program or activity receiving federal financial assistance. Unlike section 503, there is no monetary minimum amount of financial assistance required for coverage under section 504. It has been estimated that three million firms—about half the businesses in the country—are covered by the Act, either as government contractors or recipients of federal funding.[5]

By regulation,[6] procedures for enforcement of section 504 by each federal agency must be the same as those used to implement Title VI of the Civil Rights Act of 1964. Under HEW (now Health and Human Services—HHS) and Department of Education model regulations, persons who believe they were discriminated against may file a complaint with the responsible official of the Department within 180 days of the alleged discrimination. If an investigation determines there is merit to the complaint, and voluntary conciliation cannot be reached, a hearing is held before an ALJ. Rulings of the ALJ may be appealed to the Secretaries of HHS or Education, but the appeal is not as a matter of right. The final decision may provide for the suspension or termination of, or refusal to grant or continue, federal financial assistance.

Although the Supreme Court has not yet specifically addressed the issue,[7] it has been widely held that section 504 impliedly confers a private right of action on behalf of otherwise qualified individuals who are injured by the discriminatory practices of federal financial recipients.[8] The courts have also held that administrative remedies need not be exhausted before the private action may be brought.[9] Nevertheless, several courts have held that handicapped persons cannot bring private claims for employment discrimination under section 504 against recipients of federal assistance unless a primary objective of the federal financial assistance is to provide employment.[10] The Supreme Court is currently considering this issue.[11]

Unlike section 503, which statutorily mandates affirmative action with respect to the handicapped, section 504 only prohibits discrimination against otherwise qualified individuals on the basis of handicap. The guideline regulations implementing section 504, however, adopted some affirmative action requirements, such as the requirement that recipients of federal funds make "reasonable accommodation" to the limitations of the handicapped unless the accommodation would impose an undue hardship.

In *Southeastern Community College v. Davis*,[12] the Supreme Court, although not striking down HEW's regulations, cast doubt on the extent to which they may impose affirmative action. According to the Court, section 504 does not require a recipient to make "substantial modifications" to its programs in order to allow handicapped individuals to participate. If the regulations attempt to do so "they would do more than clarify the meaning of 504 . . . , they would constitute an unauthorized extension of the obligations imposed by that statute."[13]

9.2 Medical Screening

Under the regulations promulgated to implement section 504, an employer receiving federal financial assistance may not make preemployment inquiry about whether the applicant is handicapped or about the nature and severity of an existent handicap unless (1) a preemployment medical examination is required of all applicants and (2) the information obtained from the examination is relevant to the applicant's ability to perform job-related functions.[14] Under the section 503 regulations a federal contractor may require a preemployment medical examination of a handicapped applicant, even if an examination is not required of the nonhandicapped.[15] Nevertheless, if the employer's job qualification requirements "tend to screen out qualified handicapped individuals, the requirements shall be related to the specific job or jobs for which the individual is being considered and shall be consistent with business necessity and the safe performance of the job."

At first glance, it might appear that the section 504 regulation, by prohibiting recipients from requiring medical examinations of only handicapped applicants, provides greater protection to the handicapped than the section 503 regulation. This is not the case. An employer's decision whether to conduct a preemployment medical examination is most likely to be based upon the size and nature of the employer's enterprise. Those employers using medical examinations would undoubtedly prefer to give them to all employees because the hazards that are customarily viewed as necessitating preemployment medical examinations often act upon medical conditions that can only be detected through a comprehensive examination. In addition, the regulation does not mandate that all medical examinations involve identical procedures. Thus, nothing would preclude an employer from requiring all employees to submit to *some* medical examination, but requiring handicapped applicants to submit to more complete examinations.

By contrast, the section 503 regulation provides additional substantive protections to handicapped applicants. Any procedure tending to screen out "qualified" handicapped individuals must be shown by the employer to be "job-related" and "consistent with business necessity and the safe performance of the job." The job-relatedness requirement in the section 504 regulation is explained to mean that the medical information must be "relevant" to the applicant's ability to perform the job. There is no requirement that the medical procedure must have a high predictive value or be within accepted medical practice.

Significantly, the section 503 regulation connects "job-relatedness" to the employment discrimination law concept of "business necessity." As defined by the Fourth Circuit in *Robinson v. Lorillard Corp.*:[16]

> The test is whether there exists an overriding legitimate business purpose such that the practice is necessary to the safe and efficient operation of the business. Thus, the business purpose must be sufficiently compelling to override any [adverse] impact; the challenged practice must effectively carry out the business purpose it is alleged to serve; and there must be available no acceptable alternative policies or practices which would better accomplish it equally well with a lesser differential [adverse] impact.[17]

Thus, under the section 503 regulation, the specific medical examination and screening procedures used (1) must have a scientifically valid basis, (2) must have a high predictive value, and (3) must be the most accurate and least onerous alternative.

Despite the subtle differences between the section 503 and section 504 regulations, both serve to limit the use of baseless and discriminatory preemployment examinations. This, however, is only the first of numerous legal issues concerning the rights of high-risk individuals under the Rehabilitation Act.

An employer's ability to engage in unlimited medical screening of applicants and employees may become curtailed by new state laws. For example, a 1981 amendment to the New Jersey state employment discrimination law[18] specifically prohibits employment discrimination based on an individual's "atypical hereditary cellular or blood trait." This is defined to include sickle cell trait, hemoglobin C trait, thalassemia trait, Tay-Sachs trait, or cystic fibrosis trait. Thus, New Jersey has become the first jurisdiction to expressly proscribe the use of multiple forms of biochemical genetic screening. Florida, Louisiana, and North Carolina prohibit discrimination in employment based on sickle cell trait.[19]

9.3 Are High-Risk Workers "Handicapped"?

The statutory definition of "handicapped individual" applicable to both section 503 and section 504 is any person who has a physical or mental impairment which substantially limits one or more of such person's major life activities, has a record of such an impairment, or is regarded as having such an impairment. Basically, the definition includes persons who are, were, or are believed to be suffering from an impairment. High-risk or susceptible individuals are not presently impaired, but they are likely to become impaired, or, at least, are believed to be more likely to become impaired in the future. An important threshold question is whether these individuals are "handicapped" and thereby protected by the Rehabilitation Act.

In *OFCCP v. E. E. Black, Ltd.*,[20] a carpenter's apprentice was required to submit to a preemployment medical examination, including a low-back x-ray, which revealed a lower back anomaly known as sacralization of the transitional vertebra. This is a congenital condition found in 8% to 9% of the population. Although its disabling long-term effects are in dispute in the medical profession, the employer conceded that the condition did not affect the applicant's current capability to perform the duties of a carpenter's apprentice. Nonetheless, relying on its medical officer's conclusions, the company determined that the applicant's spinal formation made him a poor risk in terms of possible later development of back problems, and denied him employment. The apprentice filed a complaint with the OFCCP, charging the employer with violating section 503.

The Labor Department found in favor of the carpenter's apprentice and ruled that the company's use of preemployment medical examinations tended to disqualify handicapped applicants despite their current capability to perform the job. The Labor Department refused to define "impairment," as used in the definitional section of the Act, to be limited to permanent disabilities such as blindness or deafness. Instead, the term impairment was held to be "any condition which weakens, restricts or otherwise damages an individual's health or physical or mental activity"[21] resulting in a current bar to employment that the individual is currently capable of performing.

On judicial review, the United States District Court for the District of Hawaii agreed with the Labor Department that the Rehabilitation Act's coverage was intended to be broad, but it held that the Assistant Secretary of Labor's interpretation was overly broad.[22] According to the court, section 706(7)(B) of title 29 of the United States Code contains critical language that restricts the Act's coverage to handicapped individuals who are "substantially limited" in pursuit of a major life activity. Thus, to be protected by the Act, an individual must have been rejected for a position for which he or she was qualified because of an impairment or perceived impairment that constitutes, for the individual, a substantial handicap to employment. The court discussed several factors to be considered in determining whether an impairment substantially limits employability, including the number and types of jobs from which the individual is disqualified, the location or accessibility of similar opportunities, and the individual's own job expectations and training.

Based on this definition, the court still concluded that the applicant was subject to the protections of the Act. First, the applicant's back condition was found to be an impairment or, at least, was regarded as such by the employer. Second, the impairment was found to constitute a substantial handicap to employment because the applicant would have been disqualified from all or substantially all apprenticeship programs in carpentry. Third, the court rejected the employer's contention that Congress did not intend to protect job applicants denied employment based on risk of future injury. The case was subsequently remanded to the Department of Labor [23] and later settled. The company gave the employee $7,500 in back pay and promised not to exclude any apprentice carpenter solely on the basis of a radiological finding of a transitional lumbrosacral vertebra.

The only other federal case as of this writing to raise the question of whether an employee with increased sensitivity to a workplace hazard was "handicapped" is *Vickers v. Veterans Administration*.[24] An employee of the Veterans Administration (VA) who was "unusually sensitive to tobacco smoke" brought an action under section 504 for damages and equitable relief requiring the VA "to make reasonable accommodations to his physical handicap by providing a work environment that is free of tobacco smoke."[25] The court held that the plaintiff was "handicapped" within the meaning of the Act because his "hypersensitivity does in fact limit one of his major life activities, that is, his capacity to work in an environment which is not completely smoke free."[26] Nevertheless, the court held that the VA was under no duty to provide an environment wholly free of tobacco smoke, and even if there were such a duty, the VA had satisfied it. Specifically, the VA had, among other things, separated smokers from nonsmokers in the office, installed two vents and an air purifier, and offered the employee an alternative job.

The various state handicap discrimination laws differ in the definition of "handicapped." For example, the Louisiana statute excludes from the definition of "handicapped" chronic alcoholism, drug addiction, cosmetic disfigurement, and anatomical loss of body systems.[27] In other states, the courts have addressed the issue and the cases have reached widely divergent results. The following handicaps have been recognized as being covered under the applicable state law: high blood pressure (California);[28] pseudofolliculitis barbae (Michigan);[29] Hodgkins disease (New York);[30] glaucoma (North Carolina);[31] allergic rhinitis (Pennsylvania);[32] cerebral palsy (Washington);[33] having only one kidney (Wisconsin);[34] alcoholism (Wisconsin);[35] deviated septum (Wisconsin);[36] and rheumatoid arthritis (Wisconsin).[37] By contrast, the following handicaps have *not* been recognized as being covered under the applicable state law: cancer of the uterus (Illinois);[38] transplanted kidney (Illinois);[39] obesity (Pennsylvania);[40] "whiplash" (Rhode Island);[41] borderline hypertension and morbid obesity (Washington);[42] and small stature (Wisconsin).[43]

The preceding federal and state cases demonstrate one of the ironies of the handicap discrimination laws. Because a handicapped individual is defined as a person who has an impairment which substantially limits one or more major life activities, the most arbitrary, illogical, and baseless forms of discrimination—such as an individual's slight medical or genetic differentiation—may not be prohibited. This irony may be explained by the fact that, at least as to the federal law, the Rehabilitation Act was only designed to prevent discrimination against the *severely* handicapped.[44] Thus, unless "regarded as having an impairment" is broadly construed,[45] the Rehabilitation Act and its state analogs may not even cover many of the theoretically high-risk workers discussed in earlier chapters.

9.4   Medical Screening and "Job-Relatedness"

Determining that a high-risk individual is covered by the Rehabilitation Act is only the beginning step in analyzing a case such as *Black*. After all, the Act protects *otherwise qualified* handicapped individuals. It still must be decided whether the handicapped individual is otherwise qualified; if not, the employer would not be in violation of the Act to refuse to hire the individual.

The Labor Department's decision in *Black* conceded that employers could exclude handicapped individuals from jobs on the basis of legitimate job requirements, but it held that only an individual's current capability to perform could be the subject of inquiry in preemployment medical examinations. The district court termed this interpretation "clearly contrary to law."[46] The court posed the situation where, if a particular person were given a job, he would have a 90% chance of suffering a heart attack within one month. "A job requirement that screened out such an individual would be consistent both with business necessity and the safe performance of the job. Yet, it could be argued that the individual had a current capacity to perform the job, and thus was a qualified handicapped individual."[47]

The court did not formulate its own legal standard for *when* possible future injury can be the basis of denying employment. Nevertheless, the basic principle that a job requirement that screens out qualified handicapped individuals on the basis of possible future injury may be lawful is in agreement with some cases decided under state handicap discrimination laws, discussed later. In addition, it is clear that the burden is on the employer to justify the denial of employment, regardless of whether the problem is viewed as (1) whether the employee is "otherwise qualified" or (2) whether the employer has made out a "business necessity" defense to the OFCCP's prima facie case.

In *Black* the employer's avowed interests in screening out persons likely to experience back problems were to avoid increased insurance or workers' compensation costs and to comply with its "occupational safety and health obligations." Certainly, other economic reasons could be offered by other employers, such as the increased costs of hiring and training replacements when there is a high turnover of employees, absenteeism and increased use of sick leave, additional medical expenses (such as more frequent monitoring or increased medical insurance premiums), the fear of potential civil liability, and the possible loss of good will.

The Assistant Secretary of Labor in *Black* ruled that higher insurance or workers' compensation costs were irrelevant to the employability of the applicant. Without addressing the cost issue per se, the district court held that an applicant's risk of future injury could be considered by the employer. Thus, the court analyzed the problem purely in terms of the applicant's present and future ability to perform the job. The quantification of any possible interference with or disruption of the business was not pertinent. In other words, the court assumed the business necessity of having healthy, capable workers without considering the adverse consequences of failing to have such a work force.

The legality of the screening procedure, however, should not be determined by the employer's asserted motivation. The focus should be on the screening procedure itself and on whether the employer has proven the necessity for the screening, the scientific validity of the procedure, and legitimacy of the resulting employment decisionmaking. To sustain a business necessity defense for using medical procedures which screen out qualified handicapped individuals, the employer should be required to prove the following.

A. The Examination, Test, or Procedure Upon Which the Employment Decision Was Based Is Job-Related.

In *Albemarle Paper Co. v. Moody*,[48] the Supreme Court cited with approval to the Equal Employment Opportunity Commission's

(EEOC's) Uniform Guidelines on Employee Selection Procedures and held that "discriminatory tests are impermissible unless shown, by professionally acceptable methods, to be 'predictive of or significantly correlated with important elements of work behavior which comprise or are relevant to the job or jobs for which candidates are being evaluated.' "[49] Based on the job-relatedness principle, employers have refused to hire:

- an employee with a heart and nervous condition for the arduous job of park technician;[50]
- an applicant who had two knee operations for the job of railroad brakeman;[51]
- an individual who had a prior back injury requiring surgery for the jobs of pipe fitter, wirer, and similar positions;[52]
- an applicant lacking a right hand and forearm for the job of taxi driver;[53]
- a man with vision in only one eye for the job of railroad "trackman."[54]

In *Western Weighing Bureau v. Wisconsin Department of Industry, Labor & Human Relations*,[55] a former employee sought reemployment after his discharge from the Army. The employer was a company working with rail cargo, and the individual applied for the job of inspector. Although the job involved some climbing and getting down on his hands and knees, it did not involve lifting or strenuous work and was less strenuous than the job the individual had performed satisfactorily before he joined the Army.

The individual was hired as an inspector but was discharged after only one and one-half days. A back x-ray taken at a required physical examination revealed spondylolisthesis, a congenital condition in which the last lumbar vertebra slips forward. Based solely on this x-ray, the company doctor recommended that the individual not be employed as an inspector.

Neither the state human relations commission nor the Wisconsin Circuit Court had much difficulty in finding that the employer had violated the state fair employment act. Because the inspector's job did not involve lifting or strenuous work, disqualification on the basis of spondylolisthesis was simply not job-related.

Job-relatedness is much more difficult to apply in cases involving predictive medical screening. Even in a relatively uncomplicated case such as *Black*, the key issues were whether the applicant, in fact, was likely to have back problems and whether the x-rays given the applicant were a medically valid way of assessing the likely future condition of the applicant's back. Although not resolving the ultimate issue, the job-relatedness concept operated to frame the issue in *Black*. It was first necessary for the employer to prove that an important part of the job required the lifting of heavy objects and that individuals with back problems would not be able to perform the job. Thus, to the extent that the x-rays sought to determine the condition of the applicant's back, the procedure was job-related.

B.   *The Examination, Test, or Procedure Has a High Predictive Value and Is the Most Accurate Test That Is Feasible to Use.*

The statistical significance of a test's sensitivity, specificity, and predictive value has been discussed earlier. Similarly, limitations on the accuracy of medical screening procedures have been explored. To justify using any medical examination, test, or procedure, the employer must prove that it is a valid, scientifically accepted measure that accurately predicts an applicant's present or future job-related functions. In addition, the employer must also show that there is no other medical procedure that is more accurate in making such an assessment, except where the other medical procedure is not feasible to use because of time, cost, or other factors.

A 1982 New Jersey case illustrates that employment decisions must have a sound medical basis. In *Rogers v. Campbell Foundry Co.*,[56] it was held that an employer could not refuse to hire an applicant whose chest x-ray showed a prominent hilar shadow on the lung. The credible medical evidence was that this condition was caused by a normal calcification process and would not predispose the applicant to silicosis or pneumoconiosis from working in the employer's foundry.

C.   *The Examination, Test, or Procedure Indicates That the Applicant Has a Strong Likelihood of Developing a Serious Injury or Illness in the Foreseeable Future and That the Applicant's Likelihood of Injury or Illness Represents a Significant Variation From the General Worker Population.*

This determination poses the most difficult medical and legal issues and is really composed of five elements.

First, the results of the test or procedure are unequivocal. An employer will have a difficult time in screening out "borderline" high-risk workers. Also, if the test results are unclear, there should be retesting and reexamination, and further medical consultation should be sought.

Second, the injury or illness to which the applicant is predisposed is severe. An employer cannot screen out individuals whose only heightened health risk involves sneezing, tearing, a mild rash, or the like. Applicants should, however, be advised of such risks. As mentioned previously, these individuals may not be protected by the Rehabilitation Act because they are not "impaired"—substantially limited in pursuit of a major life activity. Nevertheless, prudence suggests that the severity of any resultant injury or illness be considered in any screening program.

Third, there is a high probability that the applicant will develop an injury or illness. This is known as "absolute risk." For example, the general population of healthy workers may contract a specific occupational disease (have a rate of incidence) of one in 10,000. Medical studies may show that individuals with a deficiency in a certain enzyme have an incidence rate of one in 1,000. Although an individual with this enzyme deficiency may be at a 10 times greater risk of disease, an employer would not be justified in refusing to hire that individual, because the absolute risk for the individual is still so low.

Fourth, the adverse effects on the health of the applicant will be manifested in the reasonably foreseeable future. Unless there is an overwhelming likelihood of the individual's contracting an extremely serious disease, such as cancer, illnesses with long latency periods should be disregarded in medical screening, although the applicant should be advised of the risk. For example, an individual aged 25 should not be denied employment as a bricklayer because of a heightened risk of developing arthritis at age 60.

Fifth, the applicant's individual risk of illness, upon which the exclusionary practice is based, represents a significant variation from the general population. This is known as "relative risk." For example, a medical examination may indicate that an applicant for the job of coal miner has an 85% chance of suffering some lung impairment. If all coal miners have an 80% chance of becoming impaired, employment should not be denied to this mildly high-risk individual. This is similar to consideration number one.

In *Bentivegna v. United States*,[57] the City of Los Angeles hired Mr. Bentivegna as a "building repairer." Bentivegna had indicated on an application form that he had diabetes mellitus. As a condition of employment, applicants were required to pass a physical examination. Applicants with diabetes were required to demonstrate "control," meaning blood sugar levels below a certain level. Bentivegna was terminated when it was learned that his blood sugar was above the level. In holding that Bentivegna's termination violated section 504 of the Rehabilitation Act, the Ninth Circuit found, among other things, that "the testimony could not establish that the difference between controlled and uncontrolled diabetics was sufficient to make the control requirement 'related to the performance of the job and . . . consistent with business necessity. . . .' "[58] The court, however, noted the following:

> A requirement more directly tied to increased risk of injury, such as the exclusion of diabetics with demonstrated nervous or circulatory problems—something all physicians testifying in this case agreed would markedly increase the risks from injury—might present a different case if applied to applicants for a job that carries elevated risks of injury.[59]

Some of the other five requirements have already been addressed in state decisions interpreting state handicap discrimination laws. The results have varied widely. In Wisconsin, in order to justify an exclusionary practice the employer must show that there is a "reasonable probability" that the characteristics of the employee will result in future hazards to the employee or co-workers.[60] No statistical criteria have been established for defining "reasonable probability," but the employer's burden would appear to be quite difficult to satisfy.

For example, in one case[61] the employer excluded an epileptic welder by relying on evidence that 10% to 30% of epileptics under medication will still have seizures. The Wisconsin Supreme Court termed this degree of future risk "a mere possibility" and held that the employer's action was illegal. In another case,[62] the Wisconsin Supreme Court indicated that categorical reliance on the opinion of the company physician is not enough to satisfy the statute. There must be some specific finding regarding the statistical probability of future injury.

Other cases from Wisconsin also recognize that "present ability to perform" is the most important consideration. Thus, it has been held that an employer could not reject an applicant with acute lymphocytic leukemia because he would be unable to perform the job in the future,[63] and an employee with a history of asthma could not be terminated from his job in a railroad's diesel house because fumes *might* endanger his health.[64]

In an Oregon case,[65] an applicant for the job of heavy appliance salesperson was rejected on the advice of the company physician because he had suffered a subendocardial infarction six years earlier and had subsequently complained of sporadic angina. The Supreme Court of Oregon upheld the Bureau of Labor's ruling that the disqualification was unjustified because the employer failed to show a "high probability" of future risk of heart attack.[66]

California also has established a difficult burden for an employer to meet in rejecting an otherwise qualified individual because of a heightened risk of future injury or illness. In *Sterling Transit Co. v. Fair Employment Practice Commission*,[67] the employer discharged a truck driver with scoliosis, a congenital but not disabling back condition. The court held that a mere possibility that the employee might endanger his health sometime in the future was inadequate justification for the employer's action. "While such [screening] procedures may be in an employer's economic interest in some cases, such a blanket exclusion eviscerates the legislative policy by erecting employment barriers more difficult to scale than Mount Rainier."[68]

Where there is a strong likelihood that a *preexisting* condition will be aggravated by exposure in the workplace, the employer's exclusionary practice is more likely to be upheld. Thus, in a New York case,[69] the Appellate Division upheld an employer's refusal to hire an applicant who was suffering from dermatitis, where the company physician concluded that exposure to the chemical elements in the plant would so exacerbate the dermatitis as to render the applicant unable to perform his duties.

It should also be pointed out that employee exclusionary practices are much more likely to be upheld where the employee's health risk could endanger the health or safety of others.[70] This has been especially true in cases involving common carriers.[71]

D. The Disqualification or Other Adverse Personnel Action Was Based on an Individualized Determination of Fitness.

Even though there have been fewer handicap cases to address this issue, it is clear that the exclusion of entire groups of individuals with certain disabilities from job consideration constitutes illegal discrimination under handicap discrimination laws. This accords with the well-established principle of employment discrimination law that "[i]ndividual risks, like individual performance, may not be predicted by resort to [proscribed] classifications...."[72]

This principle is illustrated in several state handicap discrimination cases. For example, in *Anderson v. Exxon Co.*,[73] the New Jersey Supreme Court held that an applicant who had a spinal fusion and a lumbar disc removed was unlawfully rejected for the job of heating oil driver. According to the court, the employer could not presume, but had to prove, that the applicant's handicap precluded his adequate performance of the job.

The Colorado Court of Appeals has held to be unlawful a hospital policy that excluded all epileptics from direct patient care positions.[74] There must be an individual determination of fitness based on the applicant's employment history and medical needs. The Connecticut Supreme Court held that a school for the blind could not refuse to hire a teacher's aide who had impaired vision.[75] Similarly, the Illinois Court of Appeals held that the presumption that a mental handicap necessarily disqualifies an applicant contravenes the state handicap statute.[76] The employer must prove that the individual cannot adequately perform the job duties.

The Wisconsin Supreme Court has held that an employer could not dismiss a truck driver simply because his visual acuity fell below standards mandated for drivers hauling goods in interstate commerce, which did not apply to the employee.[77] The employer failed to show that the individual had a disability that interfered with his ability to perform the job. Similarly, the Maine Supreme Court held that an employer failed to prove that a cook trainee who wore a leg brace, a trainman who had a laminectomy, and a heavy laborer with a heart murmur were unable to perform their jobs without endangering the safety and health of others.[78]

These principles also apply to the Rehabilitation Act. In *Coleman v. Casey County Board of Education*,[79] an otherwise qualified applicant who had a leg amputated was denied a job as a school bus driver and brought an action under section 504 of the Rehabilitation Act. A federal court in Kentucky struck down as violative of the Rehabilitation Act a state administrative regulation requiring that school bus drivers have both natural legs. In *Costner v. United States*,[80] a constitutional challenge was brought against a federal motor carrier safety regulation which prohibits any person with an established history or clinical diagnosis of epilepsy from driving a motor vehicle in interstate or foreign commerce. The district court, in striking down the regulation, noted that the plaintiff had not had a seizure in 22 years and had been driving trucks safely for 15 years. The Eighth Circuit reversed. The court held that the individual qualifications of the plaintiff are immaterial to the validity of the regulation and that because the regulation was rationally related to a legitimate state interest, it was constitutional.

E.   *No Reasonable Accommodation Will Permit the Handicapped Individual to Perform the Necessary Job Functions.*

The law is not well settled on what degree of accommodation is required in employment. In *Southeastern Community College v. Davis*,[81] the Supreme Court held that under section 504 a recipient of federal funds need not make major modifications of its program to accommodate the handicapped. Nevertheless, "surmountable barrier" discrimination is prohibited[82] and the employer will be required to accommodate the handicapped if doing so will not impose undue burdens on the employer.

Similar duties of reasonable accommodation exist under many state handicap discrimination laws.[83] The burden of proving that the physical criteria of the job are job-related rests with the employer. The Fifth Circuit in *Prewitt v. United States Postal Service*[84] explained the rationale for placing this burden on the employer.

> The employer has greater knowledge of the essentials of the job than does the handicapped applicant. The employer can look to its own experience, or, if that is not helpful, to that of other employers who have provided jobs to individuals with handicaps similar to those of the applicant in question. Furthermore, the employer may be able to obtain advice concerning possible accommodations from private and government sources.[85]

According to the section 503 regulations, employers must make "reasonable accommodation," but the term is not otherwise defined. It is likely, however, that it would include making facilities accessible, restructuring the job, arranging part-time or modified work schedules, acquiring or modifying equipment or devices, adjusting or modifying examinations, providing readers and interpreters, and taking other similar actions. Even with regard to safety hazards, the extent of necessary accommodation is not clear. For example, if an otherwise qualified handicapped individual is not capable of lifting the 50-pound bags of cement used by the employer, will the employer be required to use 20-pound bags? Will the employer be required to designate an employee to perform all the required heavy lifting, while assigning the handicapped employee some less strenuous duties? What would be the response of the union?

As with other issues, reasonable accommodation to health hazards may be even more complicated. It is likely that accommodation will focus on administrative practices, such as shift rotation and other "administrative controls," dividing maximum exposure time, more frequent monitoring and medical surveillance, and the added use of personal protective equipment. It is doubtful that an employer will be required to reduce exposure levels beneath OSHA permissible exposure limits (PELs) to accommodate a sensitive handicapped employee.

CHAPTER 10

TITLE VII AND THE ADEA

10.1 Background and Procedure

Title VII of the Civil Rights Act of 1964, as amended, prohibits discrimination in hiring, discharge, compensation, or other terms, conditions, or privileges of employment because of an individual's race, color, religion, sex, or national origin. It is the most comprehensive and important law prohibiting discrimination in employment. The Act applies to employers, labor unions, and employment agencies. To be an "employer" under the Act, an entity must have employed 15 or more persons for at least 20 weeks in either the current or preceding calendar year and be engaged in an industry affecting commerce. State and local government employees and certain federal government employees also are covered by Title VII.

Aggrieved individuals must file a charge (complaint) with the Equal Employment Opportunity Commission (EEOC) within 180 days of the alleged discriminatory act. After a period of up to 180 days for investigation and conciliation by EEOC, the charging party may file an action in district court. In states with their own fair employment laws, the appropriate state agency must be given 60 days to resolve the complaint before procedures are begun with EEOC. Prevailing plaintiffs are entitled to back pay, reinstatement, other equitable relief, and attorney fees.

Unlawful employment discrimination is usually considered to involve one of two types of practices, "disparate treatment" or "disparate impact." The Supreme Court has provided a good working definition of these terms:

> "Disparate treatment" . . . is the most easily understood type of discrimination. The employer simply treats some people less favorably than others because of their race, color, religion, sex, or national origin. Proof of discriminatory motive is critical, although it can in some

130

situations be inferred from the mere fact of differences in treatment. . . . Claims of disparate treatment may be distinguished from claims that stress "disparate impact." The latter involve employment practices that are facially neutral in their treatment of different groups but that in fact fall more harshly on one group than another and cannot be justified by business necessity. . . . Proof of discriminatory motive, we have held, is not required under a disparate impact theory.[1]

Discrimination in employment because of the presence of or a perceived predisposition to occupational illness is, for Title VII purposes, most likely to be disparate impact rather than disparate treatment discrimination. Thus, an employer is unlikely to refuse to hire or promote members of one racial or ethnic group because members of that group are considered to be prone to occupational illness. The discrimination usually involves the use of neutral medical criteria or screening tests that have a disparate impact on a particular class of persons because of race, color, religion, sex, or national origin.

In the landmark case of *Griggs v. Duke Power Co.,*[2] the Supreme Court held that Title VII prohibits not only overt discrimination, but also practices that are fair in form but discriminatory in operation. According to a unanimous Court, "good intent does not redeem employment procedures or testing mechanisms that operate as 'built-in head-winds' for minority groups and are unrelated to measuring job capability."[3] In *Griggs,* the employer's use of the Wonderlic Personnel Test and the Bennett Mechanical Comprehension Test (as well as the requirement of a high school diploma) were struck down because they operated to disqualify black applicants at a substantially higher rate than white applicants and were unrelated to measuring job capability.

In *Albemarle Paper Co. v. Moody,*[4] the Court clarified *Griggs* and held that a plaintiff may establish a prima facie case of disparate impact by showing that "the tests in question select applicants for hire or promotion in a racial pattern significantly different from that of the pool of applicants."[5] The burden is then on the employer to show that "any given requirement (has) . . . a manifest relationship to the employment in question."[6] The plaintiff may still rebut this evidence, however, by demonstrating that "other tests or selection devices, without a similarly undesirable racial effect, would also serve the employer's legitimate interest in efficient and trustworthy workmanship."[7]

A crucial but still unresolved issue is how substantially or significantly different the comparative test results must be in order to support a finding that there was a disparate impact. In a footnote in *Castenada v. Partida*[8] there is dictum that disparate impact would be

established where there was a difference of two or three standard de-
viations. Most Supreme Court and lower court decisions, however,
have considered disparate impact on an ad hoc basis.[9] According to
EEOC, ''[a] selection rate for any racial, ethnic or sex group which is
less than four-fifths (4/5) (or 80%) of the rate for the group with the
highest rate will generally be regarded . . . as evidence of adverse
impact.''[10] This formula, however, as an administrative interpretation of a statutory requirement, is not binding on the courts.[11]

10.2   Race, Color, Religion, and National Origin

As discussed in section 6.3, most biochemical genetic conditions
have prevalence rates which differ markedly along racial or ethnic
lines. Applying the disparate impact approach of Title VII, the use of
genetic screening for such a trait would establish a prima facie case of
discrimination. For example, based on Table 4–1, if 1,000 individuals from each of the following groups were tested, the following
numbers of individuals would display G-6-PD deficiency:

Black Americans (male)	160	European Jews	10
Filipinos	120	British	10
Mediterranean Jews	110	White Americans	1

In this example, the use of G-6-PD screening would certainly
fall more harshly on Black Americans, Filipinos, and Mediterranean
Jews. Could the employer justify G-6-PD screening and refute a
claim of employment discrimination by showing that these racial and
ethnic groups were represented in the work force in numbers at least
equal to their percentage of the population? The answer is no.

In *Connecticut v. Teal*,[12] the Supreme Court considered this ''bot-
tom line'' defense in a slightly different context. The Court held that
a written examination for promotion to supervisor violated Title VII
because of its disproportionate racial effect, regardless of the ''bot-
tom line'' composition of the work force.

> It is clear that Congress never intended to give an employer li-
> cense to discriminate against some employees on the basis of race or sex
> merely because he favorably treats other members of the employees'
> group. . . .
>   . . . Title VII does not permit the victim of a facially discrimina-
> tory policy to be told that he has not been wronged because other per-
> sons of his or her race or sex were hired. That answer is no more satis-
> factory when it is given to victims of a policy that is facially neutral but

practically discriminatory. Every *individual* employee is protected against both discriminatory treatment and against "practices that are fair in form, but discriminatory in operation."[13]

Besides genetic screening, there are a variety of other neutral employment criteria designed to screen out poor health risks that may have a disparate impact on the basis of race, color, religion, or national origin. The criteria may be based on the immutable biological makeup of the individual or result from diet, life-style, or other behavior-based factors. So long as there is a disparate impact, a prima facie case under Title VII would be established. Cytogenetic monitoring for chromosomal damage, however, has not yet been shown to have a disparate impact by race.[14]

Religious discrimination based on medical screening would most likely involve religion in its ethnic sense. For example, Mediterranean Jews are more likely to be G-6-PD deficient than either European Jews or Mediterranean non-Jews (*e.g.*, Greeks). Religious beliefs, to the extent that they affect diet, dress, life-style, and other behavorial factors, could also influence an individual's susceptibility to occupational illness. Where religion has conflicted with workplace safety and health, the interests of safety and health usually have prevailed.

For instance, in one case EEOC determined that an employer's "no beard" rule and hard hat requirement did not constitute religious discrimination against a Sikh employee because OSHA required the use of hard hats and respirators.[15] In another case the Missouri Court of Appeals held that it was not discriminatory for an employer to fire a woman who worked around machinery when she refused to wear slacks because of her religious beliefs.[16]

Once a plaintiff proves that an employment practice has a disparate impact, the burden shifts to the employer to justify the practice. In *Griggs,* the Supreme Court, in discussing employer defenses, indicated that "[t]he touchstone is business necessity. If an employment practice which operates to exclude Negroes cannot be shown to be related to job performance, the practice is prohibited."[17]

Based on *Griggs,* two intertwined defenses have emerged, "business necessity" and "job-relatedness." *Griggs* used the terms in the same sentence and did not differentiate between the two. Some subsequent decisions have attempted to distinguish the two defenses in the following way. "Business necessity" applies when a general employment practice is used whose purpose is not to determine whether an applicant or employee is capable of performing the job requirements. For example, an employer would attempt to use a business

necessity defense to justify not hiring someone who had been con-
victed of a crime,[18] not hiring an employee whose wages were subject
to garnishment,[19] or using a seniority system that had a racially discriminatory impact.[20] "Job-relatedness," which has a somewhat
narrower scope, concerns whether an employer's criteria used in determining whether an applicant or employee is qualified for employment bear a reasonable relationship to the demands of the job. For
example, the requirement of a high school diploma,[21] an employer's
height and weight requirements,[22] and the requirement of passing
scores on standardized tests[23] would be evaluated under job-relatedness.

The standards used for determining the merits of the business
necessity and job-relatedness defenses are similar. The key to resolving the question of business necessity is "whether there exists an
overriding legitimate business purpose such that the practice is necessary to the safe and efficient operation of the business."[24] Once the
employer presents evidence to show that its employment practice is
grounded upon business necessity, courts balance all the relevant
factors to determine whether the need for the practice sufficiently
outweighs any disparate impact. According to one court,[25] the balancing involves a consideration of the nature of the business involved, the business practice at issue, and the degree of discriminatory impact. Where the job requires a high degree of skill and
responsibility, however, the courts may be more likely to permit an
employer to use narrow selection criteria.[26]

In *Smith v. Olin Chemical Corp.*,[27] the plaintiff was discharged
from his position of manual laborer after an x-ray revealed bone degeneration of the spine with a prognosis of possible further degeneration. The employee alleged that his condition was due to sickle cell
anemia, and, therefore, the employer's policy had a disparate impact
on blacks. In a questionable decision, the Fifth Circuit affirmed the
district court's granting of summary judgment for the company. Despite the disparate impact of the employer's policy, the manifest job-
relatedness of the rule was considered to be so apparent that the employer was not even required to present a business necessity defense.
According to an EEOC decision,[28] however, an employer violated
Title VII when it refused to hire a black woman for the job of telephone operator because she had sickle cell anemia. The employer
had argued that it rejects all applicants, regardless of race, with sickle
cell anemia or other chronic blood conditions that render the applicant medically unfit. Because the case involved summer employment, however, no lawsuit was ever filed in court.

In *EEOC v. Trailways, Inc.*,[29] a black employee who suffered from pseudofolliculitis barbae, a skin disorder resulting from in-grown hairs when the person is clean-shaven, brought an action challenging the employer's ''no beard'' policy. The plaintiff made out a prima facie case of disparate impact by introducing medical testimony that the disorder is found in 25% of black males but in far less than 1% of white males. The employer failed to rebut this evidence with a showing of business necessity.[30]

Job-relatedness essentially involves a determination of a job's requirements and a comparison of the job requirements with the employer's method for assessing fitness. In *Albemarle Paper Co. v. Moody*,[31] the Supreme Court held that ''discriminatory tests are impermissible unless shown, by professionally acceptable methods, to be 'predictive of or significantly correlated with important elements of work behavior which comprise or are relevant to the job or jobs for which candidates are being evaluated.' ''[32]

Cases involving the business necessity and job-relatedness defenses are usually difficult in any event.[33] When the issue of susceptibility to illness enters the picture, the legal uncertainties become even more pronounced. Any thin line that could be drawn to distinguish between the defenses of business necessity and job-relatedness becomes virtually obscured in the context of predictive genetic and biological screening of workers and applicants. An employer's justification for using these procedures would necessarily involve elements of both defenses.

Although there have been no cases decided on this precise issue, a court would be likely to require an employer's defense to include proof of the following:

1. There is a valid basis for excluding workers who are presently capable of performing the required work but who may become physically unable or impaired at some point in the future.

2. It is essential to the business that employees not suffer or be suffering from an illness.

3. There is a high correlation between a specific genetic, cytogenetic, biological, or behavioral trait and the individual's increased risk of disease.

4. The specific screening procedure used to determine the presence of the trait has a high predictive value.

5. No other medical procedure or work rule can achieve the desired goal with less discriminatory impact.

10.3 Sex

There are several ways in which a woman's actual or believed predisposition to occupational illness could result in adverse treatment by employers.

- First, an employer might presume that women in general lack the physical strength, stamina, or dexterity to perform the job and, therefore, are more likely to become injured on the job.
- Second, an employer might conclude that women in general are more susceptible to occupational illness where there are exposures to certain toxic substances, such as lead and benzene.
- Third, an employer might consider that some women are predisposed to occupational illness because of the combined effects of workplace exposure and another factor uniquely affecting a subclass of women, such as those women taking oral contraceptives.[34]
- Fourth, an employer may use a neutral biological marker in preemployment medical screening which has a disparate impact on women.

The first illustration represents disparate treatment discrimination and is the classic stereotypical reasoning that Title VII was intended to prohibit. In *Rosenfeld v. Southern Pacific Co.*,[35] the employer refused to consider a woman for a certain position because it believed that the arduous nature of the work rendered women unsuited for the job. The Ninth Circuit affirmed the finding of a Title VII violation.

> The premise of Title VII, the wisdom of which is not in question here, is that women are now to be on equal footing with men. The footing is not equal if a male employee may be appointed to a particular position on a showing that he is physically qualified, but a female employee is denied an opportunity to demonstrate personal physical qualification. Equality of footing is established only if employees otherwise entitled to the position, whether male or female, are excluded only upon a showing of individual incapacity. This alone accords with Congressional purpose to eliminate subjective assumptions and traditional stereotyped conceptions regarding the physical ability of women to do particular work.[36]

Disparate treatment sex discrimination also may be more closely related to occupational medical practices. For example, in *Wroblewski v. Lexington Gardens, Inc.*,[37] the Supreme Court of Connecticut held that the state fair employment law was violated when an employer required only female applicants to answer urogenital and reproductive health questions on a medical questionnaire.

The second illustration (increased sensitivity to workplace chemicals) also involves disparate treatment, in that all women are excluded from employment. It is somewhat different from the first illustration, however, because the employer's decision is based on *some* scientific evidence. This is a particular problem in the occupational health area, where definitive scientific conclusions often lag well behind the first available data. The danger is that scant data will be used to justify a sweeping exclusionary policy. Even where there are better data, however, the principle of individualized determination would apply.

In *City of Los Angeles v. Manhart*,[38] the Supreme Court held that an employer violated Title VII when it required its female employees to make larger contributions to its pension fund than its male employees. Even though, as a class, women live longer than men, not all of the women will live longer than all of the men in the class. Therefore, as applied to individuals (whose life expectancy obviously cannot be calculated prospectively), the use of sex-based mortality tables violated Title VII.

> The statute's focus on the individual is unambiguous. It precludes treatment of individuals as simply components of a racial, religious, sexual, or national class. . . . Even a true generalization about the class is an insufficient reason for disqualifying an individual to whom the generalization does not apply.[39]

Based on *Manhart*, sex-based studies of injury and illness rates[40] may not be used to support disparate treatment.

The third illustration involves "sex-plus" discrimination, in which "the employer does not discriminate against the class of men or women as a whole, but rather disparately treats a subclass of men or women."[41] In the leading case of *Phillips v. Martin Marietta Corp.*,[42] the employer had a policy of not hiring women with pre-school-age children but did not have a similar rule with respect to men. The Supreme Court held that disparate treatment of a subclass of one sex can be unlawful sex discrimination. Other forms of sex-plus discrimination, such as "no marriage" rules for women but not men[43] and requiring married women to use their husbands' surnames,[44] also have been held to violate Title VII. These same principles would apply to occupational safety- and health-related sex-plus discrimination.

The fourth factor, use of neutral medical criteria with a disparate impact on women, raises legal issues virtually identical to disparate impact discrimination based on race, color, religion, and national origin, which have been discussed earlier. Disparate impact discrimination based on sex has been found in a variety of other Title VII cases, such as minimum height and weight requirements[45] and "no spouse" rules.[46] This theory would certainly apply to safety- and health-related employer practices.

Section 703(e) of Title VII provides that it is not unlawful for an employer to differentiate in hiring on the basis of religion, sex, or national origin "in those certain instances where religion, sex, or national origin is a bona fide occupational qualification reasonably necessary to the normal operation of that particular business or enterprise." Both EEOC's Interpretive Guidelines[47] and judicial decisions[48] have made it clear that in its application to differentiation on the basis of sex, the defense is only available where members of one sex are unable to perform the duties essential to the job.

To sustain a bona fide occupational qualification (BFOQ) defense to a charge of sex discrimination, the employer must prove that it "had reasonable cause to believe, that is, a factual basis for believing, that all or substantially all women would be unable to perform safely and efficiently the duties of the job involved."[49] This defense is difficult to sustain and has been successful principally when the hiring of a member of a particular sex was essential to maintaining security and order,[50] to protect legitimate privacy interests,[51] or because of the need for sex authenticity.[52] It is not clear whether the BFOQ defense applies where an individual is presently capable of performing the job, but may not be able to perform in the future.[53]

Business necessity and job-relatedness, the principal defenses to disparate impact discrimination, have been discussed earlier in the context of discrimination based on race, color, religion, and national origin. Sex discrimination cases also have followed the business necessity principles of *Griggs*. Therefore, whether the employer's action in the fourth illustration (disparate impact medical procedures) constitutes sex discrimination should be determined by applying the same factors mentioned earlier. At least for the present, it would appear that the medical evidence is too insubstantial to justify the use of medical screening procedures with a disparate impact by sex.

10.4   Pregnancy

There are two related health concerns when pregnant women are exposed to toxic substances in the workplace. The first is the danger to the woman herself at a time of possibly increased susceptibility to occupational illness. The second is the danger to the fetus. Although pregnancy-related employment decisions invariably consider both concerns, it is the danger to the fetus that has been given primary attention.

In 1978, Title VII was amended to prohibit discrimination in employment based on pregnancy, childbirth, or related medical conditions. The amendment provides in pertinent part:

> (k) The terms "because of sex" or "on the basis of sex" include, but are not limited to, because of or on the basis of pregnancy, childbirth, or related medical conditions; and women affected by pregnancy, childbirth, or related medical conditions shall be treated the same for all employment-related purposes, including receipt of benefits under fringe benefit programs, as other persons not so affected but similar in their ability or inability to work, and nothing in section 2000e-2(h) of this title shall be interpreted to permit otherwise.

Based on this language, any treatment of women who are pregnant must be consistent with treatment accorded other persons. Because an employee's heightened risk of illness justifies excluding an employee from the workplace, a pregnant woman could be excluded, but only by applying the same standards used for nonpregnant persons with current or potential impairments.

There are three possible bases for excluding pregnant women: Continued employment could injure the woman, it could injure co-workers or the public, or it could injure the fetus. Different legal standards have been applied to each of these situations.

In *Meyer v. Brown & Root Construction Co.*,[54] a woman employee whose duties involved preparing accounting records, reports, and inventories and performing light work in a warehouse informed her supervisor that she was pregnant. Although she was told she would be granted a leave of absence when she was ready, she was unexpectedly replaced from her former position and assigned to a heavy manual labor position in the warehouse. The woman feared that this type of work could injure her or her unborn child. When the company refused to change her assignment, she quit. The Fifth Circuit held that the woman was constructively discharged in violation of Title VII and affirmed an award of $23,620 in back pay and $3,500 in attorney fees.

Where the concern is for co-worker or public safety and health, the courts are more inclined to uphold the removal of pregnant employees. For example, in *Harriss v. Pan American World Airways, Inc.*,[55] the Ninth Circuit upheld the airline's policy of requiring that female flight attendants take maternity leave immediately upon learning of their pregnancy. The court based its decision on evidence that a flight attendant's ability to perform her emergency functions might be impaired by fatigue, nausea and vomiting, or spontaneous abortion. Passenger safety was considered to be a business necessity for the challenge based on the company's pre-1978 policy. (Before the Pregnancy Amendment, which expressly made any discrimination based on pregnancy sex discrimination, discrimination based on pregnancy merely was considered "facially neutral" treatment adversely affecting women under *General Electric Co. v. Gilbert*[56]). Passenger safety was considered a BFOQ for the post-1978 policy. Nevertheless, it is essential that safety claims be supported by evidence adduced at the trial. In another airline case a district court observed that "the incantation of safety rationale is not an abracadabra to which this court must defer."[57]

Employers may have a more difficult time in justifying the removal of pregnant employees where the sole concern is the health of the fetus. In *Zuniga v. Kleberg County Hospital*,[58] the Fifth Circuit held that Title VII was violated when a hospital terminated a pregnant x-ray technician.

> Even if the business necessity defense does extend to the preservation of fetal health or the avoidance of tort liability, we find that Zuniga has effectively revealed the alleged business necessity to be a mere pretext for discrimination by showing that the Hospital failed to utilize an available, alternative, less discriminatory means of achieving its business purpose. . . . The Hospital could have avoided terminating Zuniga's employment while protecting itself and the fetus by granting Zuniga a leave of absence in accordance with its own established policies.[59]

In another case holding that the termination of a pregnant x-ray technician was unlawful, *Hayes v. Shelby Memorial Hospital*,[60] the district court issued an even more sweeping opinion. The court implied that fetal health may *never* constitute a business necessity and flatly rejected the BFOQ defense as being inapplicable.

> The defendant would have the court extend the concept of a business purpose "necessary to the safe and efficient operation of the business" to include the avoidance of possible future liability to the fetus. Such an unwarranted extension would shift the focus of the business necessity defense from a focus of concern for the safety of hospital patients to a focus of concern for hospital finances. Even if the court were to extend the concept of business purpose to include avoidance of possible litigation and consequent potential liability, the defendant has not met the second requirement of the defense—that there were no acceptable alternatives that would accomplish the purpose with a less discriminatory impact. . . . Hospital officials did not seriously look into other duties

within the hospital that the plaintiff could perform, nor did they consider rearranging the plaintiff's duties within the Radiology Department.[61]

In rejecting the applicability of the BFOQ defense the court noted that there are two requirements for the defense:

(1)   The qualification invoked must be reasonably necessary to the essence of the employer's business, and
(2)   The employer has a reasonable factual basis for believing that substantially all women would be unable to safely and efficiently perform the duties of the job.[62]

Because both aspects of the defense focus on job performance, the court held that to sustain a BFOQ defense the employer must show a nexus between pregnancy and an inability to perform the job. ''Potential for fetal harm, unless it adversely affects a mother's job performance, is irrelevant to the BFOQ issue.''[63]

Two additional points related to pregnancy discrimination should be mentioned. First, the employer's policies for dealing with pregnant employees may be the subject of a collective bargaining agreement. For example, in *Amoco Oil Co.*,[64] an arbitrator upheld a contract provision requiring female employees to inform the employer at the first sign of pregnancy and requiring the discharge or transfer of pregnant employees because of potential exposure to teratogens.

Second, it is a violation of Title VII for an employer to discriminate against an employee seeking to return from a pregnancy leave of absence. In *Fancher v. Nimmo*,[65] the Veterans Administration was held to have violated Title VII by refusing to reassign a woman to her former position in the Nuclear Medicine Department. Her removal, which occurred prior to her leave of absence, also violated Title VII even though it was done to avoid exposing her to radiation.

10.5   Fertility

The medical basis of reproductive hazards and the frequent employer response—exclusion of fertile women from high-risk jobs—have been discussed earlier (sections 5.3, 6.4). The legality of these practices under Title VII is a controversial and unresolved issue.[66]

In 1980 the Office of Federal Contract Compliance Programs (OFCCP) and the EEOC jointly published Proposed Interpretive Guidelines on Employment Discrimination and Reproductive Hazards.[67] The proposed guidelines, which were withdrawn in 1981,[68] prohibited the exclusion of all women of childbearing capacity.

In 1982, in *Wright v. Olin Corp.*,[69] the Fourth Circuit decided the first Title VII case involving an exclusionary policy. The employer's "female employment and fetal vulnerability" program created three job classifications, described by the court as follows:

> 1) Restricted jobs are those which "may require contact with and exposure to known or suspected abortifacient or teratogenic agents." Fertile women are excluded from such jobs. Any woman age 5 through 63 is assumed to be fertile and can be placed in a restricted job only after consulting with Olin's medical doctors to confirm the woman cannot bear children and will sustain no other adverse physiological effects from the environment. 2) Controlled jobs may require very limited contact with the harmful chemicals. Pregnant women may work at such jobs only after individual case-by-case evaluations. Nonpregnant women may work in controlled jobs after signing a form stating that they recognize that the job presents "some risk, although slight." Olin encourages women in controlled jobs to bid for other jobs if they intend to become pregnant. 3) Unrestricted jobs are those which do "not present a hazard to the pregnant female or the fetus." They are open to all women.[70]

The first problem faced by the court was to decide whether the program should be considered as disparate treatment or disparate impact discrimination. The court observed that the fact situation "does not fit with absolute precision into any of the developed theories."[71] The court rejected the disparate treatment theory as "wholly inappropriate"[72] and chose to view the case as one of disparate impact—largely because the business necessity defense is more flexible and would permit the evaluation of all relevant considerations.

The court determined that evidence of the existence of the fetal vulnerability program established a prima facie case of a Title VII violation. This is hardly disputable. The question is whether the program was compelled by business necessity. According to the court, the health of unborn children of its workers is a legitimate business concern of an employer. Therefore, "under appropriate circumstances an employer may, as a matter of business necessity, impose otherwise impermissible restrictions on employment opportunity that are reasonably required to protect the health of unborn children of women workers against hazards of the workplace."[73]

The employer's burden of proving this business necessity defense, however, is a difficult one. Essentially, the employer must prove that:

1. There are significant risks of harm to the unborn children of female workers from exposure during pregnancy.
2. There are no similar risks to the unborn children of male workers.
3. Objective scientific evidence (probably requiring expert testimony) supports the employer's decision to restrict only fertile women.
4. The employer's program is effective in eliminating the risk.

The plaintiff may rebut this prima facie defense by showing that an acceptable alternative would accomplish the protective purpose equally well with less differential impact or that underlying the employer's program is a discriminatory intent.

The Fourth Circuit in *Olin* established a burden of proof consistent with Title VII case law, but one that, as a practical matter, few employers would ever be able to meet. The current state of medical knowledge does not support the notion that there are significant teratologic risks to the offspring of women workers but not mutagenic risks to the offspring of men workers.

The likely effect of this burden of proof would be to find that the fetal protection program violates Title VII. The remedy, however, of prohibiting the exclusion of fertile women from exposure to possible reproductive hazards is unsatisfactory. Without other coordinate efforts to improve reproductive health in the workplace, prohibiting the exclusion of fertile women merely equalizes, or widens, the risks.

New efforts are needed to minimize the dangers of reproductive hazards in the workplace, and these new efforts must include a larger role for the affected employees. The following six recommendations should be implemented:

1. All employees who are working in areas where there are possible reproductive hazards must be informed in writing of this fact and notified of the specific substances.
2. Employees must be advised in writing of the possible short-term and long-term effects of exposure and must be provided with available literature on the substances and the nature of the hazards.
3. No employer may condition employment on the employee's being sterilized.
4. Pregnancy and fertility testing must be made available by the employer.

5. Medical removal protection must be provided for pregnant employees as well as those employees attempting to become parents.

6. There must be ongoing efforts to reduce exposure levels through improved control technologies, substitution of substances, and better personal protective equipment.

The Connecticut Reproductive Hazards Act[74] is the first state law to address many of these issues. Among other things, it requires employers to give employees notice if they are working with reproductive hazards, prohibits conditioning employment on an employee's being sterilized, and requires employers to make reasonable efforts to transfer a pregnant employee to a temporary job or take other reasonable measures to protect the reproductive health of employees.

Even these recommendations cannot totally eliminate the possibility that a woman would become pregnant and not discover she was pregnant until after some teratogenic effect had occurred. The issue may ultimately revert to one of risk acceptability and balancing the competing public policy interests discussed in section 6.4. Meanwhile, most employers are determined to maintain their exclusionary policies. They prefer to litigate (and even lose) Title VII sex discrimination claims rather than face the prospect of a lawsuit brought by a child as a result of maternal exposures, with its attendant adverse publicity, loss of good will, increased insurance costs, and other consequences.

Ironically, the impetus for changing these exclusionary reproductive policies may well be the first lawsuits brought by children damaged by paternal exposures. Only then will some employers realize that single-sex exclusionary policies do not even accomplish their primary objective of protecting the health of workers' offspring and eliminating possible civil liability.

10.6   Age

The Age Discrimination in Employment Act (ADEA) prohibits age discrimination in the employment, discharge, promotion, or treatment of persons between the ages of 40 and 70. Thirty-eight states, the District of Columbia, and Puerto Rico also have laws prohibiting age discrimination in employment.

The ADEA applies to every employer engaged in an enterprise affecting commerce that has 20 or more employees for each working day in each of 20 or more calendar weeks in the current or preceding calendar year. The ADEA also applies to employment agencies, unions, and state and local political subdivisions. As of 1978, enforcement of the ADEA is vested in EEOC, but private actions also may be brought by aggrieved individuals. A wide range of relief is available to prevailing plaintiffs, including compensatory and punitive damages, reinstatement, injunctive and declaratory relief, and attorney fees. The procedures are the same as for Title VII cases, except that under the ADEA there is a right to a jury trial.

Nearly all reported ADEA cases involve alleged disparate treatment discrimination and concern matters other than susceptibility to occupational illness. Nevertheless, it is possible that the ADEA could afford an avenue for relief to individuals subjected to adverse treatment because of increased risk of occupational disease associated with age.

Some OSHA health standards, such as those regulating arsenic and coke oven emissions, require that older employees be given medical examinations more frequently. In addition, older workers may be more susceptible to certain occupational diseases. Based on these two factors, an employer might refuse to hire older employees because of a fear that it would increase costs. Such action would certainly constitute disparate treatment age discrimination, and the defense of increased costs would almost assuredly fail.[75]

It is much more likely that discrimination against older workers would involve neutral medical or employment criteria that have an adverse impact upon older workers. For example, in *McIntosh v. U.S. Home Corp.*,[76] the plaintiff alleged that he was discharged because he was suffering from Paget's disease, which is more prevalent in older persons. Without ruling on whether an action may be based on an employee's disease with a higher prevalence rate within the protected class, the court granted a dismissal under rule 41(b) of the Federal Rules of Civil Procedure. The evidence presented at the trial indicated that the plaintiff was discharged because of poor performance, an unwillingness to submit to discipline, and the company's intention to "wind down" the plaintiff's division. It is possible, however, that under a different set of facts, a violation of the ADEA could be found where there was discriminatory treatment of a person within the protected class because of an age-related susceptibility to occupational disease.

In *Geller v. Markham*,[77] the Hartford, Connecticut school board adopted a cost-reduction plan whereby all new hires had to have less than five years of teaching experience. The board reasoned that because base pay increased with the level of experience, costs could be lowered significantly by hiring less-experienced teachers. The plaintiff was denied a position in favor of a less-experienced 25-year-old and brought an action under the ADEA, claiming that the policy had a disparate impact on members of the protected class. Among the evidence presented by the plaintiff were statistics showing that 92.6% of teachers over the age of 40 had five or more years of experience, but only 60% of teachers under the age of 40 had comparable experience. The Second Circuit affirmed the district court's holding in favor of the plaintiff.

The *Geller* approach will be of most benefit to individuals whose increased risk is based on prior workplace exposures. Thus, if an asbestos products manufacturer adopted a policy of not hiring any individuals who had worked for five or more years at another asbestos products company, it is likely that a plaintiff within the protected class would, at least, be able to make out a prima facie case of age discrimination.

There are two main hurdles to be overcome by a plaintiff in either a *McIntosh*-type or *Geller*-type case. First, under either theory, the court must adopt the disparate treatment theory as being applicable to the ADEA. This theory was first articulated in *Griggs v. Duke Power Co.*,[78] a Title VII case, in which the Supreme Court held that an employer may not use facially neutral employment practices that have a disparate impact on the protected class. In *Geller*, the Second Circuit specifically adopted the *Griggs* approach for ADEA cases.[79] Although there is dictum in the opinions of other circuits, the Second and Eighth Circuits are the only courts to expressly adopt and apply this theory,[80] and it is not clear that other circuits or the Supreme Court would agree. In fact, in his dissent to the denial of *certiorari* in *Geller*, Justice Rehnquist expressed his view that the ADEA only prohibits intentional discrimination and does not proscribe neutral practices having a disparate impact.[81]

The second problem for any ADEA plaintiff is the possible business necessity defense of the employer. Just as BFOQ is a valid defense against a charge of disparate treatment discrimination, the business necessity defense may be used as a valid defense in a case involving alleged disparate impact discrimination. Because there are no ADEA cases that consider this issue, Title VII cases are the best reference point. As already discussed, employers have a difficult burden in proving that a practice with a discriminatory impact is essential to the safe and efficient operation of the business. In the BFOQ context, ADEA cases have held that economic considerations alone cannot sustain the defense. According to the Fourth Circuit, "[e]conomic considerations . . . cannot be the basis for a BFOQ—precisely these considerations were among the targets of the act."[82]

The courts are much more sympathetic to the BFOQ defense when the safety and health of the employee, co-employees, and the public are involved. The Fifth Circuit has stated: "[S]afety to fellow employees is of such humane importance that the employer must be afforded substantial discretion in selecting specific standards which, if they err at all, should err on the [side of] preservation of life and limb."[83] Many cases have concerned maximum age limitations on the hiring or continued employment of individuals in jobs where lives are dependent on employee efficiency, such as bus drivers, airline pilots, police officers, and fire fighters.[84] The cases reach widely divergent results and are difficult to reconcile.

In cases where the BFOQ defense has been rejected, the main problem has been that arbitrary age cutoffs have been used. Oddly enough, where an employer has a program of comprehensive periodic medical examinations, it may be more difficult to sustain a BFOQ defense because the individual determination of medical fitness makes arbitrary age cutoffs unnecessary.[85] Because of the uncertainty surrounding this aspect of ADEA litigation, it is unclear how these defenses would be applied in ADEA actions brought by high-risk workers.

10.7   Employee Refusals to Take Medical Tests

There is one other possible application of Title VII that may be important to the issue of medical screening of employees. Title VII may provide an applicant or employee with the right to refuse to take certain medical tests.

Section 704(a) of Title VII provides that an employer may not retaliate against an employee or applicant "because he has opposed any practice made an unlawful employment practice by this title, or because he has made a charge, testified, assisted, or participated in any manner in an investigation, proceeding or hearing under this title." Most of the cases brought under this section involve alleged employer retaliation after the filing of a charge with the EEOC.[86] Nevertheless, there are some cases based on more general employee "opposition" to violative practices of the employer.

It is generally recognized that section 704(a) protection extends to different forms of employee activity besides merely filing a charge with EEOC. For example, employees have been found to be protected when they opposed an employer's discriminatory job assignments[87] or refused to alter a minority applicant's test score so that he would be denied employment.[88] When an employee's opposition takes the form of disruptive activity, the courts will balance the competing interests of protecting persons who oppose discrimination with the employer's right to control its personnel.[89]

No court has ever resolved the question of whether section 704(a) protects employees who refuse to submit to a test that they believe is discriminatory. In the one case where the issue was raised,[90] the case was decided on other grounds. It is clear, however, that an employee need not be correct in believing that a practice (or test) is discriminatory; only a good faith belief is required.[91]

Based on these considerations, it is possible that an applicant or employee could validly refuse to submit to discriminatory medical testing and any retaliation by the employer would violate Title VII.

Chapter 11

THE NATIONAL LABOR RELATIONS ACT

11.1 Protected Activities of Employees

The National Labor Relations Act (NLRA) is the federal labor law providing the legal framework within which employees may engage in concerted activities to improve their working conditions. Section 8(a)(1) of the NLRA makes it an unfair labor practice for an employer "to interfere with, restrain or coerce employees in the exercise of" section 7 rights, including "the right to self-organization, to form, join, or assist labor organizations, to bargain collectively through representatives of their own choosing, and to engage in other concerted activities for the purpose of collective bargaining or other mutual aid or protection...." Generally, to be protected under section 8(a)(1) the employee action must take place through a union representative or be done "in concert" with other employees. Even individual employee action may be protected, however, if the employee is also furthering the interests of other employees.

In *NLRB v. Interboro Contractors, Inc.*,[1] the Second Circuit upheld the National Labor Relations Board's doctrine of "constructive concerted activity" under which "activities involving attempts to enforce the provisions of a collective bargaining agreement may be deemed to be for concerted purposes even in the absence of such interest by fellow employees."[2] The Board has applied this principle to other actions of individual employees that benefit other members of the bargaining unit, including attempts to improve workplace safety and health. In *Alleluia Cushion Co.*,[3] an employee was discharged after he filed a complaint under the California Occupational Safety and Health Act. The NLRB held that the discharge violated section 8(a)(1) of the NLRA because by asserting the rights of all employees to a safe and healthful workplace, the employee was engaged in constructive concerted activity.

In *Meyers Industries, Inc.*,[4] an employee was discharged for complaining about allegedly unsafe brakes on his truck. The Board overruled *Alleluia* and held that the discharge did not violate section 8(a)(1). In adopting a new objective standard the Board held that to be protected the activity must be ''engaged in with or on the authority of other employees, and not solely by and on behalf of the employee himself.'' *Interboro* was distinguished because it involved the attempted implementation of a collective bargaining agreement.

Even before *Meyers* the Board's *Interboro-Alleluia* rule had not been well received by the courts of appeals. For example, the Sixth Circuit has held that the employee must actually, rather than impliedly, be representing the views of other employees to be protected[5] and the Ninth Circuit has held that the filing of a safety complaint by a single employee is unprotected where there is no collective bargaining agreement in effect.[6] The Supreme Court is presently considering this issue.[7]

Section 8(a)(1) protection applies to a wide range of concerted employee activities in the area of job safety and health. The distribution of leaflets concerning safety and health hazards in the plant,[8] the meeting of employees to discuss safety,[9] the filing of safety grievances,[10] the filing of a complaint with NIOSH,[11] the filing of a complaint with OSHA,[12] and the refusal to work under extremely hazardous conditions[13] all have been held to be protected activity.

11.2   Bargaining Over Occupational Safety and Health

Sections 8(a)(5), 8(b)(3), and 8(d) of the NLRA require the employer and union to bargain in good faith with respect to wages, hours, and other terms and conditions of employment. Included within these so-called ''mandatory subjects of bargaining''[14] is occupational safety and health.[15]

One of the effects of a subject's being considered a mandatory subject of bargaining is that neither the employer nor the union may make unilateral changes in these conditions without first bargaining to impasse with the other side. Thus, it has been held to be a violation of section 8(a)(5) for an employer to decide unilaterally what kind of respirator employees must wear[16] or what disciplinary action may be taken against employees for refusing to wear safety glasses.[17]

In *Johns-Manville Sales Corp. v. International Association of Machinists, Local Lodge 1609*,[18] the employer adopted a work rule prohibiting smoking in the plant because of the increased health risks that smoking poses to employees working with asbestos. The union filed a grievance, arguing that the new rule constituted a unilateral change in working conditions without bargaining with the union. The arbitrator agreed with the union. There are limited grounds on which the merits of an arbitration decision may be reviewed by the courts, but the company attempted to obtain such a review by asserting that the decision was against public policy. The Fifth Circuit affirmed the district court's refusal to set aside the arbitrator's decision. According to the court, the arbitration decision was not contrary to public policy. "If smoking in such plants should be prohibited even at the cost of employee discharge, there are governmental agencies with authority to promulgate such a rule with the force of the law."[19] The employer could not institute such a policy in the middle of a contract's term without bargaining with the union.

As part of the duty to bargain in good faith, an employer must provide information needed by the union for the proper performance of its duty as the representative of the employees.[20] This duty extends beyond the period of contract negotiation to cover the entire term of the contract.[21] Recently, unions have attempted to invoke this principle to obtain detailed information about conditions in the workplace. Unions frequently have requested employee medical records and the identities, properties, and health hazards of various chemicals used in the workplace. Employers objecting to the release of this information have asserted a variety of defenses including trade secrets, a proprietary interest in the information, physician-patient privilege, confidentiality, and undue burden.

In *Johns-Manville Sales Corp.*,[22] for example, the International Chemical Workers Union requested a variety of medical information including the results of sputum cytology tests, chest x-rays, blood tests, and pulmonary function tests. The union wanted the information to aid it in developing a health program to protect employees identified by the employer as being partially disabled by occupational pneumoconiosis. The NLRB ordered the company to provide the union with the requested information.

In 1977, in response to the discovery of sterility among union members working with the pesticide DBCP at an Occidental Chemical plant in California, the Oil, Chemical and Atomic Workers International Union (OCAW) initiated a campaign to gain disclosure of hazard information at many of its organized plants. The international union sent 560 locals a form letter requesting company disclosure; 110 of these locals chose to send the letter on their own stationery to the company representatives.

The letter requested the following data:

1. morbidity and mortality statistics on all past and present employees;
2. the generic name (chemical name, as opposed to trade name or code number) of all substances used and produced at the plant;
3. results of clinical and laboratory studies of any employee undertaken by the company, including the results of toxicological investigations regarding agents to which employees may be exposed;
4. certain health information derived from insurance programs covering employees, as well as information concerning occupational illness and accident data related to workers' compensation claims;
5. a listing of contaminants monitored by the company, along with a sample protocol;
6. a description of the company's hearing conservation program, including noise level surveys;
7. radiation sources in the plant, and a listing of radiation incidents requiring notification of state and federal agencies;
8. an indication of plant work areas which exceeded proposed NIOSH heat standards and an outline of the company's control program to prevent heat disease.

More than half of the 110 companies furnished the information in some form or another. OCAW filed section 8(a)(5) charges against two of the companies that refused to supply the requested information, Minnesota Mining and Manufacturing Company and Colgate-Palmolive Company. The cases were consolidated with a third case, a section 8(a)(5) charge against Borden Chemical Company, based on its failure to supply the International Chemical Workers Union with a list of the generic names of all materials and chemicals handled by union members.

In *Minnesota Mining & Manufacturing Co.*[23] and the two companion cases,[24] the NLRB held that the unions had the right to obtain all of the requested information. According to the Board, "[f]ew matters can be of greater legitimate concern to individuals in the workplace, and thus to the bargaining agent representing them, than exposure to conditions potentially threatening their health, well-being, or their very lives."[25] The Board rejected the employer's proprietary interest claim as irrelevant and the undue burden claim as unsubstantiated. With respect to physician-patient privilege and confidentiality, the Board noted that the union did not request the names of individual employees and that confidentiality would be safeguarded by having physicians interpret and analyze the documents. Moreover, the Board held that even where supplying the union with statistical or aggregate medical data may result in identification of some individual employees, the important need for the data outweighs any minimal intrusion on employee privacy. Finally, as to trade secrets, the Board ordered the parties to bargain about conditions of disclosure, but stated that, if necessary, the Board would strike the balance between the competing claims of the parties.

On judicial review, the Board's decision in each of the three consolidated cases was enforced in all respects.[26] According to the D.C. Circuit,

> the goals of occupational health and safety are inadequately served if employers do not fully share with unions available information on working conditions and employees' medical histories. Requiring the release of exposure and medical data in such cases will facilitate the identification of workplace hazards, promote meaningful bargaining calculated to remove or reduce those hazards, and enable unions effectively to police the performance of employers' contractual obligations as well as to carry out their own responsibilities under the respective collective bargaining agreements.[27]

One would be tempted to ask why unions would seek to use the NLRA to obtain exposure and medical records when OSHA's Access Regulation mandates disclosure. There are at least four reasons. First, the OSHA regulation is limited to employees exposed to certain toxic substances. Second, the OSHA regulation could be amended, repealed, or struck down in court. In fact, already there is a proposal to, among other things, reduce the number of covered substances from 39,000 to 3,492.[28] Third, the OSHA regulation does not require that any records be maintained, but only that those records generated by the employer be retained and made available. Union discovery of existing records may be the first step in efforts to require employers to collect additional information. Fourth, under OSHA's access regulation individual employee consent is needed before medical records are given to the union. The likely inability of the union to obtain unanimous employee consent would cripple its ability to perform epidemiological research.

Perhaps the best way for a union to learn about workplace safety and health hazards is for the union to have its own experts conduct an inspection. Not surprisingly, many employers would view the prospect of union safety and health inspectors with considerable trepidation. In *Winona Industries, Inc.*,[29] the employer prohibited employees from wearing "tank tops" on the grounds that it was contrary to OSHA requirements and could cause industrial dermatitis. The union challenged the rule and sought to have its own industrial hygienist conduct an inspection. The NLRB held that the employer's refusal to permit the inspection constituted a violation of section 8(a)(5) because the inspection was relevant to the union's discharge of its bargaining obligation.

Safety and health provisions have been included in collective bargaining agreements for many years, but the passage of OSHA in 1970 served to promote greater awareness of workplace hazards and to increase the importance attached to safety and health in union contracts. According to a 1983 study, 82% of union contracts contained occupational safety and health clauses.[30] As shown in Table 11-1, the subjects most often covered were safety and health committees and safety equipment.

It is now widely believed that the collective bargaining process offers great hope in fostering the improvement of workplace safety and health. Nevertheless, despite the greater importance attached to safety and health in recent years, collective bargaining on these issues traditionally has not been looked upon with much interest by either employers or rank-and-file employees.

Union lawyer George Cohen wrote in 1972: "Generally speaking, union efforts at the bargaining table to impose more stringent controls over safety and health have been beaten back as cost conscious companies continue to guard zealously their 'managerial pre-

Table 11-1.   Safety and Health Provisions in Collective Bargaining Agreements, 1983

Clause	Occurrence in Contracts (%)
Safety equipment	46
Safety and health committees	45
Employee obligations	37
Physical examinations	30
Hazardous work	25
First aid	20
Accident investigation	17
Government inspection participation	12

Source: Adapted from The Bureau of National Affairs, Inc., Basic Patterns in Union Contracts 108–11 (10th ed. 1983).

rogatives' over these subject areas against erosion from any source."[31] There is little to suggest a change in management's position since then. As indicated in Tables 11-2 and 11-3, however, union members have not given safety and health matters a high priority, either.

Table 11-2 indicates that only one-third of workers would forego a 10% pay raise for "a little more safety and health." This figure would obviously vary by industry and would no doubt increase if the improvement in safety and health were more than "a little." The interesting thing, however, is that safety and health ranks below all other subjects commonly negotiated in collective bargaining agreements. The only subjects below safety and health (besides greater comfort at work) are permissive (or nonmandatory) subjects, included far less frequently. This finding is consistent with the priorities of union members for union performance.

Table 11-3 is consistent with Table 11-2 in that the only areas of union concern ranking below occupational safety and health are permissive subjects of bargaining. Bernard Kleiman, general counsel of the United Steelworkers of America, has summed up the problem: "Safety is a very tough thing to negotiate. There are so many levels of consciousness to it. Both sides have to be hit over the head a good deal before they develop the consciousness that permits them to move."[32]

The argument also has been made that OSHA operates as a disincentive to bargaining. Where gains can be achieved politically

Table 11-2. Benefits for Which Union Members Were Willing to Forego a 10% Pay Raise

Benefit	Percent of Workers
Increased retirement benefits	65.9
More medical insurance	58.1
More paid vacation	57.5
Shorter workweek	42.4
Greater chance for promotion	40.6
Greater job security	33.7
A little more safety and health	33.1
Greater comfort at work	28.7
More interesting work	27.5
Greater freedom to decide work	18.2

Source: Frenkel, Priest, & Ashford, *Occupational Safety and Health: A Report on Worker Perceptions*, 103 Monthly Lab. Rev. No. 9, at 11, 12 (Sept. 1980) (based on 1977 study at University of Michigan).

Table 11-3.   Union Members' Priorities for Union Activities

Area of Union Concern	Effort Ranking
Handling grievances	1
Keeping membership informed of union action	2
Improving fringe benefits	3
Increasing membership input in union direction	4
Increasing job security	5
Increasing wages	6
Increasing occupational safety and health	7
Increasing worker "say" in how the job is performed	8
Increasing job interest	9
Increasing worker input in business decisions	10

Source: Frenkel, Priest, & Ashford, *Occupational Safety and Health: A Report on Worker Perceptions*, 103 Monthly Lab. Rev. No. 9, at 11, 13 (Sept. 1980) (based on 1977 study at University of Michigan).

through governmental regulation, unions are free to use their limited economic weapons to achieve traditional union objectives. According to Dr. Lawrence S. Bacow of MIT:

> The existence of OSHA discourages some bargaining over safety and health issues by offering a relatively cheap alternative to negotiated hazard abatement. Health and safety issues do not command a high position on union bargaining agendas because there is little political return on cleaning up the workplace; changes are often not recognized for years and the individuals most likely to benefit tend to be underrepresented. In addition, unions prefer standardized regulations to negotiated agreements that may place organized employers at a competitive disadvantage.[33]

Perhaps the most troubling aspect of the attitudes exemplified by Tables 11-2 and 11-3 is that in times of high unemployment and economic recession it may be assumed that in collective bargaining, employees would give the highest priority to wages, hours, and job security. The final limitation on the efficacy of collective bargaining for job safety and health is that only about 20% of American workers are union members.

Notwithstanding the practical constraints limiting the expansion of safety and health provisions, existing provisions remain important. Included within the group of common safety and health items are provisions for medical examinations. According to one study,[34] medical examinations are required in 30% of all contracts. Petroleum (86%), mining (83%), transportation (68%), rubber (67%), and transportation equipment (54%) are the product industries whose contracts have the highest percentage of these provisions. Of collective bargaining agreements containing medical examination provisions, 31% require physical exams for new hires, 31% require physical exams when employees are rehired or return to work from layoff or leave, and 76% require physical exams periodically or at management's request. In 46% of these provisions employees may appeal an unfavorable medical opinion.

There are two possible medical exam provisions that could affect high-risk employees which have been notably absent from collective bargaining agreements. First is the right of employees to refuse medical examination. The following provision has been suggested, but there is no evidence that it has ever been included.

> If an employee refuses any medical examination or biological monitoring process, the employer shall inform the employee of the possible health consequences involved. In no circumstances shall an employee be required to sign a release statement or any language purporting to release the employer from any liability under any law as a result of refusal to take the medical examinations or refusal to be involved in any biological monitoring activity. The employee should not be disciplined in any way.[35]

One explanation for the absence of provisions such as this is that because medical examinations are most often used in hazardous industries, they are viewed by management as an important entrepreneurial prerogative in selecting fit workers and viewed by employees as a valuable benefit and as an aid in detecting occupational illness. Consequently, provisions actually in effect regarding medical examinations are limited to detailing when and where examinations are performed, who pays for them, who conducts them, whether the union has access to the information, and similar matters.[36]

At least one study, however, refutes the theory that employees perceive medical examinations as a "benefit." The study found that as many as 30% of employees refused to submit to OSHA-mandated postemployment medical examinations. Included in the survey were several firms in the vinyl chloride industry. The resistance to postemployment examinations was based on the dislike of physicians, distrust of company doctors, and the desire not to know what, if anything, was medically wrong.[37]

A concerted refusal by employees to undergo medical examinations that was made in good faith may be considered protected activity under section 8(a)(1) of the NLRA. The determining factor may be the motivation of the employees. Refusals based on legitimate fears of the hazards of the examinations themselves will probably be considered protected activity.[38] Unreasonable refusals and refusals aimed at achieving other objectives will probably not be considered protected activity.[39] In the latter situation, the employees would be refusing to perform work because of a dispute about working conditions. Therefore, their legal status would be that of economic strikers who may not be discharged but who may be permanently replaced. (The Supreme Court has held that although an employer may hire permanent replacements for economic strikers, the strikers retain certain rights under the NLRA, such as the right to vote in a union representation election, and any striker who files an application for reinstatement must be placed on a preferential hiring list.[40])

The second broad area of bargaining that might be pursued is prescribing the permissible medical procedures of company medical departments. Collective bargaining agreements do not usually specify what tests are to be performed and, perhaps more importantly, they do not specify what tests may *not* be performed. One possible explanation for this is that a detailing of medical procedures is beyond the competence of the contract negotiators, and, in any event, the determination of the specifics of medical examinations is considered a matter for the sound professional judgment of the physician. An example of a provision which does, however, require the use of a specific test is an agreement first entered into in 1975 between the United Farm Workers of America and Inter-Harvest, Inc. "One baseline cholinesterase test and other necessary cholinesterase tests shall be taken on those workers employed as applicators at Company's expense when organo-phosphates are used. Union shall be given results of said tests immediately."[41] Provisions in other collective bargaining agreements require chest x-rays, pulmonary function tests, and other hazard-specific procedures.

The extent to which collective bargaining agreements address the issue of the employability of medically impaired individuals depends on whether the medical condition is detected at the preemployment examination of an applicant or is detected at a periodic or return-to-work examination of a present employee. While present employees may be accorded a wide range of protections, job applicants have virtually none.

Two main reasons may be postulated to explain why few collective bargaining agreements address the issue of medical screening of new employees. First, at common law an employer could hire any person for any reason or no reason at all, including the employer's opinion of the medical suitability of the individual. Even today, the only limitations on employee selection are specific statutes proscribing discrimination based on membership in a specific class determined by factors such as age, race, color, sex, religion, national origin, handicap, veteran status, or union activity. Thus, employee selection is an important management prerogative that would not be easily relinquished in collective bargaining.

Second, applicants for employment frequently are not union members, or if they are, they are not presently within the bargaining unit. Because applicants are considered "employees" under the NLRA,[42] employee selection is a mandatory subject of bargaining. Nevertheless, employee selection is not likely to be viewed as an important concern by union negotiators. Unions are much more likely to use their economic leverage on issues directly affecting present unit employees. This fact is important to the employability of applicants whose increased risk is based on prior exposure at another workplace.

Once an individual is hired, a variety of collective bargaining provisions could have a bearing on the employer's decisionmaking about the continued medical suitability of the individual. Disputes over medical findings may be subject to a multiphysician review or medical arbitration. Employees unable to continue work in a particular work environment may have medical removal protection. This permits the employee to transfer to another job at the company where there is a more healthful environment. In many cases, the agreement will provide for rate retention, allowing the employee to retain a higher paying job classification after transfer, a maintenance of seniority rights, and even "bumping" rights to obtain the new position.

11.3   Contract Enforcement and Arbitration

Many collective bargaining agreements contain broad arbitration clauses requiring arbitration of all disputes. This includes disputes arising out of the refusal to hire, transfer, demotion, layoff, or termination of individuals because of medical determinations. Arbitration decisions are based on specific contract language and employer practices. Therefore, one must be cautious about applying a particular decision to another factual situation or drawing conclusions from only a few cases. Nevertheless, it is valuable to see how some recent grievances related to occupational medical practices have been resolved.

As discussed earlier, employers may make the truthful completion of medical questionnaires and a satisfactory physical examination valid conditions of employment. Applicants who refuse to take a physical examination need not be hired. Employees also may be required to take periodic physical examinations. In *Rollins Environmental Services, Inc.*,[43] the arbitrator ruled that the time spent by an employee in taking a required annual physical examination, given by a company doctor at the beginning of a work day, was not compensable because there was no contractual requirement or past practice of paying employees. It would probably be compensable under the Fair Labor Standards Act, however, inasmuch as the medical examination was a condition of employment and performed for the benefit of the employer.[44] Compensation also must be given employees for time spent in taking OSHA-required medical examinations.

Medical examinations often are required when employees return to work after a leave of absence or layoff. In *Maple Meadow Mining Co.*,[45] an arbitrator held that a company was not authorized to require employees seeking recall from a layoff to sign an ''Authorization for Release of Medical Information.'' This form gave the employer broad access to past, present, and future medical records, information, x-rays, and other health data. The employer was held to have a right only to information reasonably related to the employee's employment, such as the results of a prerecall physical exam.

Employers often are given wide leeway in prescribing the medical criteria for a particular job. Sometimes, these criteria are quite controversial. In *Olin Corp.*,[46] the employer was engaged in making metal products, including lead shot and bullets. Because of possible reproductive hazards, the employer adopted a rule prohibiting fertile female employees aged 18 to 50 from working in bullet manufacturing. Two fertile female employees were working in the exposed area at the time the new rule was announced. One transferred to another job and the other had a tubal ligation performed and returned to work. The union filed a grievance but the arbitrator upheld the company action.

> The contract specifically provides that the Company is responsible for the occupational health of its employees. Further, it is the Company, not OSHA, which bears the financial responsibility for occupational damage to employee health. . . . If the Arbitrator were to judge the Company's medical evaluations and conclusions to be overly cautious and unnecessary, he could be jeopardizing the future health and safety of the Company's employees.[47]

Work rules adopted by employers, such as the required use of personal protective equipment, usually have been upheld where reasonable and clearly related to employee safety and health.[48] Two work rules which have been widely challenged are "no beard" rules and "no smoking" rules. Although such policies may be adopted for reasons other than occupational safety and health (*e.g.*, product contamination, fire hazards), the following discussion is limited to the rules established solely for employee safety and health reasons.

As detailed in Chapter 3, the presence of facial hair makes it extremely difficult to get a good respirator seal. Consequently, some employers have adopted rules prohibiting employees from having beards when respirator usage is required. In *J.R. Simplot Co.*,[49] such a rule was upheld. Similar respirator and "no beard" rules also have been upheld. For example, in *Teledyne Wah Chang Albany*,[50] a sand chlorination worker was unable to wear a company-supplied respirator because of severe weight loss in his face. The arbitrator ruled that the employee was properly sent home without pay. In *Phoenix Forging Co.*,[51] a "no beard" rule was upheld because there was a danger that flying sparks in the forge shop would cause beards to catch fire.

Not all "no beard" rules, however, have been upheld. In *United Parcel Service*,[52] the employer had a rule prohibiting maintenance employees from having beards because of the possibility that air masks might be needed to clean up hazardous material spills. The arbitrator held that the rule was invalid. The *possibility* of such spills was found to be remote, and even if masks were needed, the chemicals involved were not lethal and therefore an absolutely perfect respirator fit was not needed.

In *E. & J. Gallo Winery & Distillery*,[53] the employer adopted a "no beard" rule because respirators were required to protect against exposure to ammonia, chlorine, sulfur dioxide, and various acids, caustics, and other substances. An arbitrator struck down the rule because the employer had not instituted feasible engineering controls as mandated by California (Cal.) OSHA. If the controls were used there would be no need for the respirators.

"No smoking" rules have been adopted by several employers that manufacture or handle asbestos products because of the synergistic effect of cigarette smoking and asbestos. The Fifth Circuit's *Johns-Manville* decision, discussed in section 11.2, was based on the employer's unilateral action. Other arbitration cases have focused on other aspects of this complex problem.

In *Nicolet Industries, Inc.*,[54] the arbitrator decided that the employer's absolute ban on smoking in an asbestos plant was invalid for four main reasons. First, long-term employees addicted to cigarettes might not be able to break the habit and would be dismissed without any other career possibilities. Second, even a total cessation of smoking would not be a cure-all for the problem. The damage from prior exposures already may have been done, and the hazards from future asbestos exposure, even without cigarette smoking, were still significant. Third, the employer's rule did not address the problem of increased risk for employees who continued smoking at home. Fourth, the arbitrator concluded that the decision whether to stop smoking should be left to the employee. While striking down the total ban on smoking, the arbitrator ruled that smoking *could* be limited to designated areas and during nonwork time (*i.e.*, breaks, lunch).

In reaching his decision in *Nicolet*, the arbitrator considered two unpublished arbitration awards involving Johns-Manville Sales Corp. In the first case, Arbitrator Brown's decision, followed in *Nicolet* by Arbitrator Rock, invalidated the total ban but permitted time and place restrictions on smoking. In the other case, Arbitrator Gregory upheld the company rule as necessary to protect employee safety and health.

Another controversial medical rule involves the screening of employees to detect drug usage, including marijuana. In *Griffin Pipe Products Co.*,[55] the company adopted a rule requiring a drug screen urine test of all employees reporting for medical treatment. The purpose of the rule was to reduce accidents. An arbitrator upheld the drug screen rule, but added two conditions. First, employees suspended under the rule where the test is later found negative must be reimbursed for lost wages. Second, employees taking prescription medication may not be subject to discipline.

In *Wabco Division of American Standard*,[56] the arbitrator ruled that an employee's refusal to take a drug screen test amounted to insubordination and warranted discharge. The employee was observed as being unsteady and disoriented, with slow and slurred speech. The employer was aware of the employee's dependence on barbiturates because of a medical problem.

A number of arbitration decisions involve the important issue of what employment actions the company may take when an employee becomes disabled and no longer able to perform the job safely and efficiently. Although a wide range of results have been reached, arbitrators tend to view the plight of employees with greater sympathy when their disabilities are work-related.

Where employee injuries or illnesses are not directly related to work, the decisions focus simply on whether the employee can perform the necessary job functions. Employers are often given considerable deference in the area, with the result being that the employer action is usually upheld. For example, arbitrators have upheld the termination of an armed race track security guard who was blind in one eye,[57] the termination of a moving company employee who had fainting spells,[58] the discharge of a plant cleaner with ulcers and a bad back,[59] the discharge of a miner with emphysema,[60] and the denial of reinstatement to a maintenance employee whose knee injury made for frequent and unpredictable instability.[61]

In situations where continued exposure would adversely affect the employee's health, arbitrators often have sanctioned transfers but not dismissals. For example, in *Schmeller Aluminum Foundry Co.*,[62] the arbitrator upheld intermittent transfers at the same basic pay rate to reduce an employee's exposure to the hazard of silicosis. A similar result, permitting transfer but not dismissal in the face of a silicosis hazard, was reached in *Arketex Ceramic Corp.*[63]

In *Ormet Corp.*,[64] however, a somewhat different result was reached. The employee, a pipe fitter, developed a skin irritation to coal tar pitch. The issue was whether the company could remove the employee from further exposure, despite his objections. The arbitrator ruled that the decision was within the company's prerogative.

> Considering the fact that the Company has not only the responsibility to protect its employees "from recognized hazards," but also the liability for payment (directly or indirectly) of the costs of any ailments caused as a result of working at the plant, it must have the right to determine whether an employee, who by his own admission is affected by pitch, should be permitted to work in areas where he could be exposed to the irritant, pitch.[65]

Similar results were reached in *Eaton Corp.*,[66] where a machine tender with dermatitis was held not to be entitled to a material handler job and in *Joy Manufacturing Co.*,[67] where a materials assembler with psoriasis was not permitted to return to his job.

In *Stauffer Chemicals Co.*,[68] employees were exposed to toxic and embryofetotoxic substances, including hydrogen sulfide, nitrous oxide, sulfuric acid, and sulfuric dioxide. A pregnant employee, fearful of the effects of exposure on her child, requested temporary reassignment to an available light duty position where there were no toxic chemicals. When the company refused, she took sick leave. The arbitrator ruled that the company should have permitted her to transfer, and therefore he held that she was entitled to sickness and accident benefits under the disability provision of the contract. It is not clear what result would have been reached if there had been no "safe" position available.

One final group of arbitration cases raises the question of whether arbitrators are willing to accept the determinations of company physicians at face value or prefer to make a searching inquiry to decide whether the medical conclusions are reasonable. In *Colgate-Palmolive Co.*,[69] the arbitrator rejected the company doctor's assessment that an employee was unable to resume work because of a back problem. The medical restriction was based on the woman's medical history rather than her present condition. Similarly, in *Bethlehem Steel Corp.*,[70] the arbitrator ruled that a medical restriction on a diabetic employee was not justified. Contrary to the employer's contention, there was only a remote possibility that others would be injured if the employee went into insulin shock and, in fact, the employee's physician stated that the employee had never been in diabetic ketoacidosis or insulin shock.

In contrast to these cases, in which arbitrators reversed the determinations of overrestrictive company medical departments, is the recent case of *Miles Laboratories, Inc.*[71] A chemical worker was misdiagnosed by both a hospital and a company physician as having an acute anaphylactoid reaction with laryngeal edema based on exposure to protease powder. The incident was later correctly diagnosed as an asthma attack. The arbitrator ruled that despite the misdiagnosis the employee was not wrongfully laid off because the company had acted in good faith and the employee had failed to indicate a history of asthma.

11.4   Union's Duty of Fair Representation

When a union gets a majority of employee votes in a representation election and thereby becomes certified by the NLRB as the bargaining agent or when an employer privately accords the union such recognition, the union becomes the exclusive bargaining representative of all employees in the bargaining unit. The countervailing principle to exclusivity is the duty of fair representation. A union with the status of exclusive bargaining representative must act on behalf of all employees in the unit and must do so fairly, impartially, and in good faith. The duty of fair representation exists during collective bargaining and the administration of the contract, including the processing of grievances.

Coincidentally, the leading case to define the duty of fair representation, *Vaca v. Sipes*,[72] involved a dispute about whether an employee was medically fit to work. An employee who had been in the hospital on sick leave obtained his doctor's approval and attempted to return to work. The company doctor, however, refused to allow the employee to return to work, fearing that the employee's high blood pressure would endanger his health. The employee was discharged and the union filed a grievance. After a union-retained doctor concurred with the company doctor's assessment, the union refused to arbitrate the grievance. Thereupon, the employee sued the union in a Missouri state court for breaching its duty of fair representation.

A verdict of $10,000 in favor of the employee was reversed by the United States Supreme Court. According to the Court, employees do not have an absolute right to have every grievance taken to arbitration. Moreover, a breach of the duty of fair representation requires more than simple negligence; it only occurs where the union's action or inaction is "arbitrary, discriminatory, or in bad faith."[73] The Court held that in this case the union did not act in bad faith because it had processed the employee's grievance to the fourth step, attempted to get less strenuous work for the employee and to have him rehabilitated, and did not act out of any personal hostility.

With respect to medical screening, two questions arise. First, does the duty of fair representation extend to *employees* who are at an increased risk of occupational illness? Second, does a union's duty of fair representation extend to *applicants* who are refused employment on the basis of medical screening?

Employees predisposed to occupational illness are entitled to fair representation, as are all the other employees in the bargaining unit. Nevertheless, the union is not prohibited from negotiating a contract which may adversely affect some members of the bargaining unit. In *Ford Motor Co. v. Huffman*,[74] the Supreme Court stated:

> The complete satisfaction of all who are represented is hardly to be expected. A wide range of reasonableness must be allowed a statutory bargaining representative in serving the unit it represents, subject always to complete good faith and honesty of purpose in the exercise of its discretion.[75]

It is unlikely that an action for breach of duty of fair representation based on contract negotiation would be successful. In one survey of federal cases from 1962 to 1980 only 11 actions were shown as brought alleging a breach of the duty of fair representation in negotiations, and not a single one was successful.[76] Consequently, a union would not breach any duty by refusing to bargain for a reduction in the permissible exposure limit to levels where the most susceptible employee in the unit would be safe or for medical removal protection and rate retention provisions to protect the jobs of such individuals.

The union could legally decide to use its limited economic leverage to obtain employer concessions which would benefit the largest number of employees.

The second question posed, dealing with the rights of applicants, is less clear. Applicants are considered "employees" under the NLRA,[77] and the union would probably have a duty to enforce an existing agreement containing a provision dealing with preemployment medical exams. Without such a provision, however, there probably would be no duty on the part of the union, and it is unlikely that the union would have as great a duty to negotiate a contract with such a provision.[78]

A practice of some employers is to refuse to hire even asymptomatic applicants with prior workplace exposures. For example, an asbestos worker with 10 years of service at company A may not be hired by company B. If the union representing company B failed to act on this worker's behalf, would it breach the duty of fair representation? Would it matter whether the individual was a union member?

Although company policies of refusing to hire previously exposed workers exist in several industries, there are no reported cases with these precise facts. In one case, *Gray v. International Association of Heat & Frost Insulators & Asbestos Workers, Local 51,*[79] the Sixth Circuit held that a job applicant, even though a union member, was owed no duty of fair representation in his efforts to secure employment. The NLRB has held, however, that the duty of fair representation is owed to applicants for referral through an exclusive hiring hall.[80]

Because a union that has breached its duty of fair representation may be liable for damages to the employee, some employees who have been injured on the job have sued their union, alleging that the union breached its duty of fair representation by not acting to ensure safe and healthful working conditions. This theory has been unsuccessful because there is no legal duty for a union to insure against workplace injuries[81] and because mere negligence is not enough to constitute a breach of the duty of fair representation.[82]

A second theory of union liability is that the existence of specific contract language giving safety and health responsibilities to the union creates a common law duty, the breach of which can lead to liability. This theory has a slight chance of success. In *Helton v. Hake,*[83] an iron worker was electrocuted when an angle iron which he was handling came into contact with a high-tension power line. The worker had made prior unsuccessful attempts to get the union steward or foreman to take steps to have the power line turned off, as required by the union contract. An action for wrongful death was brought against the local union and the union steward. A trial court jury found for the plaintiffs based on the union's negligent failure to perform a duty owed to the decedent under the collective bargaining contract. In affirming the trial court, the court of appeals held that usually a union assumes only an advisory role with respect to safety and health matters and is only charged with the duty of fair representation. In this case, however, the collective bargaining agreement provided that the union steward had reponsibility for enforcing safety rules without interference from the employer. Therefore, the union assumed a heightened duty and was liable in tort for breach of the duty.

The possibilities for recovery under the contract-common law theory, however, may be diminished by other important considerations. To begin with, the union's safety responsibility must be clearly set out in the contract; general language is not enough to establish a legal duty.[84] Next, if safety is solely the responsibility of the union local, then only the local may be sued.[85] Finally, any cognizable common law action may be preempted by federal labor law. In *Condon v. Local 2944, United Steelworkers of America*,[86] the First Circuit stated:

> [E]ven if a union had a duty of due care in conducting safety inspections as a matter of New Hampshire common law, federal law would preempt imposing it unless it could be shown to arise wholly outside the ambit of those obligations circumscribed by a union's duty of fair representation under the collective bargaining agreement: that is, unless it involved union activity that was peripheral to the concern of the applicable federal statutes and presented only a tangential or remote potential conflict with the federal regulatory scheme.[87]

Although the potential for union liability thus appears slim, Hawaii[88] and Michigan[89] nevertheless have enacted laws immunizing unions from civil liability for all employee injuries covered by workers' compensation.

CHAPTER 12

WORKERS' COMPENSATION AND COMMON LAW PERSONAL INJURY ACTIONS

12.1 Workers' Compensation Coverage and Remedies

At common law, employees who suffered a work-related injury or illness had a right of action for damages against their employer. Because these actions were based on negligence, the employers were usually able to escape liability by invoking the common law defenses of contributory negligence, assumption of risk, and the fellow servant rule.[1] Thus, if the injury or illness was caused in any part by the negligence of the injured worker or any co-worker, or if the employee expressly or impliedly assumed the risk of working in a hazardous occupation, there was no recovery.[2]

Beginning in 1910 in New York, the states made the first efforts to give to individual workers and their families relief from the hardship of industrial accidents. By 1921, 46 states had passed workers' compensation laws, and today there is a statute in every jurisdiction. The six basic objectives of workers' compensation are to:

1. provide sure, prompt, and reasonable income and medical benefits to injured workers or income benefits to their dependents, regardless of fault;
2. provide a single remedy and reduce court delays, costs, and work loads arising out of personal injury litigation;
3. relieve public and private charities of financial drains incident to uncompensated industrial accidents;
4. eliminate payment of fees to lawyers and witnesses, as well as the expense of time-consuming trials and appeals;
5. encourage maximum employer interest in safety and rehabilitation through an appropriate experience-rating mechanism; and
6. promote frank study of the causes of accidents to prevent future accidents.[3]

Workers' compensation is a form of strict liability whereby the employer is charged with the injuries arising out of its business, with-

168

out regard to fault. Common law damage actions are precluded, but
so too are common law defenses. The employee is assured of medical
expenses and income maintenance; employers are protected against
personal injury judgments and are assured of relatively fixed production costs that can be passed along to consumers. Resort to the compensation system is the "exclusive remedy" of injured workers.

Virtually all private sector employees are covered by state workers' compensation laws, and government employees are protected by
similar laws. Although the specific coverage provisions vary by state,
domestic servants, casual employees, and farm laborers are often excluded. In other job classifications, coverage may be elective at the
option of the employer. Where the statute does not apply, injured
employees retain their common law rights and remedies.

Workers' compensation laws have been criticized frequently,
and in 1972 the Report of the National Commission on State Workmen's Compensation Laws concluded that the laws were, in general,
inadequate and inequitable. The Commission submitted 84 recommendations for improvements which, if made, would make the system operate fairly and efficiently, the Commission maintained.

One of the most troubling areas of workers' compensation law is
occupational disease. Most of the early laws excluded occupational
diseases from coverage. Today, even though all states now include
occupational illnesses, claimants still must prove "causation" and
that the disease from which they suffer is work-related and not one of
the "ordinary diseases of life." Consequently, occupational disease
cases are six times more likely to be contested[4] and relatively few
claimants prevail.[5]

The initial problem with occupational disease cases is that workers often fail to apply for benefits. According to a 1981 survey,[6] only
21.8% of individuals who attributed their main disability to bad
working conditions had ever applied for workers' compensation. By
comparison, 64.4% of those who suffered an injury on the job applied for workers' compensation.

Even where workers seek compensation for illness, a time-
consuming contest is much more likely. According to data compiled
by Peter S. Barth and H. Allen Hunt,[7] the contest rate for accident
cases is 9.8%. For occupational illness cases, especially where work-
relatedness is more difficult to prove, the contest rate is much higher:
for cancer, 45.5%; for respiratory conditions due to toxic agents,
78.5%; for repeated trauma disorders, 85.8%; and for dust diseases,
88.2%. In 76% of these contested cases the main issue is whether the
illness is compensable.

Individuals seeking workers' compensation for occupational illness are often thwarted by legal doctrines bearing no relationship to modern medicine. For example, some states require that the worker be exposed to a health hazard for a specified period of time to be eligible for compensation. Thus, in *Carr v. Homestake Mining Co.*,[8] an individual totally disabled by silicosis was denied compensation because the South Dakota statute requires at least five years of exposure to silica dust during the 10 years immediately preceding disablement.

Another obstacle is that a statute of limitations may preclude the filing of a claim. For example, in *State v. Tallman*,[9] an individual was exposed to bentonite dust from 1937 to 1948. In 1976 it was determined that the employee was suffering from pulmonary fibrosis caused by his bentonite exposure. The Supreme Court of Wyoming held that the claim was barred by a provision in the state workers' compensation law that a claim must be filed within one year after diagnosis or within three years of last exposure, whichever comes first.[10] Obviously, this harsh rule would preclude any compensation for the numerous occupational illnesses with long latency periods.

A similar harsh result was reached in *Garafolo v. Arms Hills Supermarkets.*[11] The individual's job required her to wrap meat in a polyvinyl chloride film, which was cut and sealed with a thin hot wire, causing the release of fumes. Although she had been treated for 10 years by her physician for asthma, it was not until almost three years after her last employment that she and her physician learned of "meat wrapper's asthma"—a type of hypersensitivity pneumonitis—and the work-related nature of her illness. The New York court held that the claim was barred because she contracted the disease more than 12 months prior to the date of disablement.

The final problem, and one that affects both occupational injury and illness cases, is that the benefit levels are inconsistent among jurisdictions and, with few exceptions, grossly inadequate. Each state law sets its own eligibility requirements, benefit levels, and administrative mechanisms for claim processing. The result is a wide range in eligibility and benefit levels. For example, benefits for total disability are based on 60% to 80% of the employee's average weekly wage (depending on the state) with a minimum and maximum payment. As of January 1, 1983, the minimum payment in Arkansas was $15 per week; in North Dakota it was $157 per week. The maximum payment in Mississippi was $112 per week; in Alaska it was $996 per week.[12] In Colorado, a worker who loses his or her hearing in both ears receives a scheduled payment of $11,676; in Iowa the award is $87,325.[13] Most states do not provide for automatic cost-of-living increases.

12.2   Medical Screening and Workers' Compensation

The primary motivating factor in employer efforts to screen out high-risk individuals from the work force is the fear that these individuals are more likely to suffer from an occupational injury or illness, thereby becoming an added cost to the employer. One obvious increased cost could come from higher workers' compensation insurance rates. The question is therefore raised whether high-risk employees are entitled to workers' compensation when they are subsequently found to be suffering from the condition to which they were predisposed.

The majority view is that a claimant will not be denied compensation because of a preexisting allergy, weakness, disease, or susceptibility.[14] According to Professor Arthur Larson of Duke University "the employer takes the employee as he finds him. . . ."[15] Nevertheless, compensation will not be granted unless there is medical evidence that the worker's condition was caused by workplace exposures.[16] In a minority of jurisdictions, occupational diseases are not compensable if the claimant's individual allergy contributed to the result.[17]

A similar issue concerns whether an employee who is forced to quit work because of job-related health problems is entitled to unemployment compensation. As with workers' compensation, eligibility for unemployment compensation depends on the wording of the state statute and judicial construction of state law. The majority rule appears to be that individuals who quit work because of job-related health problems are entitled to unemployment compensation, even if the employees are sensitive to the workplace environment.[18]

As discussed earlier, one basis of increased risk is the behavior of the individual, including diet, smoking, and drinking. The question thus arises whether these nonoccupational factors should affect a claimant's right to workers' compensation.

In general, claimants are entitled to full compensation if they can prove that they are suffering from an occupational illness that arose out of their employment and the disease is not an "ordinary disease of life." In cases involving claimants whose cigarette smoking contributed to their occupational illness, some courts have awarded full compensation,[19] while others have apportioned the claimant's award.[20] Compensation has been denied entirely where the illness was found to be related solely to nonoccupational factors.[21]

A similar approach has been adopted under federal compensation acts. In *General Dynamics Corp. v. Sacchetti*,[22] the widow of an employee who was a moderate smoker until ten years before his death was held to be entitled to death benefits under the Longshoremen's and Harbor Workers' Compensation Act (LHWCA). The Second Circuit held that although prior smoking may have increased his risk of fibrotic changes from asbestos exposure, it was not a "prior permanent partial disability" which would limit liability under section 8(f) of the LHWCA. "[S]moking cannot become a qualifying disability until it results in medically cognizable symptoms that physically impair the employee. To apply the rule for limited liability to socially pervasive risks would require a new novel definition of 'disability' and would broaden the rule beyond its intended scope."[23]

Employers may be reluctant to hire individuals with preexisting infirmities or disabilities, because they fear liability for future workers' compensation. To dissipate this reluctance, five states permit, with workers' compensation agency approval, individuals to sign general waivers of their rights, and another 15 states permit waivers for aggravation of an existing condition or under special circumstances.[24] An example of a general waiver is the following Connecticut law:[25]

> Whenever any person . . . has any physical defect which imposes upon his employer or future employer a further or unusual hazard, it shall be permissible for such person to execute in writing for himself or his dependents, or both, an acknowledgement of physical defect.

Importantly, the waiver may not apply to any occupationally related illness. In addition, the law provides that " 'physical defect' shall not be construed to include an occupational disease, susceptibility thereto, or a recurrence thereof." Other states, such as Massachusetts,[26] expressly provide that any agreement purporting to waive an employee's right to compensation is invalid.

Prior occupational exposures to toxic substances can establish a susceptibility to occupational illness from further exposures. The willingness of employers to hire individuals with prior occupational exposures and persons who are otherwise at increased risk of occupational injury or illness may depend on how the workers' compensation law of a particular state provides for the compensation of individuals with "successive disabilities."

The first of the three approaches to this problem is the "full responsibility" rule, which imposes liability for the entire resulting disability on the present employer.[27] This rule has been criticized as placing an unfair burden on the employer to make full compensation for an employee's injury or illness even when the employer is only partially responsible.[28] In addition, one effect of the rule is that employers are unwilling to hire any employees thought to be impaired or predisposed to illness because of the fear that they will be responsible for any successive injuries.[29]

The second approach, the "apportionment statute," divides the compensation liability between the present employer and another party.[30] The "other party" may be a prior employer or its compensation carrier, a second injury fund, or the employee, if the final disabling result was caused by a prior personal disability.[31] An important question is what prior disabilities are apportionable. The general rule is that "disability" does not include a prior nondisabling defect, disease, or latent condition.[32] A number of cases have held that a preexisting asymptomatic back condition will not lead to the apportionment of compensation for a subsequent work-related back injury.[33] This same reasoning would appear to apply to all types of increased risks.

Under the third approach, the "second injury fund," the present employer is liable for the amount of disability attributable to the present employment, with the fund paying the difference up to the total amount of compensation to which the employee is entitled.[34] Many of the state special injury funds restrict their applicability to instances where the employer had knowledge of the prior injury.[35] The theory underlying this restriction is that the laws were enacted to encourage the hiring of handicapped workers, and if the employer did not know of the prior injury, the employee would not be disadvantaged in seeking employment. This rule, however, operates as an incentive for employers to engage in increased medical screening of applicants.

An increasingly important area of workers' compensation, and one with particular relevance to medical screening, is the problem of cumulative injury. The number of cumulative injury claims and their costs have been increasing dramatically. For example, in California, between 1975 and 1977 the number of cumulative injury claims rose from 8,974 to 13,393.[36] The average benefit for each of these claims was more than four times the amount awarded for noncumulative injuries.[37] Back injuries, heart and vascular problems, and hearing loss make up a high percentage of the cumulative injury claims. Table 12–1 indicates which disabling conditions are most likely to contain cumulative injuries.

Table 12-1.   Cumulative Injuries in California in 1978

Condition	Percent of all Disabling Injuries	Percent of Cumulative Injuries
Back	24.9	34.3
Heart/Vascular	7.4	22.7
Hearing loss	0.2	13.2
Extremities	54.1	14.4
Neuroses	N.A.	5.9
Pulmonary	0.6	1.9
All other	12.6	7.6

Source: California Workers' Compensation Institute, *Cumulative Injury in California: The Continuing Dilemma* 9 (1978), *cited in* La Dou, Mulryan, & McCarthy, *Cumulative Injury or Disease Claims: An Attempt to Define Employers' Liability for Workers' Compensation*, 6 Am. J.L. & Med. 1, 9 (1980). Reprinted by permission.

Not surprisingly, more than 50% of cumulative injury claimants are over age 50.[38] This fact suggests two possible employer actions. First, preemployment or preplacement predictive screening may be increasingly concerned with the likelihood of developing long-term cumulative injuries; and second, there may be increased monitoring of workers over 40 so that they can be screened out at the first signs of cumulative injury. Both of these prospects are troubling: the first because of the inaccuracy of any long-term prediction, the second because of the inequity and inefficiency of discharging productive middle-aged workers based on fear of possible workers' compensation liability. Possible protection against age discrimination in employment is discussed in section 10.6.

12.3   Federal Workers' Compensation Laws

The first compensation program for federal employees, enacted in 1908, actually predates the earliest state workers' compensation laws. Today, there are a number of federal compensation laws that apply to federal government and private sector employees.

The Federal Employees Compensation Act (FECA), originally passed in 1916, ensures federal civilian employees compensation for work-related injuries and illnesses. The FECA is quite similar to state workers' compensation laws in providing compensation for lost wages and reduced earning capacity. The FECA is administered by the Office of Workers' Compensation Programs in the U.S. Department of Labor. Disputed claims are adjudicated by the Employees' Compensation Appeals Board.

The Longshoremen's and Harbor Workers' Compensation Act (LHWCA) provides workers' compensation benefits to employees, other than seamen, of private employers whose employees work in maritime employment upon the navigable waters of the United States. The LHWCA provides benefits for injury and illness, medical benefits, and death benefits. The LHWCA is the exclusive remedy for injuries to covered employees. The Act is administered by the Office of Workers' Compensation Programs (OWCP) in the U.S. Department of Labor. All disputed LHWCA claims are adjudicated by the Benefits Review Board.

The Federal Employers' Liability Act (FELA) provides the exclusive remedy for the injury or death of interstate railroad employees caused by the negligence of the employer. Unlike the FECA and LHWCA, which provide for compensation benefits regardless of fault, the FELA provides for the recovery of damages—including pecuniary loss, medical expenses, and pain and suffering. The employer is usually permitted to assert the comparative negligence of the employee to mitigate the damage award. FELA actions may be brought in federal or state court. The Jones Act extends to seamen the same rights to sue their employers that are extended to railroad employees under the FELA.

The most important new federal compensation system provides benefits for victims of coal miners' pneumoconiosis or "black lung." Title IV of the Federal Coal Mine Health and Safety Act of 1969 was designed to provide benefits for miners who were totally disabled because of pneumoconiosis and for survivors of those who had died from the disease. Amended in 1972, 1977, and 1981, the benefits for newly filed claims are now funded by a federal excise tax on each ton of coal mined, paid by the employer into the Black Lung Disability Trust Fund. Claims for benefits are adjudicated as claims under the LHWCA.[39] From 1969 to 1980 a total of $10 billion in payments was made to 500,000 claimants.[40]

Pursuant to regulations of the U.S. Department of Labor,[41] there are several legal presumptions concerning the relationship between employment and disease. Two such presumptions are (1) the rebuttable presumption that if a miner suffering from pneumoconiosis was employed for 10 or more years in one or more coal mines, then the disease arose from such employment,[42] and (2) the irrebuttable presumption that a miner suffering from pneumoconiosis is totally disabled.[43] To determine a claimant's entitlement to benefits, the OWCP performs a complete pulmonary evaluation, including a chest x-ray, physical examination, pulmonary function tests, and blood-gas studies.[44]

The federal government's legislative response to the black lung problem represents an important new attempt to compensate victims of a specific occupational disease through an employer-supported, government-administered program. Congressional consideration also has been given to proposed legislation to create a compensation system for victims of asbestos-related diseases.

12.4   Tort Actions Against Employers

Workers' compensation awards provide limited benefits to ill or injured workers. The awards are based on disability—the loss of earning capacity. Thus, in addition to medical expenses, workers' compensation represents a fractional replacement for lost income. By comparison, awards to plaintiffs in civil actions include special damages (*i.e.*, medical expenses, lost income) and general damages (*i.e.*, impairment or loss of physical capacity, pain and suffering) and may also include punitive damages to punish willful, wanton, or reckless misconduct by the defendant and to deter similar actions by others.

Table 12-2 illustrates the great disparity between workers' compensation awards and recoveries for similar injuries in civil actions based on products liability.

Based on the figures in Table 12-2, it is obvious why employees suffering from work-related injury or illness would seek to avoid workers' compensation and pursue common law damage actions. Nevertheless, workers' compensation is the exclusive remedy of an employee against his or her employer unless the employee can invoke one of the statutory or judicial exceptions to the exclusivity rule.

Table 12-2.   Comparison of Average Award for Product Liability and Workers' Compensation

Severity of Injury	Product Liability (Injury and Disease*)	Workers' Compensation (Injury)
Death	$133,000	$57,000
Permanent total	255,000	23,000
Permanent partial	157,000	6,000
Temporary total	17,000	2,000

Source: U.S. Department of Labor, Assistant Secretary for Policy, Evaluation, and Research (ASPER), An Interim Report to Congress on Occupational Disease 94 (1980).
    *Includes a very small number of disease cases.

The first broad group of exceptions involves situations where there is a gap in workers' compensation coverage for one of the following reasons:

- The employer failed to take out insurance or qualify as a self-insured.
- The employee's job classification is not covered by the state workers' compensation law (*e.g.*, agricultural workers, domestic servants, charitable workers).
- The injury or illness complained of is noncompensable.
- The state law permits actions against company officials in their individual capacity.

The two most important exceptions related to medical screening, however, are medical malpractice actions and actions for willful and intentional torts.

A. Medical Malpractice

Medical malpractice actions based on employer-provided medical services are very complicated and, besides the variation in state laws, depend on the type of service performed. The first thing to consider is the employment status of the physician or other health professional who rendered the medical services. In general, if the physician is an employee of the company, the statutory co-employee immunity will apply.[45] This means that no common law action may be brought against the employer or the physician. In the few states that do not grant immunity to co-employees, however, the physician could be sued.[46]

Even where co-employee immunity exists, an action may be based on the dual capacity rule. The dual capacity or dual persona doctrine permits an employee to recover from his or her employer if the employer "possesses a second persona so completely independent from and unrelated to his status as employer that by established standards the law recognizes it as a separate person."[47]

In the leading case of *Duprey v. Shane*,[48] a nurse employed by a chiropractor was injured in the course of her employment and then was negligently treated by her chiropractor-employer. The California Supreme Court held that the employee could maintain a cause of action because her employer's negligent treatment occurred when the employer was acting in his second capacity as a chiropractor.

Judicial reaction to *Duprey* has varied widely. While some jurisdictions have followed it,[49] others have rejected it outright[50] or have
limited it to situations where the employer's negligence aggravated a
compensable injury or illness, where the employer was not required
to render medical treatment, or where the injury or illness for which
treatment was initially sought was noncompensable under workers'
compensation.[51]

Two recent cases demonstrate the divergence of judicial opinion
about the dual capacity doctrine as applied to medical malpractice
cases. In *Therrell v. Scott Paper Co.*,[52] the Supreme Court of Alabama
held that the dual capacity doctrine did not apply to medical treatment rendered at an employer's medical facility after an accident.
According to the court, the provision of emergency medical services
is an obligation flowing from the company's role as employer.

By contrast, the Supreme Court of Colorado's decision in
Wright v. District Court[53] makes malpractice by a company doctor actionable per se, without regard for the traditionally used dual capacity considerations. In this case a company-employed physician
treated an employee for back injuries suffered on the job. Several
days after returning to work the employee reinjured his back. He
then brought a malpractice action against the physician, alleging that
the physician misdiagnosed his injury and advised him to return to
work before he had fully recovered. The court held that the relationship between the parties was identical to the private doctor-patient
relationship. Furthermore, the employer was not required to provide
the medical services.

> Colorado's Workmen's Compensation Act does not require [an em-
> ployer] to maintain and operate a clinic. When an employer voluntar-
> ily undertakes to directly render medical treatment to its injured
> employees, it ... generates obligations that are unrelated to the em-
> ployment relationship and that create a new doctor-patient relation-
> ship.[54]

Another important extension of the dual capacity doctrine involves the failure of the company physician to detect or to inform the
employee of illness after an examination performed for the employer's benefit. In *Bednarski v. General Motors Corp.*,[55] a wrongful death
action was permitted to be brought based on the company's failure to
diagnose lung cancer or else failure to inform the plaintiff's decedent
that he had lung cancer, after performing a series of physical examinations and x-rays. Only if the injury were noncompensable, however, could the plaintiff recover. Many of these failure-to-diagnose or

failure-to-inform cases are based on non-work-related illnesses that were allegedly detectable during preemployment examinations.[56]

An employer might also be found liable for negligently failing to discover an employee's propensity to contract a compensable, work-related illness, thereby permitting the employee to be exposed to conditions that bring about the disease.[57] In such a case, however, the plaintiff would be required to prove that a reasonably prudent company doctor exercising ordinary skill and judgment would have detected the employee's likelihood of contracting an occupational disease. It is unlikely, at least at the present time, that an employer would be liable where the employee's predisposition was slight or could only be detected through sophisticated biochemical or cytogenetic procedures.

If the physician rendering the medical services is an independent contractor, a different analysis is used. Because independent contractors do not have co-employee immunity they are amenable to suit. The problem is that there may not be a physician-patient relationship between an employer-retained independent contractor and the employee. In such event, the only duty owed to the employee would be the duty not to injure the employee in the course of the examination.

In general, the legal relationship between the independent contractor-physician and the employee depends on the nature of the services provided. Where the service is for the benefit of the employee, a physician-patient relationship exists and the physician may be sued. Where the only benefit is for the employer, however, no action may lie. For example, in *Rogers v. Horvath*,[58] the employer hired a physician to examine the plaintiff to determine whether the employee's petition for a continuation of workers' compensation benefits had merit. The court held that because the examination was not performed for the purpose of diagnosis or treatment, no physician-patient relationship existed and the special duty of a doctor to the patient did not arise.

In most cases, when the physician is sued as an independent contractor, only the physician is liable.[59] When the physician is sued as an employee of the company, the employer may be liable based on the principle of *respondeat superior*[60] or based on the breach of an independent duty because of negligent practices and procedures used by the company medical department.[61]

One of the most interesting medical malpractice actions against an independent contractor was filed in 1979 by 10 lead workers employed by NL Industries of Indianapolis, Indiana.[62] The complaint alleged that Dr. Frederic A. Rice, who was retained by NL Industries, gave the employees numerous injections of calcium disodium versenate, a chelating drug, from 1971 to 1979. The plaintiffs alleged that Dr. Rice was negligent in administering a chelating drug to workers who were continuing to be exposed to lead and that he failed to warn them of the harmful side effects. The injuries alleged to have resulted from this treatment include the death of one worker, neurological disorders, kidney problems, and lead encephalopathy. The case was scheduled for trial in 1984.

It is even possible that a physician may be liable when neither employed by the company nor working as an independent contractor for the company. In *Willitzer v. McCloud*,[63] the Supreme Court of Ohio held that an independent physician examining workers' compensation claimants at the request of the Industrial Commission for the purpose of reporting their medical conditions is not immune from a suit based on alleged intentional misrepresentations of their conditions which resulted in a denial or reduction of their benefits. The court rejected the defendant's argument that he was immune from suit because of his role in the quasi-judicial workers' compensation process. There was no discussion of the physician-patient issue, presumably because the action was not based on malpractice.

B. Willful and Intentional Torts

In every jurisdiction, either by statute or case law, an exception to the exclusivity rule is recognized for an employer's willful or intentional acts. In most states, however, this exception has been construed very narrowly to cover only assault and battery and other acts where there was a deliberate attempt to injure the employee.

Even in situations that would seem to fall clearly within the category of intentional torts, some courts have held that workers' compensation was the employee's exclusive remedy. For example, in *Hood v. Trans World Airlines, Inc.*,[64] while a supervisor was reprimanding an employee for failing to perform his duties the supervisor deliberately spat in the employee's face. The Missouri Court of Appeals held that an action against the employer was barred because the supervisor's "offensive act did not arise out of a private quarrel personal to [the supervisor] and the plaintiff, but rather out of the employer-employee relationship itself and was based solely upon plaintiff's performance as an employee."[65]

In ruling that the plaintiff could proceed only against the supervisor individually the court ignored well-settled principles of agency law, including the fact that the supervisor was acting within the scope of his employment and was furthering the interests of the company. If the holding was influenced by the trivial nature of the injury, one wonders whether the court would have reached the same result if the supervisor had beaten the employee with a club for failing to perform his job properly.[66]

Despite cases like *Hood*, there is actually a trend to expand employer liability for willful and intentional torts. In *Mandolidis v. Elkins Industries, Inc.*,[67] the plaintiff, a machine operator for a furniture manufacturing business, was operating a 10-inch table saw not equipped with a safety guard. When his right hand came in contact with the saw blade, two fingers and a part of his hand were cut off. The employee brought an action for damages against his employer and alleged that the employer knew of the hazards of the unguarded saw, that other employees had suffered similar injuries, that the unguarded machine had been recently cited by OSHA, that the employer put a guard on the machine for a time but then ordered it removed, and that after the plaintiff objected to working without a guard he was told to operate the machine or be fired. The employee alleged that these acts were so deliberate, willful, and wanton as to constitute an intentional act.

The West Virginia Supreme Court of Appeals held that the employee stated a valid claim. It expanded the intentional injury exception to hold that an employer is liable for employee injuries resulting from the employer's willful, wanton, or reckless misconduct. "[W]hen death or injury results from willful, wanton, or reckless misconduct, such injury is no longer accidental in any meaningful sense of the word, and must be taken as having been inflicted with deliberate intention for the purposes of the Workmen's Compensation Act."[68] Although the *Mandolidis* theory has been urged in other cases, it usually has been rejected.[69] It has been followed only in Ohio.[70]

Actions for fraudulent concealment also may be based on the employer's intentionally failing to disclose an employee's state of impaired health. In *Delamotte v. Unitcast Division of Midland Ross Corp.*,[71] the employee was given periodic chest x-rays by his employer beginning in 1952. Although the x-rays revealed a progressively worsening case of silicosis, it was not until 1972 that the employee was informed of his condition and advised to consult his own physician.

The Ohio Court of Appeals held that an action based on fraudulent, malicious, and willful concealment was not barred by workers' compensation.

In *Johns-Manville Products Corp. v. Contra Costa Superior Court* (also known as the *Rudkin* case),[72] an asbestos worker died of work-related lung cancer. His heirs brought an action against the decedent's employer alleging that the employer fraudulently concealed from the decedent, doctors retained to treat the decedent, and the state government that the decedent was suffering from asbestos-related disease. The Supreme Court of California held that these allegations stated a valid cause of action for aggravation of the disease, although an action for contracting the disease would be barred by workers' compensation.

12.5   Tort Actions Against Third Parties

The "exclusive remedy" provisions of workers' compensation laws only apply to actions brought by injured employees against *their* employer. "Third party actions" are permitted in some jurisdictions against other employers and individuals. Some examples of these kinds of actions are those brought (1) by employees against co-employers; (2) by employees of subcontractors against general contractors; (3) by employees of general contractors against subcontractors; (4) by employees against co-employees; and (5) by employees against property owners.[73] These negligence actions are based on the theory that workers engaged in a common undertaking are owed a duty of reasonable care.

In another group of actions, individuals or entities, by contract or voluntarily, have assumed duties that would not otherwise exist. Most of these cases arise where some arrangement is made for the third party to provide safety and health information, supervision, or services. For example, in *Caldwell v. Bechtel, Inc.*,[74] an employee who contracted silicosis while working on a subway tunnel under construction brought an action against the consulting engineering firm, which had a contractual obligation to provide safety engineering services. The D.C. Circuit held that the contractual authority created a special relationship between the worker and the firm, breach of which gave rise to an action for damages.

Liability may also be based on the "Good Samaritan" rule, which permits recovery against one who voluntarily assumes a duty and then breaches that duty. This rule has been adopted by the *Re-*

statement (Second) of Torts section 324A. In *Heinrich v. Goodyear Tire & Rubber Co.*,[75] an employee of Kelly-Springfield Tire Company, a wholly owned subsidiary of Goodyear, contracted an unspecified occupational disease. The employee and his wife then brought an action against Goodyear alleging, among other things, that Goodyear undertook to provide Kelly with health and safety information and services and that Goodyear's failure to do so resulted in the employee's disease. Although acknowledging that an action could be based on section 324A, the court held that the plaintiffs failed to allege that Goodyear completely assumed this duty, as required by section 324A(b). Other actions based on section 324A have been brought against insurors and government agencies who allegedly conducted negligent safety and health inspections.[76]

The fastest growing area of third-party litigation is products liability—where the employee alleges that an injury or illness was caused by a product manufactured by the defendant and distributed or supplied to the employee's employer. The allegation that the product is unreasonably dangerous is often based on the manufacturer's failure to warn of the hazardous nature of the product. In the leading case of *Borel v. Fibreboard Paper Products Corp.*,[77] an industrial insulation worker who had contracted asbestosis and mesothelioma sued the manufacturers of the insulation materials. The Fifth Circuit held that the defendants breached their duty to warn of the foreseeable dangers associated with handling asbestos. "This duty to warn extends to all users and consumers, including the common worker in the shop or in the field."[78]

Although most of the products liability actions have been brought against manufacturers of products used in the work or production process, the same theory could be used for actions against the manufacturers of safety or even medical equipment. For example, in *Porter v. American Optical Corp.*,[79] a successful products liability action was brought against the manufacturer of a defectively designed respirator and filter apparatus. The plaintiff's decedent, an employee in a gypsum plant, had contracted asbestosis while using the defective respirator.

It is important to distinguish third-party products liability actions from dual capacity products liability actions. In the latter situation injured employees sue their own employer (rather than a third-party manufacturer) for injuries caused by a product manufactured by the employer for sale to the general public. While a few states recognize such actions,[80] most of the states to consider the issue have not.[81]

12.6   Tort Actions for Reproductive Injuries

The scientific basis and the equal employment implications of reproductive hazards in the workplace already have been discussed. There is also a great potential for tort liability where injury is caused by reproductive hazards. Where an employee is exposed to gameto-toxins and sterilization results, the injury to the employee probably would be considered, for liability purposes, as any other occupational illness. The unique legal issues surround the injury, illness, or death of offspring of an exposed parent or parents.

At common law, no cause of action was recognized for negligently inflicted prenatal injuries.[82] Beginning in 1946,[83] the earlier view was overruled, and by 1967 every jurisdiction in the United States had adopted the position that if a child is born alive, the child is permitted to maintain an action for prenatal injuries, and if the child dies of prenatal injuries after birth, an action will lie for wrongful death.[84]

The jurisdictions are very closely divided on the question of whether a cause of action will lie for prenatal injuries where the child is stillborn. A slight majority of jurisdictions recognize such actions,[85] but there is a substantial minority.[86] Moreover, of those jurisdictions permitting recovery, virtually all of them require that the child be ''viable'' at the time of the injury.[87] ''Viable'' has been defined as that stage of development, usually after the second trimester, when the child could survive if separated from the mother.[88]

Where the child is born alive, it must be determined whether the harm to the child resulted from preconception exposure of the mother or father or postconception exposure of the mother. Postconception harms are actionable, regardless of whether the child was viable at the time of injury, so long as the child is born alive.[89] Where the injury to the child results from preconception parental exposure, however, the law is less well settled.

In the leading case of *Renslow v. Mennonite Hospital*,[90] when the child's mother was 13 years old she was negligently given two 500-c.c. transfusions of incompatible Rh-positive blood. Although the hospital knew of the error, it never informed her or her family. Eight years later, when the woman had a baby, the child was born prematurely and suffering from jaundice and hyperbilirubinemia. Consequently, the child had brain damage and other defects caused by the prenatal damage to her hemolitic process. The Supreme Court of Illinois held that the child had a cause of action against the hospital for injuries resulting from the negligent transfusion.

Other courts have permitted recovery for preconception injuries arising from a physician's negligence in performing a Caesarean section on the mother several years before the child's birth[91] and based on products liability where birth control pills altered the mother's chromosomal structure and the woman gave birth to twins with Down's syndrome.[92]

Although there are no reported cases involving preconception exposure to toxic substances in the workplace, employer liability is certainly possible. For example, in *Dillon v. S.S. Kresge Co.*,[93] a pregnant employee of the defendant contracted rubella, allegedly as a result of the defendant's negligence in failing to maintain sanitary conditions. The child, who was born with unspecified serious and permanent injuries, was held to have an actionable case against the defendant. It is not clear, however, how the plaintiff could *prove* how sanitation could influence the transmission of rubella, a viral disease that is contagious from person to person.

Perhaps the best known example of widespread reproductive damages from workplace exposures is the DBCP exposure of Occidental Chemical Company employees in Lathrop, California in 1977. DBCP, a liquid pesticide, is a known gametotoxin, mutagen, and carcinogen.[94] As a result of the reproductive harms to the workers (largely sterility of male employees), 57 lawsuits were brought by the workers against their employer based on intentional tort theory and against the manufacturers of the DBCP, Dow Chemical and Shell, for products liability based on failure-to-warn theory. Forty-nine of the cases were settled before trial for a total of over $10 million. Seven cases were tried, with verdicts for the plaintiffs of $4.99 million. One case involving a worker who contracted cancer was still pending.

In addition to the cases brought by the employees, eight cases were brought in 1983 by the children of exposed workers. Among the birth defects allegedly caused by the DBCP exposure of their fathers are Down's syndrome, missing bones in toes, in-turned feet, genital problems, and being born with a single, damaged kidney. These cases are still pending.

Applying the general principles of recovery for prenatal injuries to the occupational setting raises a number of legal and factual issues.[95] First, the right to maintain an action for wrongful death may depend on whether the fetus was viable at the time of the injury. Because most stillbirths and miscarriages from toxic insults are caused during the early stages of pregnancy, this may be a bar to recovery. Second, in cases brought to recover for birth defects, the specific theory of liability must be determined. If an action for birth defects is based on negligence, the court must be willing to accept the theory that a duty is owed to a child even before conception. Moreover, it is not clear what effect compliance with an OSHA standard would have on such an action. Under a strict liability theory, the plaintiff would have to prove that the activity (use of a toxic substance) was "abnormally dangerous" or "ultra-hazardous."

The third set of issues surrounds the burden of proof. Because of the frequent lack of medical evidence regarding birth defects, it may be difficult to prove that the injuries were caused by the workplace exposures. In some jurisdictions it may be important to prove that the injuries occurred after conception, but because many toxic substances are both mutagenic and teratogenic, this also may be difficult to prove.

Finally there is the question of whether any defenses are available to the employer. It is clear that a parent's contributory negligence cannot be imputed to the child,[96] nor can the child be said to have assumed the risk.[97] The employer's best argument would be that the parent's negligence was a superseding cause of the injury, thereby relieving the employer of liability.[98] Closely related to this is the notion that responsibility had shifted from the employer to the parent.[99] The raising of defenses relating to proximate cause invariably requires an inquiry into public policy, which, in this area, has yet to be spelled out.

As discussed in Chapter 10, Title VII may preclude employers from implementing policies which exclude workers from exposure to reproductive hazards. If these reproductive risks are deemed acceptable by society (see section 6.4), the risk should not fall entirely on the employer. It would be unduly harsh for employers who acted in good faith to be exposed to the full panoply of civil liability in the event of a birth defect.

Where an employer has complied with applicable OSHA standards, the employer has provided affected employees with all available information, and the employee has knowingly and voluntarily consented to work in an environment containing reproductive hazards, any recovery by an injured child should be limited to compensatory damages. Punitive damages should not be recoverable, nor should separate causes of action by the parents (*e.g.*, loss of companionship, emotional distress) be available. Compensatory damages should be borne by the company and passed along to consumers as a cost of using a dangerous product. The prohibition on additional liability is not only equitable but will encourage employers to comply with OSHA and to make full disclosure of reproductive hazards to employees.

12.7   Medical Screening and Personal Injury Litigation

One of the supposed benefits of workers' compensation is that companies are given an incentive to prevent occupational injuries and illnesses. Although this may be true to a limited extent with larger, experience-rated companies, there is inadequate support for the broad hypothesis that the fear of increased workers' compensation rates is a significant factor in improving workplace safety and health.

The same is not true with regard to the fear of civil liability. On August 26, 1982, the Manville Corporation, the world's largest asbestos mining and manufacturing firm, filed a petition for reorganization under Chapter 11 of the Federal Bankruptcy Code. Manville cited the fact that it was involved in more than 16,500 asbestos-related lawsuits and estimated an additional 32,000 lawsuits (with over $2 billion in estimated potential liability) over the next 20 years.

When a company the size of Manville, with over $2 billion in annual sales and over $1 billion in assets, files a Chapter 11 petition, other companies surely take note. A number of corporate responses to the Manville situation have a direct bearing on occupational medical practices. The extent to which any of the following company actions have been implemented is difficult, if not impossible, to determine. Nevertheless, anecdotal reports abound.

On the positive side, many companies are reevaluating the literature on the potential health effects of substances currently in use. They are justifiably concerned that a substance common to their workplaces, such as benzene or formaldehyde, will become the next asbestos. When new substances are to be used, some companies are performing more detailed pretesting and they are demanding more detailed information from suppliers—beyond material safety data sheets.

Although reports are impossible to confirm, some companies assert that they are taking more active steps to improve workplace conditions. Certainly, there is no question that employers are performing more detailed medical surveillance of employees.

Not all of the new initiatives in the occupational health area are calculated solely to improve employee health; some are designed exclusively to avoid potential civil liability without regard for employee health.

As noted earlier, there is a potential for employers to engage in increased medical screening to avoid the hiring of higher risk workers. Employers also could focus more on employee life-style factors in medical screening. The refusal of some asbestos companies to hire smokers is an example of such a practice already in use. Corporate medical departments also are practicing defensive medicine, concerned that the failure to perform certain tests could be evidence of negligence.

Perhaps the greatest use of defensive medicine in hiring and placement is by the railroads. Under the Federal Employers Liability Act (FELA) injured railroad employees are permitted to sue their employers for negligence. Many of the cases are based on the alleged negligence of the company in assigning the employee to a particular job. For example, in *Emmons v. Southern Pacific Transportation Co.*,[100] an employee who had contracted polio when he was four years old (which left him with a limp) was hired as a railroad clerk. After working at this job for seven months the employee applied for and was hired at the higher paying job of switchman-brakeman. Because he had been with the company less than a year he was not given another physical. This new job injured the employee's right ankle (which had been operated on for polio). A jury found that the company was negligent in assigning the employee to the job of switchman-brakeman and awarded him $100,000, although the railroad ultimately won the case on the ground that the statute of limitations had run.

In a similar case, *Ybarra v. Burlington Northern, Inc.*,[101] an employee was required to lift a 40 to 50 pound bucket of oil with one hand from below the level of his feet while squatting and then twisting on the side of the locomotive, all the time holding onto the engine with the other hand. After a number of prior minor back injuries, the employee eventually suffered a serious back injury which required a laminectomy, the wearing of a back brace, and the periodic receipt of pain-relieving injections.

The injured worker brought an action under the FELA, alleging that the railroad was negligent in (1) requiring the use of a lifting procedure which caused excessive stress on the back and (2) assigning him to do lifting work beyond his physical capacity. The Eighth Circuit affirmed a jury's award of $185,000 in damages.

The threat of civil liability in cases like *Emmons* and *Ybarra* may have a bearing on corporate medical practices. Employees with impairments might be denied employment altogether, they might not be promoted or given a chance to prove that they can perform demanding work, or employers might perform continuous and detailed medical screening of workers. The fear of FELA liability has caused the railroads to practice defensive medicine, including the use of low-back x-rays. According to Wiley Mitchell, General Solicitor of the Southern Railway Company: "If you fail to give a preemployment back x-ray and as a result of that unnecessarily expose the particular employee to a hazard that he would have avoided had you given him the x-ray, you're wide open to an unlimited liability under the Federal Employers Liability Act in the event the employee is in fact injured."[102]

Another negative consequence of employers attempting to avoid civil liability is that employees who show symptoms of occupational disease or who are diagnosed as having an occupational illness are sometimes fired even if they are currently capable of performing the job. As a result, employees are often reluctant to report symptoms to the company doctor, see their personal physicians, file workers' compensation claims, seek administrative controls or personal protective equipment, or do anything that they see as possibly jeopardizing their jobs.

Two additional occupational health practices dictated by civil litigation strategy deserve mention. First, the reluctance of companies to perform epidemiological studies for fear that this could be used to show knowledge of health risks (and therefore willful exposure) was discussed in section 1.4. Second, some employers whose employees are exposed to asbestos reportedly are giving their employees written notice at the first instance that a chest x-ray shows any irregularity such as pleural thickening, pleural plaques, or fibrotic changes. Presumably, the statute of limitations begins to run upon notice of these asbestos-related conditions. Nevertheless, any lawsuit brought at this point would result in a minimal recovery because the individual is not impaired. If the employee waits until there are more severe manifestations of asbestos disease, the company would argue that the statute of limitations had run.

It is not clear, however, that such a strategy would be successful in court. For example, in *Pierce v. Johns-Manville Sales Corp.*,[103] an insulation worker who was exposed to asbestos was diagnosed in 1973 as suffering from asbestosis. In 1979 he was diagnosed as having lung cancer, and he died in 1980. The Maryland Court of Appeals held that a wrongful death and survival action brought against the asbestos manufacturer in 1980 was not barred by the state's three year statute of limitations. The court recognized that an award for possible future consequences is not permitted and therefore to hold that the action had to be brought within three years of the diagnosis of asbestosis would result in substantial unfairness and preclude any right to recover for the latent disease of lung cancer.

Finally, the concern over possible civil liability may cause larger companies to contract out the most hazardous parts of their operations to smaller, less stable, less experienced, and less solvent companies. These subcontractors may lack the resources, expertise, and commitment to protect workers exposed to the most serious hazards. Moreover, if an employee contracts a compensable illness the company would be unable to satisfy any judgment obtained in court by the employee.

CHAPTER 13

SOCIETAL PERSPECTIVES

13.1 The Human Element

On May 10, 1983, a 45-year-old employee of Hyman Viener &
Sons, a Richmond, Virginia lead smelting plant, was fired for refusing to have an OSHA-mandated blood test to determine his blood-
lead levels. The following morning, the man, who had worked for the
company for 10 years, walked up to the company office and asked to
see the co-owner about getting his job back. The man then allegedly
took out a handgun and shot and wounded the co-owner and a supervisor standing nearby. After returning to his car and getting a shot-
gun, the man allegedly shot and killed his foreman, who was attempting to help the first two men.

The former employee. was arrested later that evening and
charged with the three shootings. Chronic lead intoxication is known
to cause neurological and behavioral disorders. According to the accused man's lawyer, his client may have been suffering from lead poisoning at the time of the shootings. Ironically, that same day the Virginia Industrial Commission concluded a 10-month investigation of
the Viener smelter, finding over two dozen violations and an ''almost
total disregard for mandatory standards.''[1]

Although the causal relationship between the level of medical
surveillance and the shootings is not clear, these tragic events illustrate two important implications of medical screening programs.
First, it is inappropriate to focus on medical screening or monitoring
of employees without addressing the hazards of the workplace. Unless the physical hazards are controlled, medical surveillance will
merely chronicle the effects of exposure. Second, medical screening
programs are of vital concern to workers. Not only is their health involved, but their jobs and the economic future of their families hang
in the balance. Medical screening and surveillance programs should

not be implemented without detailed thought about the effects of such programs on the lives of affected workers.

Before discussing the economic, ethical, and policy ramifications of medical screening, it is important to reiterate the definition of medical screening set out in section 1.3. Medical screening is the process by which a work force is selected and maintained by application of medical criteria. Thus, while there are various practical and legal differences between preemployment examinations of potential employees and periodic examinations of current employees, to the extent that both types of examinations have a direct bearing on employment opportunity, both examinations are types of medical screening. Consequently, unless otherwise limited, the following discussions of medical screening apply to medical screening at all stages of employment.

13.2   Economic Considerations

Many of the legal and policy arguments about medical screening focus on the tension between the goals of occupational safety and health and equal employment opportunity. Economic considerations, however, also are very important and should not be overlooked or minimized. A company's decision whether to engage in medical screening and, if so, what type of program to implement will certainly be influenced by economic considerations. Similarly, any attempt to regulate employer medical screening must consider the possible economic consequences to employees and to society.

In 1983 Dr. Philip Jacobs and Dr. Alan Chovil of the University of South Carolina published an article in which they evaluated the literature dealing with the cost-effectiveness of corporate medical programs.[2] They concluded that absence-surveillance and alcoholism-control programs were clearly cost-effective, but that it was less clear whether preemployment and periodic medical examinations were cost-effective. Unfortunately, the "benefits" in the studies reviewed consisted only of decreases in health insurance claims, absenteeism rates, and disability payments. By contrast, the success of future medical screening programs is also likely to be assessed based on benefits from increased employee productivity, the avoidance of civil liability, and reduced OSHA compliance costs.

While economic considerations may be used by companies in deciding whether to implement medical screening programs, a purely economic model of decisionmaking has several drawbacks. In the following pages an economic model for evaluating medical screening is presented; it is followed by a discussion of the shortcomings of such an approach.

Before attempting to determine the economic effects of medical screening, it is important to define the type of medical screening being performed. Roughly speaking, medical screening may be viewed as either accurate or inaccurate, and with the employer's costs less than or greater than the benefits. On a two-by-two table, the analysis would look as shown in Table 13-1.

If one assumes that employers are informed and rational, then they certainly will not begin or continue using Type IV medical screening. Likewise, one would assume that many employers would use Type III medical screening only when necessitated by OSHA, collective bargaining, or other requirements.

From a microeconomic standpoint, Type I medical screening is efficient, even though there may be negative societal consequences associated with these programs, such as invasion of privacy, loss of autonomy, and other consequences discussed in the following section.

Type II medical screening may benefit an individual employer, but still may be economically inefficient for society or may involve substantial "transfer payments," such as higher taxes to support unemployment compensation and other governmental subsidies.

There will be net benefits to the employer when the cost to the employer of administering the medical screening (and increased costs associated with a reduced labor supply) is less than the total of the number of true positives screened out by the test multiplied by the average cost to the employer of each added case of occupational illness if the true positive employees were exposed and developed the illness.

$$\text{Cost of screening} < \text{True positives} \times \begin{array}{c} \text{Average cost per case} \\ \text{to the employer} \end{array}$$

"Inaccurate" means that there are unacceptably high percentages of false negatives and false positives identified by the test. This is

Table 13-1. Accuracy and Cost-Benefit Comparisons of Medical Screening

Benefit Analysis	Screening Accurate	Screening Inaccurate
Employer benefits outweigh employer costs	I	II
Employer costs outweigh employer benefits	III	IV

further defined in section 13.3. For example, low-back x-rays are considered worthwhile by many railroads because the cost of screening is less than the number of true positives identified by the x-rays multiplied by the average cost of a back injury case. The test is inaccurate, however, because of the low predictive value of the test, as documented in section 3.6.

In order for Type II medical screening to benefit society, the net savings from the unexposed true positives (those screened out) would have to exceed the societal costs of the false negatives and false positives.

True positives × Average net savings to society per case
> Net cost to society per case × (False positives + False negatives)

To calculate the societal net savings of preventing the exposure of the true positives, one would start with the savings to the employer and then add the increased productivity of another job, savings of health care resources, and other factors. Subtracted from this total would be the societal costs incurred relative to the true positives, including a reduction in productivity if the worker were injured on a different job and the social costs if the individual were unable to obtain another job. The unnecessary social security, welfare, and similar payments will decrease the needed transfer payments from taxpayers to recipients. Transfer payment demand would be increased by necessary unemployment compensation and other payments.

The net societal costs of the false negatives would be zero if the alternative to the medical screening program were to hire all workers (they would have been hired in any event). If the alternatives were other, more accurate tests, however, which would have identified the false negatives as true positives, then there would be societal costs from the false negatives.

Perhaps the most difficult costs to quantify are those relative to the denial of employment to the false positives. These costs could include either (1) the cost of obtaining another job, plus or minus whether the new job is a more efficient utilization of the available labor, or (2) the societal costs of long-term unemployment. This latter figure would include not only government-sponsored income replacement but also the other social costs associated with unemployment such as increased suicide, crime, alcoholism, infant mortality, and divorce.[3]

As one might expect, there is simply inadequate information available to test whether accurate medical screening is worthwhile to society or whether inaccurate medical screening may be worthwhile to a given employer but inefficient for society. Moreover, as discussed in the following section, it is not at all clear that it is appropriate or possible to use cost-benefit analysis as the primary basis for determining the suitability of occupational health policy.[4] A consideration of economic principles, however, remains important in framing many of the larger policy issues that need to be addressed.

13.3   Ethical and Public Policy Considerations

While economic considerations may be valuable to address, they are not the endpoints for an analysis of the societal implications of medical screening. Fortunately, our national employment policies are based on a different set of assumptions and values than mere economic efficiency. Without reliance on these noneconomic considerations, child labor laws, employment discrimination laws, and other remedial legislation may never have been enacted. Indeed, workplace safety and health may not be economically efficient for individual employers or society.[5] But the enactment of OSHA was for humanitarian reasons, not economics. As Senator Yarborough summed it up in the debates before passage of OSHA, "We are talking about people's lives, not the indifference of some cost accountants."[6]

Even if medical screening (accurate or inaccurate) were economically efficient, a whole set of ethical and policy considerations would still have to be analyzed. These considerations become all the more prominent if economic considerations are not given sole importance. Among the numerous ethical principles implicated by medical screening are those dealing with autonomy, paternalism, beneficence, nonmaleficence, well-being, privacy, equity, and utilitarianism.[7]

One way of subdividing the problem is first to consider the issue of inaccurate tests and then to consider accurate ones. In the preceding section, "inaccurate" was somewhat vaguely defined as not having unacceptably high percentages of false negatives and false positives. Although greater precision would eliminate many conceptual problems, it is impossible to develop a more specific definition. There is simply no numerical cutoff point of predictive values below which a test is regarded as inaccurate. Moreover, whether a test generates "unacceptably high levels" of false positives and false negatives depends greatly on the use being made of the information and the interests of the individual involved. Dr. Marvin Schneiderman illustrates this principle with the following example:

> During the war, aircraft were given identifying markings. One could merely look up and determine if it was the enemy or not. If it was an enemy plane, it was shot at. If it was one of ours, it was cheered. In the light of false positives and false negatives, what were the consequences of wrong identification? Identifying an enemy plane as one of ours was a false negative and it bombed you. Identifying the plane as one of theirs when it was really one of ours (and shooting at it) was a false positive. What was the cost? The cost to the shooters was quite different than the cost to the pilot and crew of that plane. The cost to those on the ground of failing to shoot down a plane was that they might be bombed. If the plane was shot down, those on the ground would not be bombed no matter whose plane it was. I think that some of our airplanes were shot down exactly because of that kind of cost-benefit computation. No one did it in a computer; no one did a detailed mathematical equation, but that was a cost-benefit computation which may have led to a fair number of our aircraft being shot down by "friendly fire."[8]

For the employer, the economic costs of false negatives are probably much greater than false positives (which will have an inverse relationship with the size of the available labor pool). In other words, it costs more to hire an individual who will become ill than to not hire an individual who would not become ill. For any given employee, the cost of being a false negative is both economic and noneconomic. The costs depend on the nature of exposure and other factors related to risk acceptability (*i.e.*, whether the employee would have accepted the job if he or she knew that he or she was a true positive). The risk to an employee of being a false positive is largely economic—lost income.

To paraphrase Justice Stewart's famous statement about hardcore pornography,[9] it may not be possible to define "inaccurate screening," but one knows it when one sees it. Thus, for example, a test with a predictive value of 1% would be prima facie inaccurate.

Having discussed, or at least dispensed with, the issue of defining "inaccurate screening," the next question is what the effects of such tests are. If the use of an inaccurate test results in the adverse treatment of an applicant or employee, the result is certainly unfair. The question is whether this unfairness should be remedied by the law.

Unfortunately, unfairness has never been the *sine qua non* for the law to intervene in the employment relationship. Undoubtedly, there are those who would argue that there is nothing inherently or sufficiently outrageous about unfair medical screening to warrant a further intrusion into employer prerogatives. After all, discrimination based on factors such as appearance, political affiliation, or sexual preference is not prohibited in private employment. Why should unfair medical screening be prohibited?

Regardless of whether other bases for discrimination in employment should be prohibited, there are four main reasons why unfair medical screening is different from other unregulated employment decisions and therefore should be prohibited. First, medical screening tests, like x-rays and blood tests, are intrusive procedures which violate a person's physical integrity. Second, the process of soliciting, obtaining, and maintaining medical information invades the privacy of the individual. Third, medical screening is decisionmaking based on mostly uncontrollable criteria. Fourth, there are severe consequences that attach to unfair screening, including humiliation, stigmatization, and possible long-term impairment of employment opportunities. Unlike other forms of arbitrary screening, unfair medical screening implicates all four of these considerations.

The ethical and policy implications of accurate medical screening are more difficult to evaluate. Accurate medical screening is certainly not unethical per se. Indeed, in many circumstances medical screening of workers contributes to the advancement of societal interests. Medical screening promotes the efficient utilization of labor, prevents work-related injury and illness, detects the presence of preexisting disease, and promotes the knowledge of individual employee health and occupational health generally.

An obvious distinction can be drawn between screening of workers who lack the present ability to perform the job and screening which attempts to forecast the risk of future injury or illness. When an individual's present physical condition, even with reasonable accommodation, precludes the performance of essential job functions, it is neither illegal nor unfair for the individual to be denied that particular job. It does not necessarily follow, however, that it is unethical to screen out workers based on future risks. Societal interests are not more likely to be advanced by the employment of a meat cutter with hemophilia or an outdoor lifeguard with xeroderma pigmentosa (both presently capable of performing the job) than by the employment of a blind bus driver or deaf telegrapher (both presently incapable of performing the job).

Whether accurate predictive screening to identify asymptomatic high-risk individuals is ethical is essentially a question of risk acceptance. There are three prerequisites before a paternalistic medical screening system can be ethical: (1) the risk must be unacceptable, (2) the screening criteria must be legitimate, and (3) the screening must not otherwise violate public policy.

First, the risk must be unacceptable. In order to reach such a conclusion the following eight factors must be satisfied.

1.   The threatened illness is severe.
2.   There is a high absolute risk.
3.   There is a high relative risk.
4.   The adverse effects are likely to be manifested in the reasonably forseeable future.
5.   The threatened illness is irreversible and its presence is undetectable in its early stages.
6.   The medical decision is based on an individualized determination of fitness.
7.   No reasonable accommodation is possible.
8.   Medical screening is the only practical way of eliminating the hazard.

Many of these factors are discussed in section 9.4.

Second, the screening criteria must be legitimate. In other words, the basis of the screening—genetic, prior illness, behavioral, or other factors—must not contravene societal values. Professor Barbara Underwood of Yale Law School, although not addressing the issue of medical screening, has suggested that considerations of autonomy counsel against screening programs based on both uncontrollable factors and controllable factors regarded as private and protected against official interference.[10] This accords with the law's antipathy for differentiation in treatment based on "an immutable characteristic determined solely by the accident of birth."[11] Therefore, the screening of applicants to work in an asbestos plant based on SAT deficiency is probably more objectionable than screening based on cigarette smoking.

Third, the screening must not otherwise violate public policy. This final set of factors includes a variety of wide-ranging concerns. To begin with, the applicants or employees being screened should be informed about the nature of all tests being performed, they should be given the test results, and they should be told what the results mean. Because even risks considered acceptable to employers may not be acceptable to a particular employee, individuals should be given the opportunity to make an informed choice about their own health risks, and if they accept the risk, they should be given every possible protection.

The next public policy concern is that the screening should not preclude employment in too many jobs or screen out too many people. As the unacceptable relative risk is lowered, incremental decreases may result in exponential increases in the number of workers screened out. For example, Wiley Mitchell, general solicitor of Southern Railway Company has testified that individuals with only a 5% increased risk should be kept out of railroad jobs.[12]

The combination of this ethical consideration with the biostatistical limitations on predictive screening creates a "whipsaw" effect. It is unacceptable to screen the potential work force on the basis of a commonly possessed biological trait, thereby screening out vast numbers of applicants. For example, screening out all fair-skinned applicants for sailing or farmwork would run counter to the basic tenets upon which our society is built. On the other hand, screening for conditions with very low prevalence rates makes the predictive value of the test so low as to make the test inaccurate and therefore unfair. The screening of all applicants for the presence of a genetic trait with a prevalence of 0.1% would necessarily have a very low predictive value.

Another important policy consideration is that the screening must not adversely affect groups with a history of having suffered discrimination. In the context of genetic screening, Dr. Thomas H. Murray has written:

> Genetic traits naturally fall along racial lines. When the trait in question occurs disproportionately often among members of historically mistreated groups, there is likely to be suspicion and mistrust on the one hand, and a feeling that this is just one more obstacle placed in the way of fair and equal treatment. We should scrutinize with great care any exclusionary screening program having a focus or disproportionate impact on such groups.[13]

A policy consideration discussed often in the preceding chapters is that medical screening should not be used as a substitute for eliminating or reducing hazards in the workplace. In addition, the negative consequences of medical screening should not go beyond the workplace to insurance, credit, military service, and other areas.

Finally, there is a strong public policy concern that workplace medical screening programs should not be self-perpetuating. Because of the hereditary basis of many types of predisposition to occupational disease, future generations of the same families, races, and ethnic groups could be screened out. In addition, as workplaces are more carefully screened for health risks, epidemiological data could be generated showing artificially high no-effect levels for toxic substances. This more extreme "healthy worker effect"[14] could result in permissible exposure limits being set at levels where only disease-resistant individuals can work safely. This, in turn, could lead to even more screening.

Soon we may find ourselves caught in an ever-tightening spiral: finding markers for more subtle problems, discovering larger numbers of susceptible workers, labeling more and different types of environments as hazardous. It is not inconceivable that, through screening, industry will become the modern counterpart of Diogenes as it searches for a perfect worker.[15]

Having determined that some forms of accurate predictive medical screening violate public policy, it is necessary to return to the question posed earlier in connection with inaccurate medical screening: Are the public policy interests violated by medical screening important enough to warrant legal intervention? While there are arguable bases for accurate medical screening, this type of screening may represent a greater societal threat than inaccurate medical screening. Employer use of accurate medical screening is encouraged by market forces and therefore is likely to be more prevalent. Unlike inaccurate medical screening, which would be attacked as irrational, accurate medical screening more squarely raises the legitimacy and public policy concerns discussed earlier. Consequently, unless compelled by irrefutable and crucial medical considerations, even accurate medical screening in employment is objectionable because it is intrusive, invades individual privacy, utilizes largely uncontrollable criteria, and results in severe consequences to the individual.

If public policy favors worker autonomy in deciding whether risks are acceptable, an important question is whether this policy is inconsistent with other existing public policy. For example, OSHA's scheme is essentially paternalistic. Employees may not assume the risk of working under hazardous conditions which do not comply with the Act's requirements. To illustrate this paradox, in the benzene case the industry argued that workplaces cannot be made totally risk free and, impliedly, that employees can choose to accept or refuse such employment. By contrast, in the reproductive hazards cases, the excluded fertile women employees argued that they should be free to decide whether to accept the risks of employment, while the employers argued that it was their responsibility to remove the most vulnerable employees from exposure.

Dr. Ronald Bayer of the Hastings Center has summarized this role reversal in the context of reproductive hazards.

> [B]oth corporations and opponents of exclusionary practices seem to have reversed their characteristic positions on risk assessment and its implications for industrial policy. Typically, workers and their representatives have pressed management for the most extensive reductions in exposure levels to toxic substances. Further, they have maintained that uncertainty requires the most cautious assumptions about the pos-

sibility of harmful consequences. Corporations have responded by arguing that a risk-free environment is a chimerical notion and that the existence of uncertainty requires a willingness to tolerate levels of exposure that have not been proven harmful. Yet in relation to reproductive hazards and, more especially, danger to the fetus, it is labor and its allies that have viewed with some skepticism the data on potential risk. Corporations, on the other hand, have adopted an almost alarmist perspective.[16]

Although the conflict between paternalism and autonomy is difficult to resolve and apply consistently, it is possible to justify increased autonomy for high-risk workers within the context of a paternalistic system. For typical workplace hazards, like benzene, public policy dictates that the hazard be eliminated or reduced to the lowest feasible level so that substantially all employees will be able to work without ill effects. Paternalism would preclude any employees from working under noncomplying conditions. Without mandatory standards, market forces would pressure workers to accept the risk of harmful workplace exposure.

If conditions are safe and healthful for substantially all employees, however, autonomy demands that an individual high-risk employee be permitted to decide whether to accept the increased risk based on his or her own medical condition. Only where there is clear medical evidence that exposure of the high-risk employee is quite likely to result in serious injury or illness would the interest in autonomy be outweighed and employer paternalism justified.

13.4   Problems and Proposals

Throughout the book various specific recommendations have been presented to deal with the scientific and legal issues raised by the medical screening of workers. There are, however, three general proposals in need of further discussion: (1) improvement in the quality of occupational health care; (2) increased research and development of guidelines on the use of medical screening in the workplace; and (3) legal protection for employees and applicants subject to discrimination on the basis of medical screening.

A.   Improvement in the Quality of Occupational Health Care

As mentioned in Chapter 1, there is a critical need for trained specialists in the occupational medical field. Similarly, there is a need for all medical students to receive at least some rudimentary instruc-

tion in occupational medicine. The lack of such training often results
in an inability to recognize illnesses caused by occupational exposures. For example, in 1978 and 1979 a group of board-certified pathologists was tested in a postgraduate course at the University of
California at San Diego. Only six of the 67 pathologists correctly
identified a tissue sample of asbestosis, but all of the pathologists correctly identified at least 75% of the nonoccupational diseases tested.[17]

It is unlikely that the medical school curriculum will be altered
dramatically to add a requirement of training in occupational medicine, especially if this means taking hours from more traditional, entrenched courses. More detailed treatment of occupational medicine
in courses in preventive medicine, community medicine, public
health, and the like is much more feasible. Another prospect is
increased public and private funding to subsidize residencies in occupational medicine as a way of increasing the attractiveness of the
specialty.

Another way of increasing the appeal of occupational medicine
and simultaneously eliminating the recurring conflict-of-interest
problem is to change the prevailing mode of employer-retained physicians. New physicians might be more likely to enter the occupational
health field if they knew that their medical judgments were not subject to managerial oversight. As it is now, "the appearance of conflicting loyalties may be as much a problem as the actuality, at least in
attracting physicians to the occupational medicine specialty and in
enabling them to function once there."[18]

Removing the responsibility for patient-contact services also
could help reduce unethical occupational medical practices. The
present system, under which company medical practices are controlled only by voluntary self-regulation and hortatory canons of
medical ethics, does not work well. This is, in fact, a criticism that has
been leveled at the concept of medical self-regulation in general. According to Robert C. Derbyshire, former president of the Federation
of State Medical Boards of the United States, "on the whole, medical
self-regulation is ineffective and the whole process is in a state of
disarray."[19]

There are at least three alternative models available for the delivery of occupational health services. First, physicians could render
their services as independent contractors. This model is used widely
already and often with worse results than where there is a full-time
employer-salaried physician. The main problem is that few medical
consultants devote all or even most of their time to occupational medicine. The result is frequently that the quality of health care is com-

mensurate with what would be expected from any person performing at his or her "second job."

A second possibility is the establishment of joint labor-management health clinics. This system is quite successful in Sweden and other countries and has even been tried in some experimental programs in the United States. The main problem is that only 20% of the work force is unionized and it is not clear what percentage of the unionized work force works in situations where there are sufficient funds, a commitment to safety and health, and an amicable labor-management relationship—all of which are prerequisites to a successful program.

A third option is to go to a community-based system of occupational health care provided by specialized clinics, either independently operated or run by a health maintenance organization (HMO),[20] hospital,[21] or medical school. This system permits the training of new health professionals in a teaching environment and encourages research and interdisciplinary cooperation. Yale University's program offers industrial hygiene and social work services, West Virginia University's clinic offers industrial hygiene services and legal counseling for its patients, and the University of Pittsburgh clinic has a mobile unit that can be taken to the workplace.

Under any of these alternative systems there is still a role for the employer-retained occupational health professional in first aid, risk assessment, environmental monitoring, biological monitoring, epidemiology, research, and other fields. The primary responsibility for direct patient-contact services, however, would lie elsewhere. These new systems must be careful to (1) improve upon some of the excellent existing employer health programs, rather than starting from scratch, and (2) make arrangements for the provision of services to small employers.

One crucial problem for any new system is that workers must overcome their reluctance to utilize the services when they are ill. Under the present state of the law this reluctance is understandable. Employees working without a collective bargaining agreement may be discharged for any reason, including a report to the employer about symptoms of occupational illness.

Besides the fear of retaliation, many workers seem to have a fatalistic attitude about their occupational health. Some may believe that nothing can or will be done to improve their working conditions and that nothing can be done to treat them if they are already ill. Others fear losing their only livelihood. They deal with the problem by avoiding it; they simply work as long as they are able. For example, after a study associated high lung cancer rates in Deer Lodge County, Montana with arsenic levels at a smelter in the area, the local union president remarked, ''So the studies are right, what are my options? I'm 42 years [old], I've got six kids and a high school education. If the plant closes, what do I do?''[22]

During the period from 1979 to 1982 the United Rubber Workers program of providing optional medical screening for its members was very successful in identifying workers with cancer, diabetes, elevated serum cholesterol, high blood pressure, and other medical conditions (most of which were not job-related). Even for this union-run, optional program, where there was no charge to the individual or notification given to the employer, the employee participation rate was only 25%.[23]

Which workers refuse to participate? Are they the healthy ones who know they are feeling well or the ones who are experiencing symptoms and are afraid of what an examination might disclose? Unfortunately, there is inadequate evidence from which to conclude that workers who refuse to undergo medical examinations are either more healthy or less healthy than their co-workers. A 1983 study of Johnson & Johnson employees who had previously declined to participate in a voluntary medical screening program found that the nonparticipants reported medical histories and life-styles as healthful as those of the participants, except that the nonparticipants (especially women) tended to smoke more.[24]

The previous discussion of the problem of employee participation has focused only on individuals who had been hired already. The use of extensive preemployment exclusionary screening undoubtedly encourages applicants not to mention prior illnesses or exposures and to deny the presence of symptoms, thereby destroying much of the preventive value of medical screening. For example, in one British study of 516 epileptics employed by the Post Office, it was found that over one-third of the individuals had not volunteered information about their epilepsy at the preemployment medical examination.[25]

It is clear that any new system attempting to improve the delivery of occupational health care must include a program to educate workers about the importance of medical surveillance and to convince them that participation is worthwhile and not futile. At the same time, the law must prohibit discrimination against workers who seek occupational medical services. It is even possible that the ''public policy'' exception to the ''at will'' doctrine could be expanded judicially to prohibit the discharge of workers who seek occupational medical care.

B. *Increased Research and Development of Guidelines on the Use of Medical Screening in the Workplace*

The medical screening of workers in the United States has been so common for so long that it would seem there should be widespread agreement on which procedures should be used in any particular situation, what findings and results are significant both individually and collectively, and what personnel actions are appropriate based on certain findings. This, of course, is not the case.

Some medical screening procedures have been inadequately researched, despite their widespread use. Other procedures have been thoroughly researched, but are still used despite their confirmed inaccuracy. Moreover, there are no studies available detailing precisely what procedures are used by employers. Largely because of a fear of potential civil liability, this information is regarded as "top secret."

OSHA has become increasingly involved in medical screening and medical surveillance, but its efforts have been hazard-specific. Thus, the asbestos, cotton dust, lead, and other health standards require detailed medical examinations. There have been no efforts, however, to promulgate more generic medical examination standards spelling out required and prohibited practices.

The logical starting point for regulation of occupational medical practices is NIOSH research. As a result of congressional urging, NIOSH is beginning to develop guidelines and recommendations on the use of genetic testing.[26] This valuable effort should be expanded to encompass all aspects of medical screening.

As discussed earlier, NIOSH has no enforcement authority. If regulations are needed to control occupational medical practices, they must be promulgated by OSHA. It is clear that OSHA has statutory authority to require the use of medical procedures to improve employee health (*e.g.*, pulmonary function tests) and to prohibit medical procedures which are themselves hazardous to employee health (*e.g.*, prophylactic chelation). It is questionable whether OSHA's authority extends to the prohibition of medical procedures or criteria that are not of themselves directly harmful to the employee, but which may result in a denial of employment opportunities.

In order to regulate this type of medical practice (including the issuance of citations and penalties), it may be necessary to amend OSHA. Such an amendment would certainly further the societal interests in economic efficiency, fairness, and improved occupational safety and health.

C. Legal Protection for Employees Subject to Discrimination on the Basis of Medical Screening

In 22 states employers are prohibited from requiring applicants and employees to take a polygraph examination.[27] The two main reasons for these laws are that the tests are considered to be inaccurate and invasive of fundamental privacy interests. It is viewed as repugnant for employees to be asked about sensitive and irrelevant matters like venereal disease and drug usage. Yet, in the context of a medical examination, employees are often tested directly for venereal disease and drug usage—often without even being aware of it. Medical questionnaires also require the furnishing of confidential information.

As described earlier, the actual and potential abuse of medical screening demands that persons who are the potential victims of these practices be protected in their employment rights. The question remains how best to accomplish this.

It is possible that some state legislatures will adopt protective laws, probably by amending their state fair employment laws. This would be an improvement over the status quo, but the problem is a national one. There is no reason why, for example, a company with plants in two states should be permitted to use certain procedures in one state but not in the other. The prospects of NIOSH research and OSHA rulemaking also suggest that federal action is preferable.

The best solution would be to amend Title VII to prohibit discrimination on the basis of medical procedures prohibited by OSHA.[28] This would be better than amending the Rehabilitation Act or OSHA because the administrative mechanism is already in place and the Title VII procedures are already well known. The law would require the cooperation of NIOSH, OSHA, and the EEOC—NIOSH for the research, OSHA for the rulemaking and enforcement against employers, and the EEOC for developing guidelines for employers and protecting employee rights. OSHA would be directed to prohibit medical procedures which are inaccurate, dangerous, invasive of employees' privacy, or discriminatory on the basis of a classification already proscribed by Title VII (race, color, sex, religion, national origin).

The medical assessment of applicants and the continued medical surveillance of employees can play an important part in the prevention of occupational disease. The problems of occupational medicine in general and medical screening in particular have been overlooked for too long and must be addressed. Without prompt attention, the combination of increased costs of dealing with occupational health hazards and the development of new medical technologies is likely to exacerbate the current problem. While expanding our technological capabilities, we must be careful to ensure that improving the health of workers is both the primary purpose and the effect of medical screening.

LIST OF STATUTES

Administrative Procedure Act—5 U.S.C. §§551 to 559, 701 to 706 (law prescribing general rules federal agencies must follow in promulgating regulations and adjudicating administrative cases).

Age Discrimination in Employment Act—29 U.S.C. §§621 to 634 (federal law prohibiting age discrimination in employment against persons 40 to 70 years old).

Civil Rights Act of 1964, Title VI—42 U.S.C. §2000d (federal law providing that recipients of federal financial assistance may not discriminate on the basis of race, color, or national origin).

Civil Rights Act of 1964, Title VII—42 U.S.C. §2000e (federal law prohibiting discrimination in employment on the basis of race, color, religion, sex, or national origin).

Fair Credit Reporting Act—15 U.S.C. §§1681a to 1681t (federal law providing, among other things, that if an applicant or employee is rejected on the basis of a credit report, the individual has a right to be informed of the report).

Fair Labor Standards Act—29 U.S.C. §§201 to 219 (federal law regulating minimum wage, maximum hours, child labor, and other employment conditions).

Federal Coal Mine Health and Safety Act of 1969, Title IV, as amended—30 U.S.C. §§901 to 945 (federal law providing benefits for victims of "black lung").

Federal Employees' Compensation Act—5 U.S.C. §§8101 to 8193 (workers' compensation law for federal civilian employees).

Federal Employers' Liability Act—45 U.S.C. §§51 to 60 (federal law permitting railroad workers to sue their employers for work-related injury and illness).

Jones Act—46 U.S.C. §688 (federal law permitting seamen to sue their employers for work-related injury and illness).

Longshoremen's and Harbor Workers' Compensation Act—33 U.S.C. §§901 to 950 (workers' compensation law for maritime employees).

National Labor Relations Act—29 U.S.C. §§151 to 168 (federal law giving employees the right to join unions, to bargain collectively, and to engage in other concerted activity for their mutual aid and protection).

Occupational Safety and Health Act (OSHA)—29 U.S.C. §§651 to 678 (federal law requiring employers to provide employees with a safe and healthful workplace).

Privacy Act—5 U.S.C. §552a (law controlling the federal government's maintenance and disclosure of information).

Rehabilitation Act of 1973—29 U.S.C. §§701 to 796 (federal law prohibiting discrimination in employment against handicapped persons).

Toxic Substances Control Act—15 U.S.C. §§2601 to 2629 (federal law regulating environmental and public health effects of toxic substances).

Trade Secrets Act—18 U.S.C. §1905 (law prohibiting federal employees from disclosing trade secret information).

Walsh-Healey Act—41 U.S.C. §§35 to 45 (federal law requiring government contractors to provide their employees with safe and healthful workplaces).

NOTES

Introduction

1. Genetic Screening of Workers: Hearings Before the Subcommittee on Investigations and Oversight, House Committee on Science and Technology, 97th Cong., 2d Sess. (June 22, 1982), at 2.
2. See, e.g., Genetic Tests for Jobs Stir Hopes and Fears, U.S. News & World Report, April 11, 1983, at 72 ("It's just one more attempt by the employer to get away from the law to provide a safe workplace.") (statement of Sylvia Krekel of the Oil, Chemical and Atomic Workers Union); Genes and Jobs, 68 A.B.A.J. 1062, 1063 (1982) ("They are concentrating on potential victims instead of cleaning up the workplace.") (statement of Rafael Moure, formerly with the Oil, Chemical and Atomic Workers Union, currently with the United Auto Workers Union).
3. See, e.g., Genetic Screening and the Handling of High-Risk Groups in the Workplace: Hearings Before the Subcommittee on Investigations and Oversight, House Committee on Science and Technology, 97th Cong., 1st Sess. (Oct. 14, 1981), at 45 ("I believe that employers should use back x-ray screening as a tool for putting an individual in a job that he or she can safely perform.") (statement of Dr. Max P. Rogers of Southern Railway Co.); Strasser, Genetic Screening Can Be a Useful Tool to Promote Safety, Occup. Health & Safety, Jan. 1984, at 29 ("It is irresponsible . . . to allow an individual with a predisposition to a certain health problem to work in an environment that could be dangerous").

Chapter 1

1. Kaufman & MacLaury, Historical Perspectives, in U.S. Department of Labor, Protecting People at Work 24–27 (1980); Rom, The Discipline of Environmental and Occupational Medicine, in Environmental and Occupational Medicine 4 (W. Rom ed. 1983).
2. Felton, 200 Years of Occupational Medicine in the U.S., 18 J. Occup. Med. 809, 812, 814 (1976).
3. Id. at 816.
4. Walsh & Marantz, Issues of Mission, Structure, and Domain, in Industry and Health Care, vol. I, Corporate Medical Departments: A Changing Agenda? 35–36 (R. Egdahl & D. Walsh eds. 1983).
5. Levy, The Teaching of Occupational Health in American Medical Schools, 55 J. Med. Educ. 18, 20 (1980).

6.   American Occupational Medical Association, personal communication, October 11, 1983.

7.   *Id.*

8.   OSHA Access to Exposure and Medical Records Standard, Preamble, 45 Fed. Reg. 35,223 (1980) (citing testimony of Dr. Alan A. McLean of AOMA).

9.   American Board of Preventive Medicine, personal communication, October 10, 1983.

10. 43 Fed. Reg. 53,003 (1978).

11. 29 C.F.R. §1910.1025(j)(4) (1983).

12. *See* Keene, *The Credibility of Occupational Medicine,* 16 J. Occup. Med. 309 (1974).

13. *Id.* at 312.

14. Yodaiken & Robbins, *Occupational Ill-Health: A Review of the Symptoms and Signs,* 22 J. Occup. Med. 465, 469 (1980).

15. Kotin & Gaul, *Occupational Ill-Health: A Review of the Symptoms and Signs—A Critique,* 22 J. Occup. Med. 471, 472 (1980).

16. Walsh & Marantz, *The Roles of the Corporate Medical Director,* in Industry and Health Care, vol. I, Corporate Medical Departments: A Changing Agenda? 77 (R. Egdahl & D. Walsh eds. 1983).

17. *Id.* at 73.

18. *See, e.g., Chiasera v. Employers Mut. Liab. Ins. Co.,* 101 Misc. 2d 877, 422 N.Y.S.2d 341 (Sup. Ct. 1979); *Lotspeich v. Chance Vought Aircraft,* 369 S.W.2d 705 (Tex. Civ. App. 1963).

19. *See, e.g., Rogers v. Horvath,* 65 Mich. App. 644, 237 N.W.2d 595 (1975); *Lotspeich v. Chance Vought Aircraft,* 369 S.W.2d 705 (Tex. Civ. App. 1963). *See generally* Annot., 10 A.L.R.3d 1071 (1966).

20. OSHA Access to Employee Exposure and Medical Records Standard, 45 Fed. Reg. 35, 231–32 (1980).

21. *Hoesl v. United States,* 451 F. Supp. 1170, 1176–77 (N.D. Cal. 1978).

22. *Lotspeich v. Chance Vought Aircraft,* 369 S.W.2d 705, 710 (Tex. Civ. App. 1963).

23. Brown, Krieder, & Lange, *Guidelines for Employee Health Services in Hospitals, Clinics and Medical Research Institutions;* 25 J. Occup. Med. 771 (1983).

24. Roberts, *The Question of Ethical Standards in Occupational Medical Practice,* 14 J. Occup. Med. 632, 633 (1972).

25. Morton, *Are Medical Ethical Practices Sufficient in Industrial Medicine?* (letter to the editor), 15 J. Occup. Med. 860 (1973). *See generally* Bundy, *How Do We Assure That the Workers' Health Is the Occupational Physicians' Primary Concern?,* 18 J. Occup. Med. 671 (1976); Dinman, *The Loyalty of the Occupational Physician,* 54 Bull. N.Y. Acad. Med. 729 (1978); Hilker, *If Hippocrates Were Alive,* 54 Bull. N.Y. Acad. Med. 764 (1978); Tabershaw, *Whose "Agent" Is the Occupational Physician?,* 30 Archives Envtl. Health 412 (1975).

26. Walsh & Marantz, *The Roles of the Corporate Medical Director,* in Industry and Health Care, vol. I, Corporate Medical Departments: A Changing Agenda? 69 (R. Egdahl & D. Walsh eds. 1983).

27. Keene, *supra* note 12, at 311–12.

28. Mancuso, *Medical Aspects,* Proceedings of the Interdepartmental Workers' Compensation Task Force Conference on Occupational Diseases and Workers' Compensation, 1976, transcribed for Subcommittee on Labor, Senate Committee on Labor and Public Welfare and House Committee on Education and Labor, 94th Cong., 2d Sess., at 429 (Joint Comm. Print 1976).

29. 29 C.F.R. §1910.151, §1926.50 (1983). For a further discussion of OSHA requirements, see section 2.5.

30. *See, e.g., Fletcher v. Union Pac. R.R.,* 621 F.2d 902, 909 (9th Cir. 1980), *cert. denied,* 449 U.S. 1110 (1981); *Lanni v. Wyer,* 219 F.2d 701, 703 (2d Cir. 1955); *Kloman v. Doctors Hosp.,* 76 A.2d 782, 784 (D.C. 1950); *Dornak v. Lafayette Gen. Hosp.,* 368 So. 2d 1185, 1186 (La. App. 1979); *Baur v. Mesta Machine Co.,* 195 Pa. Super. 22, 32, 168 A.2d 591, 597, *rev'd on other grounds,* 405 Pa. 617, 176 A.2d 684 (1961).

31. Purposes and Objectives of the American Occupational Medical Association (1971). Full text reprinted by permission. *See generally* Howe, *Organization and Operation of an Occupational Health Program,* 17 J. Occup. Med. 362 (1975).

32. Genetic Screening and the Handling of High-Risk Groups in the Workplace: Hearings Before the Subcommittee on Investigations and Oversight, House Committee on Science and Technology, 97th Cong., 1st Sess. (Oct. 14, 1981), at 1.

33. *Id.* at 116.

34. *Id.* at 113 (statement of Wiley Mitchell, General Solicitor, Southern Railway Co.).

35. 29 C.F.R. §1910.1001(j)(3) (1983).

36. *Id.* §1910.1001(j)(4).

37. *See* section 2.5.

38. U.S. Department of Health, Education and Welfare, National Occupational Hazard Survey, vol. III (Survey Analysis and Supplemental Tables), at 80–83 (table 11) (1977).

39. *Id.*

40. *See* section 7.4.

41. *See* section 7.1.

42. Holden, *Looking at Genes in the Workplace,* 217 Science 337 (1982); Severo, *Dispute Arises Over Dow Studies on Genetic Damage in Workers,* N.Y. Times, Feb. 5, 1980, at A1, col. 1.

43. 42 U.S.C. §289l–3 (1976).

44. 45 C.F.R. Part 46 (1983).

45. *Id.* §46.116.

46. Personal communication, October 3, 1983.

47. Personal communication, September 30, 1983.

48. *See* Freedman, Industry Response to Health Risk 17–18 (1981).

49. *See* Morton, *supra* note 25; Westin, *Dilemmas Facing Occupational Health Surveillance,* in Individual Rights in the Corporation 200–202 (A. Westin & S. Salisbury eds. 1980).

50. *See* Whorton, *Accurate Occupational Illness and Injury Data in the U.S.: Can This Enigmatic Problem Ever Be Solved?,* 73 Am. J. Pub. Health 1031 (1983).

Chapter 2

1. Component Committee on Disability Criteria of the American Lung Association Pediatric and Adult Lung Disease Committee, 7 ATS News No. 3, at 20–28 (1981), *cited in* Kanner, *Impairment and Disability Evaluation: An Overview,* in Environmental and Occupational Medicine 43 (W. Rom ed. 1983). For a similar definition, *see* American Medical Association, Guides to the Evaluation of Permanent Impairment iii (1977).

2. *See* Hogan & Bernacki, *Developing Job-Related Preplacement Medical Examinations,* 23 J. Occup. Med. 469 (1981).

3. *See* W. Shepard, The Role of the Physician in Industry 19 (1976); Schussler, Kaminer, Power, & Pomper, *The Preplacement Examination*, 17 J. Occup. Med. 254, 255–56 (1975).

4. Report of the Privacy Protection Study Commission, App. III, at 82 (1977) [hereinafter cited as Privacy Commission].

5. U.S. Department of Health, Education and Welfare, National Occupational Hazard Survey, Vol. III (Survey Analysis and Supplemental Tables), at 73 (table 9) (1977) [hereinafter cited as NOHS].

6. Privacy Commission, *supra* note 4, at 11.

7. *Id.*

8. *Id.* at 40–41.

9. *Id.* at 12.

10. *Id.*

11. Finucane, *General Foods Medical and Environmental Health Systems (MEHS)*, 24 J. Occup. Med. 794 (1982).

12. *See Medical Information Systems Roundtable*, 24 J. Occup. Med. 781–866 (1982).

13. Privacy Commission, *supra* note 4, at 12; Voelz & Spickard, *Preemployment Medical Evaluation by Questionnaire*, 14 J. Occup. Med. 18 (1972).

14. Arizona Center for Occupational Safety and Health, The Occupational and Environmental History 14–15 (1980).

15. Privacy Commission, *supra* note 4, App. III, at 11.

16. *Farrens Tree Surgeons, Inc.*, 264 NLRB No. 90, 111 LRRM 1305 (1982).

17. *E.g., Interpace Corp.*, 54 LA 534 (Myers, 1970); *PPG Indus., Inc.*, 53 LA 597 (Diff, 1969); *Reynolds Metals Co.*, 53 LA 503 (Holly, 1969).

18. Schilling, *Developments in Occupational Health*, in Occupational Health Practice 15 (R. Schilling ed. 1981).

19. *Id.* at 13.

20. *See* Schussler et al., *supra* note 3.

21. Walsh, *The Future of Corporate Health Initiatives*, in Industry and Health Care, vol. I, Corporate Medical Departments: A Changing Agenda? 223 (R. Egdahl & D. Walsh eds. 1983).

22. W. Shepard, *supra* note 3, at 16.

23. *Id.* at 16–17.

24. *Id.* at 17.

25. Campione, *The Pre-employment Examination: An Evaluation*, 41 Indus. Med. 27, 29 (1972).

26. NOHS, *supra* note 5, at 77 (table 10).

27. *Id.* at 78.

28. W. Shepard, *supra* note 3, at 17.

29. Cooper, *Health Surveillance Programs in Industry*, in Patty's Industrial Hygiene and Toxicology 596 (G. Clayton & F. Clayton eds. 1979).

30. *See* Frank, *The Occupational History and Examination*, in Environmental and Occupational Medicine 21, 22–25 (W. Rom ed. 1983).

31. Lost in the Workplace: Is There An Occupational Disease Epidemic?, at 74–76 (U.S. Dept. of Labor, 1979).

32. NOHS, *supra* note 5, at 93–94 (table 14).

33. *Id.* at 97–98 (table 15).

34. *Id.* at 101–02 (table 16).

35. *Id.* at 105–06 (table 17).

36. *Id.* at 90–91 (table 13).

37. *Id.* at 86–87 (table 12).
38. *Id.* at sections 4.1, 4.2.
39. *See* section 3.7.
40. 29 C.F.R. §1910.95(j)(5) and (6) (1983).
41. 30 U.S.C. §843(a) (1976); 42 C.F.R. §37.5(b) (1983).
42. 11 OSHC 1441 (1983), *petition for review filed*, No. 83-7321 (9th Cir., May 12, 1983).
43. 11 OSHC 1464 (1983).
44. *Id.* at 1472.

Chapter 3

1. Schilling, *Prevention of Occupational Disease and Ill Health*, in Occupational Health Practice 584 (R. Schilling ed. 1981)
2. Wright & Bailey, *Screening Well People*, in Occupational Health Practice 204 (R. Schilling ed. 1981).
3. Sheridan, *Genetic Screening: Its Promise and Peril*, Occup. Hazards, April 1983, at 75, 76.
4. Omenn & Motulsky, *Eco-Genetics: Variation in Susceptibility to Environmental Agents*, in Genetic Issues in Public Health and Medicine 84 (B. Cohen, A. Lilienfeld, & P. Huang eds. 1978).
5. A. Winchester, Human Genetics 165 (1975); Motulsky, *Ecogenetics: Genetic Variation in Susceptibility to Environmental Agents*, in Human Genetics, Proceedings of the Fifth International Congress of Human Genetics 376, 377 (1977).
6. A. Scheinfeld, Heredity in Humans 4 (1972).
7. Harris, *Nature and Nurture*, 297 New Eng. J. Med. 399 (1977).
8. A. Emery, Heredity, Disease and Man—Genetics in Medicine 112 (1968); I. Potter, Heredity and Disease 23 (1968); J. Stansbury, J. Wyngarden, & D. Fredrickson, The Metabolic Basis of Inherited Disease 3 (4th ed. 1978).
9. F. Vogel & A. Motulsky, Human Genetics 259 (1979).
10. Harris, *supra* note 7, at 1399; Omenn & Motulsky, *supra* note 4, at 83.
11. Cooper, *Health Surveillance Programs in Industry*, in Patty's Industrial Hygiene and Toxicology, vol. 3, at 595, 601 (1979).
12. *Id.*
13. *Id.*
14. Stedman's Medical Dictionary 674 (4th unabr. lawyer's ed. 1974).
15. L. Cavalle-Sforza, Elements of Human Genetics 52 (1973).
16. Velazquez, *The Genetic Concept of Disease*, 31 Revista De Investigacion Clinica 1 (Enero-Marzo 1979).
17. *Id.*
18. *Id.*
19. Multiple Factors in the Causation of Environmentally Induced Disease 1 (D. Lee & P. Kotin eds. 1972).
20. *Id.* at 2.
21. *Id.* at 1.
22. *Id.* at 3.
23. Brewer, *Human Ecology, an Expanding Role for the Human Geneticist*, 23 Am. J. Human Genetics 92 (1971).

24. Stokinger, Mountain, & Scheel, *Pharmacogenetics in the Detection of the Hypersusceptible Worker*, 151 Annals N.Y. Acad. Sciences 968, 969 (1968).

25. Motulsky, *supra* note 5, at 379.

26. Occupational Safety and Health Administration (OSHA), The Identification, Classification and Regulation of Toxic Substances Posing a Potential Occupational Carcinogenic Risk, 42 Fed. Reg. 54,155–56 (1977).

27. *See* Archer & Livingston, *Environmental Carcinogenesis and Mutagenesis*, in Environmental and Occupational Medicine 63 (W. Rom ed. 1983).

28. Croce & Koprowski, *The Genetics of Human Cancer*, 238 Scientific Am. 117 (1978); Higginson, *Importance of Environmental and Occupational Factors in Cancer*, 6 J. Toxicology & Envtl. Health 941 (1980); Lynch, *Genetics, Etiology and Human Cancer*, 9 Preventive Med. 231 (1980).

29. Higginson, *supra* note 28.

30. P. Bogovski, Historical Perspective of Occupational Cancer (1980); Cole & Merletti, *Chemical Agents and Occupational Cancer*, 3 J. Envtl. Pathology & Toxicology 399 (1980); Higginson, *supra* note 28.

31. United States Congress, Office of Technology Assessment, Technologies for Determining Cancer Risks From the Environment 3 (1981) [hereinafter cited as Cancer Risks].

32. *Id.* at 88.

33. World Health Organization, Early Detection of Health Impairment in Occupational Exposure to Health Hazards (1975).

34. P. Timiras, Developmental Physiology and Aging 473 (1972).

35. *See* E. Calabrese, Pollutants and High Risk Groups 165 (1978).

36. Doll, *Cancer and Aging: The Epidemiologic Evidence*, 5 Oncology 1970—Tenth International Cancer Congress 1–28 (1971); Case, Hooker, & McDonald, *Tumors of the Urinary Bladder in Workmen Engaged in the Manufacture and Use of Certain Dyestuff Intermediates in the British Chemical Industry*, 11 Brit. J. Indus. Med. 75 (1954). *But see* Hoover & Cole, *Temporal Aspects of Occupational Bladder Carcinogenesis*, 288 New Eng. J. Med. 1041 (1973); Kahn, *The Dorn Study of Smoking and Mortality Among U.S. Veterans: Report on Eight and One-Half Years of Observation*, 19 N.C.I Monog. 1 (1966). *See generally* Whittemore, *The Age Distribution of Human Cancer for Carcinogenic Exposures of Varying Intensity*, 106 Am. J. Epidemiology 418 (1977).

37. *See* E. Calabrese, *supra* note 35, at 31. *See also* 46 Fed. Reg. 4078 (1981) (OSHA hearing conservation standard permits age correction to the audiometric tests of workers over 50).

38. Occupational illness rates for different racial and ethnic groups also may vary widely because of employment patterns, with certain groups being overrepresented in hazardous industries. *See generally* Davis, *The Impact of Workplace Health and Safety on Black Workers: Assessment and Prognosis*, 31 Lab. L.J. 723 (1980); 11 OSHR 134–35 (1981).

39. E. Calabrese, *supra* note 35, at 85.

40. Allison & Wong, *Skin Cancer: Some Ethnic Differences*, in Environments of Man 69 (J. Bresler ed. 1968); E. Calabrese, *supra* note 35, at 87; Crombie, *Racial Differences in Melanoma Incidence*, 40 Brit. J. Cancer 185 (1979).

41. Stebbings, *A Survey of Respiratory Disease Among New York City Postal and Transit Workers*, 6 Envtl. Research 147, 153 (1973). *See* Oscherwitz, Edlavitch, Baker, & Jarboe, *Differences in Pulmonary Functions in Various Racial Groups*, 96 Am. J. Epidemiology 319 (1972).

42. U.S. Department of Health, Education and Welfare, Public Health Service, Framingham Heart Study: Habits and Coronary Heart Disease (1966).
43. Stebbings, *supra* note 41.
44. 29 C.F.R. §1910.1043 (h) (3) (iii) (1983).
45. Anderson, *Familial Susceptibility*, in Persons at High Risk of Cancer 39 (J. Fraumeni, Jr. ed. 1975).
46. *Id.*
47. Fraumeni, *Clinical Patterns of Familial Cancer*, in Genetics of Human Cancer 225 (J. Mulvihill, R. Miller, & J. Fraumeni eds. 1977).
48. *Id. See* Mulvihill, *Congenital and Genetic Diseases*, in Persons at High Risk of Cancer 25 (J. Fraumeni, Jr. ed. 1975); King, Go, Elston, Lynch, & Petrakis, *Allele Increasing Susceptibility to Human Breast Cancer May Be Linked to Glutamate-Pyruvate Transaminase Locus*, 208 Science 406 (1980).
49. Noweir, Moselhi, & Amine, *Role of Family Susceptibility, Occupational and Family Histories and Individual's Blood Groups in the Development of Silicosis*, 37 Brit. J. Indus. Med. 399 (1980).
50. Genetic Screening and the Handling of High-Risk Groups in the Work Place, Hearings Before the Subcommittee on Investigations and Oversight, House Committee on Science and Technology, 97th Cong., 1st Sess. (Oct. 15, 1981), at 248 [hereinafter cited as Genetic Screening].
51. Hoover, Mason, McKay, & Fraumeni, *Geographic Patterns of Cancer Mortality in the United States*, in Persons at High Risk of Cancer 349–51 (J. Fraumeni, Jr. ed. 1975); Crombie, *Variation of Melanoma Incidence with Latitude in North America and Europe*, 40 Brit. J. Cancer 774 (1979).
52. S. Epstein, The Politics of Cancer 488 (1979).
53. *Id.*
54. *See id.*; Hoover, et al., *supra* note 51, at 357. *See generally* R. Shakman, Where You Live May Be Hazardous to Your Health (1979).
55. Cancer Risks, *supra* note 31, at 77, *citing* Doll & Peto, *The Causes of Cancer: Quantitative Estimates of Avoidable Risks of Cancer in the United States Today*, 66 J. Nat'l Cancer Inst. 1191 (1981).
56. Berg, *Diet*, in Persons at High Risk of Cancer 202–07 (J. Fraumeni, Jr. ed. 1975). *See generally* Ames, *Dietary Carcinogens and Anticarcinogens*, 221 Science 1256 (1983).
57. *Id.*
58. *See* Cancer Risks, *supra* note 31, at 78–80; Graham & Mettlin, *Fiber and Other Constituents of Vegetables in Cancer Epidemiology*, in Nutrition and Cancer: Etiology and Treatment 189 (G. Newell & N. Ellison eds. 1981); Kritchevsky & Klurfeld, *Fat and Cancer, id.*; MacLure & MacMahon, *An Epidemiologic Perspective of Environmental Carcinogenesis*, 2 Epidemiologic Rev. 19, 23–26 (1980).
59. *Id.*
60. *See* E. Calabrese, Nutrition and Environmental Health (1981); Petering, Murthy, & Cerklewski, *Role of Nutrition in Heavy Metal Toxicity*, in Biochemical Effects of Environmental Pollutants 365 (S. Lee ed. 1977).
61. Severo, *Federal Mandate for Gene Tests Disturbs U.S. Job Safety Official*, N.Y. Times, Feb. 6, 1980, at A1, col. 1, A17, col. 1 (citing Dr. Herbert E. Stokinger). The reported literature involving cruciferous vegetables, however, suggests that they may exert a protective effect against colon and possibly other cancers by inducing aryl hydrocarbon hydroxylase activity in the intes-

tinal epithelia. MacLure & MacMahon, *supra* note 58, at 24. Vinyl chloride, however, is associated with angiosarcoma, a rare cancer of the liver.

62. Calabrese, Kajola, & Carnow, *Ozone: A Possible Cause of Hemolytic Anemia in G-6-PD Deficient Individuals*, 2 J. Toxicology & Envtl. Health 709 (1977); Calabrese, Moore, & Ho, *Low G-6-PD Activity in Human and Sheep Red Blood Cells and Susceptibility to Copper Induced Oxidative Damage*, 21 Envtl. Research 366 (1980); Stokinger & Scheel, *Hypersusceptibility and Genetic Problems in Occupational Medicine—A Consensus Report*, 15 J. Occup. Med. 564 (1973).

63. *See* Z. Harsanyi & R. Hutton, Genetic Prophecy: Beyond the Double Helix 11–15 (1981).

64. U.S. Department of Health, Education and Welfare, Healthy People—The Surgeon General's Report on Health Promotion and Disease Prevention 121 (1979).

65. *Id.*

66. *Id.*

67. *Id.* at 122.

68. Hammond, *Tobacco*, in Persons at High Risk of Cancer 134 (J. Fraumeni, Jr. ed. 1975).

69. Blackwell, French, & Stein, *Adverse Health Effects of Smoking and the Occupational Environment*, NIOSH Current Intelligence Bull. No. 31, 40 Am. Indus. Hygiene A.J. A38 (1979), *cited in* Omenn, *Predictive Identification of Hypersusceptible Individuals*, 24 J. Occup. Med. 369, 373 (1982).

70. Hammond, *supra* note 68, at 131, 134–35.

71. *See* Kent & Cenci, *Smoking and the Workplace: Tobacco Smoke Health Hazards to the Involuntary Smoker*, 24 J. Occup. Med. 469 (1982).

72. *See, e.g.*, Pearle, *Smoking and Duration of Asbestos Exposure in the Production of Functional and Roentgenographic Abnormalities in Shipyard Workers*, 24 J. Occup. Med. 37 (1982); Weiss, Levin, & Goodman, *Pleural Plaques and Cigarette Smoking in Asbestos Workers*, 23 J. Occup. Med. 427 (1981); Weiss & Theodos, *Pleuropulmonary Disease Among Asbestos Workers in Relation to Smoking and Type of Exposure*, 20 J. Occup. Med. 341 (1978).

73. I. Selikoff, Disability Compensation for Asbestos-Associated Disease in the United States 333, 335 (1982) (report to U.S. Department of Labor).

74. *Id.*

75. *See* Vitale, Broitman, & Gottlieb, *Alcohol and Carcinogenesis*, in Nutrition and Cancer: Etiology and Treatment 291 (G. Newell & N. Ellison eds. 1981).

76. Rothman, *Alcohol*, in Persons at High Risk of Cancer 140 (J. Fraumeni, Jr. ed. 1975). *See* Cancer Risks, *supra* note 31, at 73–76.

77. Rothman, *supra* note 76, at 140–45.

78. *Id.*; Cancer Risks, *supra* note 31, at 73–76.

79. 9 OSHR 998 (1980).

80. Lyle, *Case History: Alcohol Interaction with a Workplace Chemical*, 31 Occup. Health 265 (1979).

81. Godard, *Alcohol and Occupation*, in Alcohol Problems in Employment (B. Hore & M. Plant eds. 1981).

82. Tabershaw, Utidjian, & Kawahara, *Chemical Hazards*, in Occupational Diseases: A Guide to Their Recognition 195 (NIOSH 1977).

83. *See* Hoover & Fraumeni, *Drugs*, in Persons at High Risk of Cancer (J. Fraumeni, Jr. ed. 1975).

84. Cancer Risks, *supra* note 31, at 95.

85. *Id.* at 101.

86. Selikoff, *Multiple Factor Interactions in Occupational Diseases*, Proceedings of the Interdepartmental Workers' Compensation Task Force Conference on Occupational Diseases and Workers' Compensation, 1976, transcribed for Subcommittee on Labor, Senate Committee on Labor and Public Welfare and House Committee on Education and Labor, 94th Cong., 2d Sess., at 310 (Joint Comm. Print 1976).

87. Hoover & Fraumeni, *supra* note 83, at 187.

88. Cancer Risks, *supra* note 31, at 98–99; S. Epstein, *supra* note 52, at 485–86.

89. Jablon, *Radiation*, in Persons at High Risk of Cancer (J. Fraumeni, Jr. ed. 1975).

90. Moss, Murray, Parr, & Conover, *Radiation*, in Occupational Diseases: A Guide to Their Recognition 471–72 (NIOSH 1977).

91. Selikoff, *supra* note 86, at 313.

92. *See* McCann, *The Impact of Hazards in Art on Female Workers*, 7 Preventive Med. 338 (1978).

93. *See* E. Calabrese, *supra* note 35, at 26–30.

94. *See* MacLure & MacMahon, *supra* note 58, at 27–28.

95. *See* Klein, Namer, & Harper, *Earthenware Containers as a Source of Fatal Lead Poisoning: Case Study and Public Health Consideration*, 283 New Eng. J. Med. 669 (1970); Kleinfeld, *Lead Intoxication From an Unexpected Source*, 24 J. Occup. Med. 146 (1982).

96. Z. Harsanyi & R. Hutton, *supra* note 62, at 116.

97. E. Calabrese, *supra* note 35, at 48–49.

98. Hyatt, Pritchard, & Richards, *Effect of Facial Hair on Respirator Performance*, 34 Am. Indus. Hygiene A.J. 135 (1973).

99. 29 C.F.R. §1910.134 (e) (5) (i) (1983).

100. *See* A. Vander, Nutrition, Stress, and Toxic Chemicals 195–252 (1981); Macek, *Of Mind and Morbidity: Can Stress and Grief Depress Immunity?*, 248 J.A.M.A. 405 (1982).

101. Davidson & Cooper, *A Model of Occupational Stress*, 23 J. Occup. Med. 564, 570 (1981). *See* Brook, *Mental Health of People at Work*, in Occupational Health Practice 541 (R. Schilling ed. 1981); La Dou, *Occupational Stress*, in Developments in Occupational Medicine 197 (C. Zenz ed. 1980).

102. *See* Chesney, Sevelius, Black, Ward, Swan, & Rosenman, *Work Environment, Type A Behavior, and Coronary Heart Disease Risk Factors*, 23 J. Occup. Med. 551 (1981).

103. *Id.* at 555. *See* Brodsky, *Psychological Factors Contributing to Somatoform Disease Attributed to the Workplace*, 25 J. Occup. Med. 459 (1983).

104. Morgan, *Psychological Problems Associated with the Wearing of Industrial Respirators: A Review*, 44 Am. Indus. Hygiene A. J. 671 (1983).

105. *Id.*; Morgan, *Psychological Correlates of Respiration: A Review*, 44 Am. Indus. Hygiene A.J. 677 (1983).

106. Morgan, *Hyperventilation Syndrome: A Review*, 44 Am. Indus. Hygiene A.J. 685 (1983).

107. Cohen, *Chronic Obstructive Pulmonary Disease: A Challenge in Genetic Epidemiology*, 112 Am. J. Epidemiology 274, 284, 286 (1980) (references omitted). Reprinted by permission.

108. Noweir et al., *supra* note 49.

109. U.S. Department of Health and Human Services, NIOSH, Work Practices

220   MEDICAL SCREENING OF WORKERS

Guide for Manual Lifting 18 (1981) [hereinafter cited as Work Practices Guide]. *Accord*, Quiet & Hadler, *Diagnosis and Treatment of Backache*, 8 Seminars in Arthritis & Rheumatism 261, 277 (1979) (no relationship between lower back pain and muscular build, lower limb form and function, scoliosis, lordosis, kyphosis, or lumbosacral angle).

110.	Work Practices Guide, *supra* note 109, at 18.

111.	Genetic Screening, *supra* note 50, at 120 (statement of Dr. Paul Rockey).

112.	*See, e.g.*, Anderson, *Occupational Aspects of Low Back Pain*, 6 Clinics in Rheumatic Diseases 17, 28–29 (1980); Gibson, Martin, & Terry, *Incidence of Low Back Pain and Pre-Placement X-Ray Screening*, 22 J. Occup. Med. 515 (1980); Quiet & Hadler, *supra* note 107, at 278–79; Snook, Campanelli, & Hart, *A Study of Three Preventive Approaches to Low Back Injury*, 20 J. Occup. Med. 478 (1978); Work Practices Guide, *supra* note 109, at 92–94.

113.	*Compare* Ford, *Orthopedic Considerations*, in Summary of Report and Proceedings of the Conference on Low Back X-Rays in Pre-employment Physical Examinations, Tucson, Arizona, Jan. 11–14, 1973, at 33, 39–40 (Missouri Pacific Railroad rejected 40% of applicants on basis of x-rays) *with* Kosiak, Aurelius, & Hartfiel, *The Low Back Problem*, 10 J. Occup. Med. 588 (1968) (29% of applicants disqualified on the basis of x-rays). *See also* Rockey, Fantel, & Omenn, *Discriminatory Aspects of Pre-Employment Screening: Low-Back X-Ray Examinations in the Railroad Industry*, 5 Am. J.L. & Med. 197 (1980).

114.	*See, e.g.*, Rowe, *Low Back Pain in Industry*, 11 J. Occup. Med. 161 (1964) (only 10% of subjects subsequently developing back pain could have been identified at screening); Redfield, *The Low Back X-Ray as a Pre-employment Screening Tool in the Forest Products Industry*, 13 J. Occup. Med. 219 (1971) (injury rate for workers screened to be at high risk actually was much lower than those screened to be at low risk).

115.	The x-rays cost between $50 and $100 each, for a total cost of $50 to $100 million. Genetic Screening, *supra* note 50, at 120.

116.	Rockey et al., *supra* note 113, at 203–04.

117.	Work Practices Guide, *supra* note 109, at 93.

118.	*See* Hogan, *The State of the Art of Strength Testing*, in Women, Work, and Health: Challenges to Corporate Policy 75 (D. Walsh & R. Egdahl eds. 1980); U.S. Department of Health and Human Services, National Institute for Occupational Safety and Health, Preemployment Strength Testing (1977); Work Practices Guide, *supra* note 109, at 95–96.

119.	*See* Work Practices Guide, *supra* note 109, at 96–98.

120.	*See* Althouse, *Revealing a True Profile of Musculoskeletal Abilities*, Occup. Health & Safety, May 1980, at 25.

121.	*See* Hogan, *supra* note 118, at 92; Work Practices Guide, *supra* note 109, at 98.

122.	*See* U.S. Department of Health, Education and Welfare, NIOSH, A Guide to the Work-Relatedness of Disease 13–17 (1977) [hereinafter cited as Work-Relatedness of Disease].

123.	Dinitrotoluene (DNT) can cause methemoglobinemia by decreasing the oxygen carrying capacity of the blood. *See* Tabershaw, Utidjian, & Kawahara, *Chemical Hazards*, in U.S. Department of Health, Education and Welfare, NIOSH, Occupational Diseases—A Guide to Their Recognition 279 (M. Key, A. Henschel, J. Butler, R. Ligo, & I. Tabershaw eds. 1977) [hereinafter cited as NIOSH Guide].

124.	Carbon dioxide intoxication can produce unconsciousness and death from oxygen deficiency. Tabershaw, Utidjian, & Kawahara, *Chemical Hazards*, in NIOSH Guide, *supra* note 123, at 416.

125. Methylene chloride exposure can lead to caroboxy hemoglobinemia, a form of oxygen deficiency. Tabershaw, Utidjian, & Kawahara, *Chemical Hazards*, in NIOSH Guide, *supra* note 123, at 210.

126. Dynamite workers with a history of coronary artery disease, when exposed to nitroglycerine have an increased risk of coronary artery spasm. *See* Hogstedt & Anderson, *A Cohort Study on Mortality Among Dynamite Workers*, 21 J. Occup. Med. 553 (1979); Hogstedt & Axelson, *Nitroglycerine-Nitroglycol Exposure and the Mortality in Cardio-Cerebrovascular Diseases Among Dynamite Workers*, 19 J. Occup. Med. 675 (1977); Lund, Haggendal, & Johnson, *Withdrawal Symptoms in Workers Exposed to Nitroglycerine*, 25 Brit. J. Indus. Med. 136 (1968).

127. Carbon disulphide increases the risk of cardiac death by accelerating the artherosclerotic process. *See* Hernberg, Partanen, Nordman, & Sumari, *Coronary Heart Disease Among Workers Exposed to Carbon Disulphide*, 27 Brit. J. Indus. Med. 313 (1970); Tiller, Schilling, & Morris, *Occupational Toxic Factor in Mortality from Coronary Heart Disease*, 4 Brit. Med. J. 407 (1968); Tolonen, Hernberg, Nurminen, & Tutola, *A Follow-up Study of Coronary Heart Disease in Viscose Rayon Workers Exposed to Carbon Disulphide*, 32 Brit. J. Indus. Med. 1 (1975).

128. *See* Sataloff, *Occupational Hearing Loss*, 15 J. Occup. Med. 360 (1973).

129. *See* Brubaker, Mackenzie, Eng, & Bates, *Vibration White Finger Disease Among Tree Fellers in British Columbia*, 25 J. Occup. Med. 403 (1983); Okada, Yamashita, Nogano, Ikeda, Yachi, & Shibata, *Studies on the Diagnosis and Pathogenesis of Raynaud's Phenomenon of Occupational Origin*, 28 Brit. J. Indus. Med. 353 (1971); Taylor, Pearson, Kell, & Keighley, *Vibration Syndrome in Forestry Commission Chain Saw Operators*, 28 Brit. J. Indus. Med. 83 (1971); Wasserman & Taylor, *Occupational Vibration*, in Environmental and Occupational Medicine 743 (W. Rom ed. 1983).

130. *See* NIOSH Guide, *supra* note 123, at 304.

131. *Id.* at 325.

132. *Id.* at 363.

133. *See* T. Harrison, Principles of Internal Medicine 4 (8th ed. 1977).

134. T. Fitzpatrick, Dermatology in General Medicine 13 (1971).

135. *Id.* at 1061–69.

136. *Id.*

137. *See* Bridbord, Wagoner, & Blejer, *Chemical Carcinogens*, in NIOSH Guide, *supra* note 123, at 443; Selikoff, *Cancer Risk of Asbestos Exposure*, in Origins of Human Cancer 1765–84 (Hiatt et al. eds. 1977); U.S. Department of Health, Education and Welfare, Public Health Service, Asbestos: An Information Resource 29 (1978); Greenberg & Lloyd-Davis, *Mesothelioma Register 1967–1968*, 31 Brit. J. Indus. Med. 91 (1974).

138. Ishimaru, Okada, & Tomeiyasu, *Occupational Factors in the Epidemiology of Leukemia in Hiroshima and Nagasaki*, 93 Am. J. Epidemiology 157 (1971).

139. Cowles, *Medical Effects of Combined Industrial Exposures*, 21 J. Occup. Med. 413, 414 (1979); Freundt, *Mixed Exposures to Chemical Hazards*, Occup. Health & Safety, Aug. 1982, at 10.

140. Cowles, *supra* note 139.

141. McJilton, *Role of Relative Humidity in the Synergistic Effect of A Sulfur Dioxide-Aerosol Mixture in the Lung*, 182 Science 503 (1973).

142. *See* Buell, *Some Biochemical Aspects of Cadmium Toxicology*, 17 J. Occup. Med. 189 (1975).

143. Daniel, *Smooth Muscle and Neural Innervation of the Airways*, in Bronchial Hyperreactivity 7–9 (1981).

144. Baer, *The Most Common Contact Allergens*, 108 Archives of Dermatology 74 (1973).

145. Adams, *High-Risk Dermatoses*, 23 J. Occup. Med. 829 (1981).

146. Birmingham, *Dermatoses*, in NIOSH Guide, *supra* note 123, at 81.

147. National Institute for Occupational Safety and Health, Criteria for a Recommended Standard—Occupational Exposure to Toluene Diisocyanate (1969); Weill, *Respiratory Effects from Toluene Diisocyanate*, in Environmental and Occupational Medicine 621 (W. Rom ed. 1983).

148. Schleuter, *Response of the Lung to Inhaled Antigens*, 57 Am. J. Med. 476 (1974).

149. Work-Relatedness of Disease, *supra* note 122, at 60.

150. Karol, *Survey of Industrial Workers for Antibodies to Toluene Diisocyanate*, 23 J. Occup. Med. 741 (1981).

151. *See* Stokinger & Scheel, *Hypersusceptibility and Genetic Problems in Occupational Medicine—A Consensus Report*, 15 J. Occup. Med. 564, 571 (1973).

152. Hanks, *The Physical Examination in Industry: A Critique*, 5 Archives Envtl. Health 365, 366 (1962).

153. *Id.* at 370.

154. *See* Rodman, *The Pre-employment Physical Examination*, 7 J. Occup. Med. 608 (1965); Schneider & McDonagh, *Experience Data on University Recruits Hired Without Pre-Employment Examinations*, 13 J. Occup. Med. 363 (1971); Williamson, *Eighteen Years Experience Without Pre-Employment Examinations*, 13 J. Occup. Med. 465 (1971). *See generally* Leckey, *Pre-employment Examinations—A Pointed Study*, 8 J. Occup. Med. 532 (1966); Michaels, *A Plea for Abandonment of the Complete History and Physical Examination*, 108 Can. Med. A. J. 299 (1973).

155. *See* Gibson, *Why the Preplacement Physical Isn't Out of Date*, 43 Int'l J. Occup. Health & Safety 31 (1974).

156. Tabershaw, *How is the Acceptability of Risks to the Health of Workers to be Determined?*, 18 J. Occup. Med. 674, 675 (1976).

157. Rockey et al., *supra* note 113, at 208–10.

158. R. Galen & S. Gambino, Beyond Normality: The Predictive Value and Efficiency of Medical Diagnosis 16 (1975).

159. *Id.* at 18.

160. *See* section 11.2.

161. Rosner & Polk, *Predictive Values of Routine Blood Pressure Measurements in Screening for Hypertension*, 117 Am. J. Epidemiology 429 (1983).

162. R. Galen & S. Gambino, *supra* note 158, at 18, 22. *Accord*, Ashenbourg, *Routine Chest X-Ray Examinations in Occupational Medicine*, 24 J. Occup. Med. 18, 19, (1982).

163. *See* R. Galen & S. Gambino, *supra* note 158, at 2–6; Kurt, *Gathering Accurate Data Ongoing Problem for Health Team*, Occup. Health & Safety, Jan. 1984, at 64; Young, *How Does One Interpret a Marginally Abnormal Serum Chemistry Test?*, 24 J. Occup. Med. 104 (1982).

164. *Chest X-Ray Examinations in Occupational Medicine*, 25 J. Occup. Med. 773 (1983).

Chapter 4

1. Stokinger & Mountain, *Tests for Hypersusceptibility to Hemolytic Chemicals*, 6 Archives Envtl. Health 495 (1963).

2. Stokinger & Scheel, *Hypersusceptibility and Genetic Problems in Occupational Medicine—A Consensus Report*, 15 J. Occup. Med. 564 (1973).

3. *Id.* at 572.

4. *Id.*

5. *Id.*

6. Reinhardt, *Chemical Hypersusceptibility*, 20 J. Occup. Med. 319 (1978).

7. United States Congress, Office of Technology Assessment, The Role of Genetic Testing in the Prevention of Occupational Illness 34 (1983) [hereinafter cited as Genetic Testing].

8. *See* Severo, *59 Top U.S. Companies Plan Genetic Screening*, N.Y. Times, June 23, 1982, at A9, col. 4 (statement of Rep. Albert Gore, Jr., Chairman of the Subcommittee on Investigations and Oversight, House Committee on Science and Technology).

9. *Id.*

10. U.S. Department of Health, Education and Welfare, Protocol for Sickle Cell Education 17 (1976).

11. Konetey-Ahula, *The Sickle Cell Diseases*, 133 Archives Internal Med. 611 (1974).

12. Lindsay, Meshel, & Patterson, *Cardiovascular Manifestations of Sickle Cell Disease*, 133 Archives Internal Med. 643 (1974).

13. *Id.*; Cooper, *Indicators of Susceptibility to Industrial Chemicals*, 15 J. Occup. Med. 355, 356 (1973).

14. Konetey-Ahula, *supra* note 11, at 612.

15. Sears, *The Morbidity of Sickle-Cell Trait: Review of the Literature*, 64 Am. J. Med. 1021, 1030 (1978).

16. Uddin, Dickson, & Brodine, *Screening of Military Recruits for Hemoglobin Variants*, 227 J.A.M.A. 1405 (1974). *See* Holden, *Air Force Challenged on Sickle Trait Policy*, 211 Science 257 (1981).

17. Reinhardt, *supra* note 6, at 320.

18. Lehman & Huntsman, *The Hemoglobinopathies*, in The Metabolic Basis of Inherited Disease 1398, 1404 (3d ed., J. Stanbury ed. 1972).

19. Stokinger & Scheel, *supra* note 2, at 572.

20. Reinhardt, *supra* note 6, at 320 (Du Pont).

21. *See* Petrakis, *Sickle-Cell Disease*, 2 Lancet 1368, 1369 (1974).

22. Lehman & Huntsman, *supra* note 18; Diggs & Flowers, *High School Athletes with Sickle-Cell Trait (HbAS)*, 68 J. Nat'l Med. A. 492 (1976); Horberg & Uddin, *Sickle-Cell Trait and Glucose-6-Phosphate Dehydrogenase Deficiency: Effects on Health and Military Performance in Black Navy Enlistees*, 141 Archives Internal Med. 1485 (1981); Murphy, *Sickle-Cell Hemaglobin (HbAS) in Black Football Players*, 225 J.A.M.A. 981 (1973).

23. *See* Stokinger & Scheel, *supra* note 2.

24. Cooper, *supra* note 13; Omenn, *Predictive Identification of Hypersusceptible Individuals*, 27 J. Occup. Med. 369, 372 (1982).

25. E. Calabrese, Pollutants and High Risk Groups 43 (1978).

26. *Id.*

27. E. Gardner, Principles of Genetics 390 (1972).
28. E. Calabrese, *supra* note 25, at 45 (1978); Omenn & Motulsky, *Eco-Genetics: Variation in Susceptibility to Environmental Agents*, in Genetic Issues in Public Health and Medicine 85 (B. Cohen, A. Lilienfeld, & P. Huang eds. 1978).
29. Cooper, *supra* note 13, at 355–56; Stokinger & Mountain, *supra* note 1.
30. E. Calabrese, *supra* note 25; Stokinger & Mountain, *supra* note 1.
31. Stokinger & Scheel, *supra* note 2.
32. *See* Calabrese, Kajola, & Carnow, *Ozone: A Possible Cause of Hemolytic Anemia in G-6-PD Deficient Individuals*, 2 J. Toxicology & Envtl. Health 709 (1977).
33. *See* Calabrese, Moore, & Ho, *Low G-6-PD Activity in Human and Sheep Red Blood Cells and Susceptibility to Copper Induced Oxidative Damage*, 21 Envtl. Research 366 (1980).
34. *See* Calabrese, Moore, & Ho, *Low Erythrocyte G-6-PD Activity and Susceptibility to Nitrite-Induced Methemoglobin Formation*, 26 Bull. Envtl. Contaminant Toxicology 837 (1980).
35. Cooper, *supra* note 13, at 356.
36. E. Calabrese, *supra* note 25, at 45.
37. K. Muensch, The Genetic Basis for Human Disease 41 (1979).
38. Uddin, Dickson, & Brodine, *supra* note 16.
39. Genetic Testing, *supra* note 7, at 90.
40. Cooper, *supra* note 13, at 356.
41. J. Stanbury, J. Wyngaarden, & D. Fredrickson, The Metabolic Basis of Inherited Disease 1375 (4th ed. 1978).
42. Cooper, *supra* note 13, at 356.
43. K. Muensch, *supra* note 37, at 41.
44. Stokinger & Mountain, *supra* note 1.
45. Stokinger & Mountain, *Progress in Detecting the Worker Hypersusceptible to Industrial Chemicals*, 9 J. Occup. Med. 537, 539 (1967).
46. E. Calabrese, *supra* note 25, at 43; Freedman, *Thalassemia: An Abnormality in Globin Chain Synthesis*, 267 Am. J. Med. Sciences 257 (1974).
47. J. Stanbury et al., *supra* note 41, at 1521.
48. *Id.*
49. E. Calabrese, *supra* note 25, at 44.
50. *Id.*
51. *Id.*
52. *Id.*
53. *Id.*
54. *Id.*
55. Minnich, Cordonnier, Williams, & Moore, *Alpha, Beta and Gamma Hemoglobin Polypeptide Chains During the Neonatal Period with a Description of the Fetal Form of Hemoglobin D (St. Louis)*, 19 Blood 137 (1962); Weatherall, *Abnormal Hemoglobins in the Neonatal Period and their Relationship to Thalassemia*, 9 Brit. J. Hematology 265 (1963).
56. E. Calabrese, *supra* note 25, at 44.
57. Pearson, O'Brien, & McIntosh, *Screening for Thalassemia Trait by Electronic Measurement of Mean Corpuscle Volume*, 288 New Eng. J. Med. 351 (1973).
58. *Id.*
59. Neel & Valentine, *The Frequency of Thalassemia*, 209 Am. J. Med. Sciences 568 (1945).

60. E. Calabrese, *supra* note 25, at 55.
61. *Id.*; Larson, *Natural History and Life Expectancy in Severe Alpha₁-Antitrypsin Deficiency, PiZ*, 204 Acta Med. Scand. 345 (1978).
62. Cooper, *supra* note 13, at 356.
63. *Id.*
64. Genetic Testing, *supra* note 7, at 93.
65. *Id.*
66. *Id*
67. *See* Lebowitz, Knudson, Morse, & Armet, *Closing Volumes and Flow Volume Abnormalities in Alpha₁ Antitrypsin Phenotype Groups in a Community Population*, 117 Am. Rev. Respiratory Disease 179 (1978).
68. *See* Evans & Bognocki, *Alpha₁-Antitrypsin Deficiency and Susceptibility to Lung Disease*, 29 Envtl. Health Perspectives 57 (1979); Mittman, *The PiMZ Phenotype: Is It a Significant Risk Factor for the Development of Chronic Obstructive Lung Disease?*, 118 Am. Rev. Respiratory Disease 649 (1978). *See also* Omenn & Motulsky, *supra* note 28, at 90.
69. Mittman, *supra* note 68. This suggests that screening programs for SAT heterozygotes would be unwarranted.
70. Mittman, *supra* note 68. Interestingly, and for as yet unexplained reasons, oral contraceptives have been shown to increase SAT levels. Laurrell & Eriksson, *The Electrophoretic Alpha₁ Globulin Pattern of Serum in Alpha₁-Antitrypsin Deficiency*, 15 Scand. J. Clinical Laboratory Investigation 132 (1963).
71. E. Calabrese, *supra* note 25, at 49.
72. *Id.* at 72.
73. J. Stanbury et al., *supra* note 41, at 1103.
74. E. Calabrese, *supra* note 25, at 83.
75. Genetic Testing, *supra* note 7, at 92–100. *See* Lappé, *Ethical Issues in Testing for Differential Sensitivity to Occupational Hazards*, 25 J. Occup. Med. 797, 798 (1983).
76. Scott & Hoskins, *Hereditary Methemoglobinemia in Alaskan Eskimos and Indians*, 13 Blood 795 (1958).
77. Balsam, Hardy, & Scott, *Hereditary Methemoglobinemia Due to Diaphorase Deficiency in Navajo Indians*, 65 J. Pediatrics 928 (1964).
78. Hseih & Joffe, *Electrophoretic and Functional Variants of NADH Methemoglobin Reductase in Hereditary Methemoglobinemia*, 50 J. Clinical Investigation 196 (1971); Schwartz, Parass, Ross, DiPillo, & Rizek, *Unstable Variant of NADH Methemoglobin Reductase in Puerto Ricans with Hereditary Methemoglobinemia*, 51 J. Clinical Investigation 1594 (1972).
79. E. Calabrese, *supra* note 25, at 66.
80. *Id.* at 190.
81. *Id.* at 75.
82. Carpenter, Raum, Glass, & Schur, *Ordering of Genes for HLA Antigens and Complement Components on the Human 6th Chromosome*, in HLA and Malignancy 9 (G. Murphy ed. 1977); Payne, *The HLA Complex: Genetics and Implications in the Immune Response*, in HLA and Disease 20, 26 (J. Dausset & A. Suejgaard eds. 1977).
83. W. Braun, HLA and Disease: A Comprehensive Review (1979).
84. Z. Harsanyi & R. Hutton, Genetic Prophecy: Beyond the Double Helix 59 (1981).

85. W. Braun, *supra* note 83, at 127.
86. W. Braun, *supra* note 83, at 127 (186); Z. Harsanyi & R. Hutton, *supra* note 84, at 58, 62–63 (more than 80).
87. W. Braun, *supra* note 83, at 31, 80, 103–04; Z. Harsanyi & R. Hutton, *supra* note 84, at 64–67.
88. Khan & Khan, *Diagnostic Value of HLA-B27 Testing in Ankylosing Spondylitis and Reiter's Syndrome*, 96 Annals Internal Med. 70 (1982).
89. Dabney, *The Role of Human Genetic Monitoring in the Workplace*, 23 J. Occup. Med. 626 (1981).
90. *See* Killian & Picciano, *Cytogenetic Surveillance of Industrial Populations*, in Chemical Mutagens: Principles and Methods for Their Detection 321 (A. Hollaender ed. 1976); Purchase, *Chromosomal Analysis of Exposed Populations: A Review of Industrial Problems*, in Mutagen-Induced Chromosome Damage in Man 258 (H. Evans & D. Lloyd eds. 1978). *See also* Buffler & Aase, *Genetic Risks and Environmental Surveillance: Epidemiological Aspects of Monitoring Industrial Populations for Environmental Mutagens*, 24 J. Occup. Med. 305 (1982). *See generally* Harnden, *Cytogenetics of Human Neoplasia*, in Genetics of Human Cancer 87 (J. Mulvihill, R. Miller, & J. Fraumeni, Jr. eds. 1977).
91. Dabney, *supra* note 89, at 628–30.
92. Genetic Testing, *supra* note 7, at 74.
93. *Id.*; Dabney, *supra* note 89, at 626, 630–31.
94. OSHA, Proposed Standard for Ethylene Oxide, Appendix C, 48 Fed. Reg. 17,315 (1983).
95. Genetic Testing, *supra* note 7, at 75.
96. *Id.* at 75–79.
97. *Id.* at 79.

Chapter 5

1. *See* W. Ganong, Review of Medical Physiology 328 (8th ed. 1977); American Industrial Hygiene Association, *Guide to Manual Lifting*, 31 Am. Indus. Hygiene A.J. 511 (1970); Chaffin, Herrin, Keyserling, & Foulke, *Preemployment Strength Testing: An Update Position*, 20 J. Occup. Med. 403 (1978).
2. Messite & Bond, *Occupational Health Considerations for Women at Work*, in Developments in Occupational Medicine 53 (C. Zenz ed. 1980).
3. OSHA Hearing Conservation Amendment, Introduction, 46 Fed. Reg. 4094–95 (1981).
4. V. Hunt, Work and the Health of Women 31 (1979).
5. Doull, *Factors Influencing Toxicity*, in General Principles of Toxicology 141–42 (L. Casarett & J. Doull eds. 1975).
6. *Id.*
7. *See* Messite & Bond, *supra* note 2, at 48–51 (reviewing literature on lead and benzene and concluding that there is inadequate evidence of sex-based susceptibility).
8. Harrington & Schilling, *Work and Health*, in Occupational Health Practice 69 (R. Schilling ed., 2d ed. 1981).
9. Hamilton & Parry, *Sex-Related Differences in Clinical Drug Response: Implications for Women's Health*, 38 J. Am. Med. Women's A. 126 (1983).

10. Ferguson, *Toxicological Problems Related to the Employment of Women*, in Health of Women Who Work 41 (M. McKiever ed. 1965); Toh, *Physiological and Biochemical Reviews of Sex Differences and Carcinogenesis with Particular Reference to the Liver*, 18 Advances in Cancer Research 209 (1973).

11. Haenszel & Taeuber, *Lung Cancer Mortality as Related to Residence and Smoking Histories*, 32 J. Nat'l Cancer Inst. 803 (1968); Toh, *supra* note 10.

12. K. Moore, The Developing Human 17 (3d ed. 1982).

13. *Id.*

14. J. Langman, Medical Embryology 9 (4th ed. 1981).

15. Strobino, Klein, & Stein, *Chemical and Physical Exposure of Parents: Effects on Human Reproduction and Offspring*, 1 Early Human Development 371 (1978).

16. W. Ganong, *supra* note 1, at 325.

17. Conibear, *Women as a High Risk Population*, in Society for Occupational and Environmental Health, Proceedings of Conference on Women and the Workplace 168, 170 (E. Bingham ed. 1976).

18. Hunt, *Occupational Radiation Exposure of Women Workers*, 7 Preventive Med. 294, 304 (1978).

19. Strobino et al., *supra* note 15, at 388.

20. Kline, *Surveillance of Spontaneous Abortions*, 106 Am. J. Epidemiology 345 (1977); Manson, *Human and Laboratory Test Systems Available for Detection of Reproductive Failure*, 7 Preventive Med. 322, 326 (1978).

21. *See* World Health Organization, Health Hazards of the Human Environment 214 (1972), *cited in* A. Hricko & M. Brunt, Working for Your Life: A Woman's Guide to Job Health Hazards at B-5 (1976). *See also* Wagoner, Infante, & Brown, *Genetic Effects Associated with Industrial Chemicals*, in Society for Occupational and Environmental Health, Proceedings of Conference on Women and the Workplace 100 (E. Bingham ed. 1976).

22. *See* Carter, Lyon, & Phillips, *Genetic Hazard of Ionizing Radiation*, 182 Nature 409 (1958).

23. Marshall, *Effects of Pesticides on Testicular Function*, 3 Urology 257 (1978); Whorton, Krauss, Marshall, & Milby, *Infertility in Male Pesticide Workers*, 2 Lancet 1259 (1977).

24. Preamble to OSHA Lead Standard, 43 Fed. Reg. 54, 388–89 (1978); Thomas & Brogan, *Some Actions of Lead on the Sperm and Upon the Male Reproduction System*, Am. J. Indus. Med. (special issue) at 127 (1982).

25. Infante, *Chloroprene: Adverse Effects on Reproduction*, in U.S. Department of Health and Human Services, Proceedings of a Workshop on Methodology for Assessing Reproductive Hazards in the Workplace 87, 89 (P. Infante & M. Legator eds. 1980).

26. Whorton et al., *supra* note 23.

27. Infante, *Genetic Risks of Vinyl Chloride*, 1 Lancet 1289 (1976).

28. Gordon, *Hypogonadism and Femininization in the Male: A Triple Effect of Alcohol*, 3 Alcoholism: Clinical & Experimental Research 210 (1979).

29. Kolodny, *Depression of Plasma Testosterone Levels After Chronic Marijuana Use*, 290 New Eng. J. Med. 872 (1974).

30. Evans, *Sperm Abnormalities and Cigarette Smoking*, 1 Lancet 627 (1981).

31. Strobino, *Chemical and Physical Exposures of Parents: Effects on Human Offspring*, 1 Early Human Development 371 (1978).

32. Schilsky, *Gonadal Dysfunction in Patients Receiving Chemotherapy for Cancer*, 93 Annals Internal Med. 109 (1980).

33. Rachootin & Olsen, *The Risk of Infertility and Delayed Conception Associated with Exposures in the Danish Workplace*, 25 J. Occup. Med. 394 (1983).

34. *Id.*

35. Messite & Bond, *Reproductive Toxicology and Occupational Exposure*, in Developments in Occupational Medicine 61 (C. Zenz ed. 1980).

36. Karrh, Carmody, Clyne, Gould, Portela-Cubria, Smith, & Freifeld, *Guidance for the Evaluation, Risk Assessment and Control of Chemical Embryo-Fetotoxins*, 23 J. Occup. Med. 397 (1981).

37. Manson, *supra* note 20, at 325.

38. *See* Welch, Barnes, Robboy, & Herbst, *Transplacental Carcinogenesis: Prenatal Diethylstilbestrol (DES) Exposure, Clear Cell Carcinoma and Related Anomalies of the Genital Tract in Young Females*, in Society for Occupational and Environmental Health, Proceedings of Conference on Women and the Workplace 47–50 (E. Bingham ed. 1976).

39. J. Langman, *supra* note 14, at 115.

40. Wilson, *Experimental Studies on Congenital Malformations*, 10 J. Chronic Diseases 111 (1959).

41. Lutwak-Mann, *Drugs and the Blastocyst*, in Fetal Pharmacology 419 (L. Boreus ed. 1973), *cited in* Messite & Bond, *supra* note 35, at 61.

42. J. Langman, *supra* note 14, at 115.

43. *Id.*

44. *See* Marshall, Hammond, Ross, Jacobson, Rayford, & Odell, *Plasma and Urinary Chorionic Gonadotropin During Early Human Pregnancy*, 32 Obstetrics & Gynecology 760 (1968).

45. Messite & Bond, *supra* note 35, at 62.

46. Langman & Welch, *Excess Vitamin A and the Development of the Cerebral Cortex*, 131 J. Comp. Neurology 15 (1967); Webster, Shimada, & Langman, *Effect of Fluorodeoxyuridine, Colcemid and Bromodeoxyuridine on Developing Neocortex of the Mouse*, 137 Am. J. Anatomy 67 (1973).

47. *See generally* J. Boyd & W. Hamilton, The Human Placenta (1970).

48. Manson & Simons, *Influence of Environmental Agents on Male Reproductive Failure*, in Work and the Health of Women 171 (V. Hunt ed. 1979).

49. Warshaw, *Employee Health Services for Women Workers*, 7 Preventive Med. 385, 387 (1978).

50. Matsumoto, Goyo, & Takeuchi, *Fetal Minamata Disease: A Neuropathological Study of Two Cases of Intrauterine Intoxification by a Methylmercury Compound*, 24 J. Neuropathology & Experimental Neurology 563 (1965).

51. *See* Preamble to OSHA Lead Standard, 43 Fed. Reg. 52, 959–66 (1978).

52. *See* Clyne, *Fetotoxicity and Fertile Female Employees*, in Women, Work, and Health: Challenges to Corporate Policy 202–03 (D. Walsh & R. Egdahl eds. 1980); Messite & Bond, *supra* note 35, at 64–69. Maternal alcoholism (Hanson, *Reproductive Hazards from Prenatal Alcohol Use: The Fetal Alcohol Syndrome*, in U.S. Department of Health and Human Services, Proceedings of a Workshop on Methodology for Assessing Reproductive Hazards in the Workplace 7 (P. Infante & M. Legator eds. 1980)) and cigarette smoking (Haas & Schottenfeld, *Risks to the Offspring From Parental Occupational Exposures*, 21 J. Occup. Med. 607, 608–09 (1979)) are frequently the causes of birth defects.

53. Manson, *supra* note 20, at 323.

54. Stellman, *The Effects of Toxic Agents on Reproduction*, Occup. Health & Safety 36, 40 (Apr. 1979).

55. Brunt & Hricko, *Problems Faced by Women Workers*, in Occupational Health 415 (B. Levy & D. Wegman eds. 1983).
56. *See* Hornstein, Crowe, & Gruppo, *Adrenal Carcinoma in Child With History of Fetal Alcohol Syndrome*, 2 Lancet 1292 (1977).
57. Clyne, *supra* note 52, at 200.
58. *Id.*
59. Greenwald, Barlow, Nasca, & Burnett, *Vaginal Cancer After Maternal Treatment With Synthetic Estrogens*, 285 New Eng. J. Med. 390 (1971); Herbst, Ulfelder, & Poskanzer, *Adenocarcinoma of the Vagina*, 284 New Eng. J. Med. 878 (1971).
60. Berger & Goldstein, *Impaired Reproductive Performance in DES-Exposed Women*, 55 Obstetrics & Gynecology 25 (1980); Rosenfeld & Bronson, *Reproductive Problems in the DES-Exposed Female*, 55 Obstetrics & Gynecology 453 (1980).
61. Bill, Schumacher, & Bibbo, *Pathological Semen and Anatomical Abnormalities of the Genital Tract in Human Male Subjects Exposed to Diethylstilbestrol in Utero*, 117 J. Urology 477 (1977).
62. *Compare* Fabia & Thuy, *Occupation of Father at Time of Birth of Children Dying of Malignant Diseases*, 28 Brit. J. Preventive & Social Med. 98 (1974), *with* Hakulinen, Salonen, & Teppo, *Cancer in the Offspring of Fathers in Hydrocarbon-Related Occupations*, 30 Brit. J. Preventive & Social Med. 138 (1976) *and* Zack, Cannon, & Loyd, *Cancer in Children of Parents Exposed to Hydrocarbon-Related Industries and Occupations*, 111 Am. J. Epidemiology 329 (1980).
63. Kantor, McCrea-Curnen, & Meigs, *Occupations of Fathers of Patients with Wilms' Tumor*, 33 J. Epidemiology & Commun. Health 253 (1979).
64. Peters, Preston-Martin, & Yu, *Brain Tumors in Children and Occupational Exposure of Parents*, 213 Science 235 (1981).
65. Gold, Diener, & Szklo, *Parental Occupations and Cancer in Children*, 24 J. Occup. Med. 578 (1982).

Chapter 6

1. Report of the Privacy Protection Study Commission 226 (1977), *citing* unpublished memorandum by Michael Baker.
2. *See* 103 LRR 236 (Mar. 24, 1980) (reporting terms of conciliation agreement between Varo Semiconductor, Inc. and the Labor Department under which 85 applicants were to receive $225,000 and 32 applicants were placed on a preferential hiring list; the action was based on §503 of Rehabilitation Act of 1973). *See generally* S. Lusterman, Industry Roles in Health Care 31 (1974), *cited in* Report of the Privacy Protection Study Commission, App. III, at 19–20 (1977) (concluding that medical examinations are used in selection and placement).
3. Weinstock & Haft, *The Effect of Illness on Employment Opportunities*, 29 Archives Envtl. Health 79 (1974).
4. *Id.* at 81.
5. *Id.*
6. *Id.* at 83.
7. *See* Severo, *Federal Mandate for Gene Tests Disturbs U.S. Job Safety Official*, N.Y. Times, Feb. 6, 1980, at A17, col. 1 (quoting Dr. John H. Weisburger of the American Health Foundation, who suggested hiring of older people for positions involving carcinogenic exposures).

8.   *See Hiring Handicapped, Not Easy*, Pittsburgh Post-Gazette, Sept. 18, 1980, §2, at 16, cols. 3–4.

9.   7 OSHR 529 (1977).

10. Whorton, *Dibromochloropropane Health Effects*, in Environmental and Occupational Medicine 573 (W. Rom ed. 1983).

11. Genetic Screening and the Handling of High-Risk Groups in the Workplace: Hearings Before the Subcommittee on Investigations and Oversight, House Committee on Science and Technology, 97th Cong., 1st Sess. (Oct. 14, 1981), at 43 [hereinafter cited as Genetic Screening].

12. *Id.* at 42. *See* Rowe, *Are Routine Spine Films on Workers in Industry Cost- Or Risk-Benefit Effective?*, 24 J. Occup. Med. 41 (1982).

13. Rockey, Fantel, & Omenn, *Discriminatory Aspects of Pre-Employment Screening: Low-Back X-Ray Examinations in the Railroad Industry*, 5 Am. J. L. & Med. 197, 210–11 (1980).

14. Genetic Screening, *supra* note 11, at 110 (statement of Dr. Max P. Rogers).

15. *Id.* at 109.

16. R. Galen & S. Gambino, Beyond Normality: The Predictive Value and Efficiency of Medical Diagnoses 3 (1975).

17. Craft, Benecki, & Shkop, *Who Hires the Seriously Handicapped?*, 19 Indus. Rel. 94 (1980).

18. *See* Chapter 10.

19. *See Joy Mfg. Co.*, 73 LA 1269 (Abrams, 1980) (dermatitis); *Ormet Corp.*, 80–1 ARB ¶8034 (Seinsheimer, 1979) (dermatitis). *But see* Walworth County, 63 LA 1203 (Moberly, 1974) (obesity).

20. *See, e.g., Checker Taxi Co.*, 57 LA 466 (Duff, 1971); *San Francisco Retailers Council*, 57 LA 482 (Wyckoff, 1971).

21. *See, e.g., Pennsylvania Tire & Rubber Co.*, 59 LA 1078 (Simon, 1972) (plant cleaner with ulcers and back injury); *Cominco American, Inc.*, 52 LA 1152 (Belcher, 1969) (miner with emphysema).

22. *Compare West Penn Power Co.*, 67 LA 1085 (Blue, 1976) (utility line worker with acrophobia entitled to transfer under contract) *with Eaton Corp.*, 73 LA 729 (Porter, 1979) (machine tender with dermatitis not entitled to transfer to material handler job).

23. Sager, *Nine in Army Select Unit Fail Marijuana Test*, Washington Post, May 19, 1983, at A1, col. 3.

24. Rodgers et al., *Homogeneous Enzyme Immunoassay for Cannabinoids in Urine*, 24 Clinical Chemistry 95, 97 (1978).

25. *See, e.g.*, O'Connor & Rejent, *EMIT Cannabinoid Assay: Confirmation by RIA and GC/MS*, 5 J. Analytical Toxicology 168 (1981).

26. 32 Morbidity & Mortality Weekly Rep. 469, 470 (1983).

27. Dackis, Pottash, Annitto, & Gold, *Persistence of Urinary Marijuana Levels After Supervised Abstinence*, 139 Am. J. Psychiatry 1196 (1982).

28. *See, e.g.*, Zeidenberg, Bourdon, & Nahas, *Marijuana Intoxication by Passive Inhalation: Documentation by Detection of Urinary Metabolites*, 134 Am. J. Psychiatry 76 (1977); *Passive Inhalation of Marijuana Smoke* (letter to the editor), 250 J.A.M.A. 898 (1983).

29. *Id.* at 100. *See also* National Institute on Drug Abuse, Cannabinoid Assays in Humans (R. Willette ed. 1976).

30. Lewy, *Preemployment Qualitative Urine Toxicology Screening*, 25 J. Occup. Med. 579, 580 (1983).

31. *Id.*

32. *See* Zeese, *Marijuana Urinalysis Tests*, 1 Drug Law Rep. 25, 29 (1983).

33. 29 U.S.C. §706(7)(B) (Supp. IV 1980).

34. 32 Morbidity & Mortality Weekly Rep. 688 (1984); 32 Morbidity & Mortality Weekly Rep. 465 (1983).

35. Cooley & Lubow, *AIDS: An Occupational Hazard?*, 107 J. Am. Dental A. 28, 29 (July 1983).

36. Of AIDS patients, 51% suffer from *Pneumocystis carinii*, 26% have Kaposi's sarcoma, 7% have both *Pneumocystis carinii* and Kaposi's sarcoma, and 16% suffer from other opportunistic infections. *Update on AIDS*, 32 Morbidity & Mortality Weekly Rep. 688 (1984).

37. *Id.; see* Francis, Curran, & Essex, *Epidemic Acquired Immune Deficiency Syndrome: Epidemiologic Evidence for a Transmissible Agent*, 71 J. Nat'l Cancer Inst. 1 (1983); Jaffe et al., *National Case-Control Study of Kaposi's Sarcoma and Pneumocystis Carinii Pneumonia in Homosexual Men: Part 1, Epidemiologic Results*, 99 Annals Internal Med. 145 (1983).

38. *Update on AIDS, supra* note 36.

39. *See, e.g., The Real Epidemic: Fear and Despair*, Time, July 4, 1983, at 56.

40. *Acquired Immunodeficiency Syndrome (AIDS): Precautions for Health-Care Workers and Allied Professionals*, 32 Morbidity & Mortality Weekly Rep. 450 (1983).

41. *The Real Epidemic, supra* note 39.

42. U.S. Department of Health, Education and Welfare, Special Report: Sickle Cell Disease (1976).

43. Va. Code §32-112.19 (1950) (repealed 1973). *See* Damme, *Controlling Genetic Disease Through Law*, 15 U. Cal. Davis L. Rev. 801, 824 (1982).

44. National Sickle Cell Anemia Control Act, 42 U.S.C. §§300b to 300b-5 (1976). *See* Z. Harsanyi & R. Hutton, Genetic Prophecy: Beyond the Double Helix 250 (1981).

45. Ariz. Rev. Stat. Ann. §§36-797.41 to .43 (1974 & Supp. 1975–1982); Cal. Health & Safety Code §§320.5 to 324.5, 325 to 327 (Deering 1982); Colo. Rev. Stat. §§23-21-201 to -204 (1973 & Supp. 1982); Conn. Gen. Stat. Ann. §§10-206 to -210 (West Supp. 1978–1982); D.C. Code Encycl. §32-322 (West Supp. 1978); Ga. Code Ann. §§88-1201.1 to .3 (Supp. 1982); Ill. Ann. Stat. ch. 40, §§204 to 205 (Smith-Hurd Supp. 1982–1983); Ind. Code Ann. §§16-2-5-1 to -9, 20-8.1-7-11, & -14 (Burns 1975 & Supp. 1982); Iowa Code Ann. §§141.1 to .6 (West Supp. 1982–1983); Kan. Stat. Ann. §§65-1,105 to -1,106 (1980); Ky. Rev. Stat. §§403.310 to .340 (Supp. 1982); La. Rev. Stat. Ann. §§40:1299 to :1299.4 (West 1977) and La. Rev. Stat. Ann. §17:170 (West 1982); Mass. Ann. Laws ch. 76, §§15A to 15B (Michie/Law Co-op. 1978); Miss. Code Ann. §§41-24-1 to -5 (1972); N.J. Stat. Ann. §§26:5B-1 to -4 (West Supp. 1982–1983) and N.J. Stat. Ann. §9:14B-1 (West 1976); N.M. Stat. Ann. §24-3-1 (1981); N.Y. Educ. Law §§903 to 904 (McKinney Supp. 1982–1983); N.C. Gen. Stat. §§143B-188 to -196 (1983); Ohio Rev. Code Ann. §3701.131 (Page 1980); S.C. Code Ann. §44-33-10 (Law. Co-op. 1976); Va. Code §§32.1-68 to -69 (1979).

46. Mass. Ann. Laws ch. 76, §15A (Michie/Law Co-op. 1978).

47. Ind. Code Ann. §20-8.1-7-14 (Burns 1975).

48. Ky. Rev. Stat. §402.310 to .340 (Supp. 1982).

49. National Academy of Sciences, Genetic Screening 117 (1975).

50. President's Commission for the Study of Ethical Problems in Medicine and Biomedical and Behavioral Research, Screening and Counseling for Genetic Conditions 21 (1983).

51. National Academy of Sciences, Genetic Screening 126 (1975) (footnotes omitted).

52. Fla. Stat. Ann. §448.075 (West 1981).

53. La. Rev. Stat. Ann. §§23:1001 to :1004 (West Supp. 1983).

54. N.C. Gen. Stat. §95-28.1 (Michie 1981).

55. Statement of Fred Bergman of the National Institute of General Medical Science, *quoted in* Z. Harsanyi & R. Hutton, *supra* note 44, at 158.

56. Stokinger & Scheel, *Hypersusceptibility and Genetic Problems in Occupational Medicine—A Consensus Report*, 15 J. Occup. Med. 564, 572 (1973); Strasser, *Genetic Screening Can Be a Useful Tool to Promote Safety*, Occup. Health & Safety, Jan. 1984, at 29.

57. Severo, *Screening of Blacks by Du Pont Sharpens Debate on Gene Tests*, N.Y. Times, Feb. 4, 1980, at A13, col. 6.

58. *Id.*; Genetic Screening, *supra* note 11, at 246–47 (testimony of Dr. Jeanne Stellman).

59. Z. Harsanyi & R. Hutton, *supra* note 44, at 149–53.

60. Introduction to Proposed Interpretive Guidelines on Employment Discrimination and Reproductive Hazards, 45 Fed. Reg. 7514 (1980), *withdrawn*, 46 Fed. Reg. 3916 (1981).

61. U.S. Department of Health and Human Services, *Health, United States, 1983* (1984), *cited in* 13 OSHR 935–36 (1984).

62. Wash. Post, Nov. 3, 1979, at A6, col. 5, *cited in* Williams, *Firing the Woman to Protect the Fetus: The Reconciliation of Fetal Protection with Employment Opportunity Goals Under Title VII*, 69 Geo. L.J. 641, 647 n.30 (1981).

63. Z. Harsanyi & R. Hutton, *supra* note 44, at 118; Mereson, *Women Workers Are Sterilized or They Lose Their Jobs*, Civil Liberties, July 1982, at 6; Williams, *supra* note 62, at 647–53.

64. *See* American Civil Liberties Union, Women's Rights Project, Comment on Interpretive Guidelines on Employment Discrimination and Reproductive Hazards, at 18 (1980) (unpublished testimony submitted to OSHA).

65. *See* United Steelworkers of America, Comment on Interpretive Guidelines on Employment Discrimination and Reproductive Hazards, at 5 (1980) (unpublished testimony submitted to OSHA).

66. National Research Council Committee on Hearing, Bioacoustics, and Biomechanics, Prenatal Effects of Exposure to High-Level Noise (1983); Schell, *Environmental Noise and Human Prenatal Growth*, 56 Am. J. Physical Anthropology 63 (1981); Westman & Walters, *Noise and Stress: A Comprehensive Approach*, 41 Envtl. Health Perspectives 291, 304 (1981).

67. K. Moore, The Developing Human 139 (2d ed. 1977); Dudgeon, *Infective Causes of Human Malformations*, 32 Brit. Med. Bull. 77 (1976).

68. U.S. Nuclear Regulatory Commission, Regulatory Guide 8.13, Instruction Concerning Prenatal Radiation Exposure (1975).

69. *Christman v. American Cyanamid Co.*, No. 80-0024 (N.D. W. Va. filed Jan. 30, 1980), second amended complaint ¶25, *cited in* Bertin, *Workplace Bias Takes the Form of "Fetal Protectionism,"* Legal Times, Aug. 1, 1983, at 18, 20 n.2.

70. *See* Petchesky, *Workers' Reproductive Hazards and the Politics of Protectionism: An Introduction*, 5 Feminist Studies 233 (1979).

71. "It is much easier to present a case, to show that this woman had a fetus in her and that is the fetus that was injured, than to try to persuade a jury that the father's sperm cell was exposed to a mutagen." Stillman, *A Legal Perspective on*

Workplace Reproductive Hazards, in Women, Work, and Health: Challenges to Corporate Policy 177–78 (D. Walsh & R. Egdahl eds. 1980).

72. *See* Genetic Screening, *supra* note 11, at 273 (testimony of Dr. Bruce Karrh of Du Pont).

73. *See* Sapolsky, *The Political Obstacles to the Control of Cigarette Smoking in the United States*, 5 J. Health Pol., Pol'y & L. 277 (1980).

Chapter 7

1. *See Adair v. United States*, 208 U.S. 161, 172–75 (1908) (union membership). *See also Coppage v. Kansas*, 236 U.S. 1, 12 (1915) (union membership; employer's "liberty of contract" a constitutional right).

2. *See Dillon v. Great Atl. & Pac. Tea Co.*, 43 Md. App. 161, 403 A.2d 406, 407–08 (Ct. Spec. App. 1979).

3. *Odell v. Humble Oil & Ref. Co.*, 201 F.2d 123 (10th Cir.), *cert. denied*, 345 U.S. 941 (1953); *Hinrichs v. Tranquilaire Hosp.*, 352 So. 2d 1130 (Ala. 1977); *Forrer v. Sears, Roebuck & Co.*, 36 Wis. 2d 388, 153 N.W.2d 587 (1967).

4. *Pearson v. Youngstown Sheet & Tube Co.*, 332 F.2d 439 (7th Cir. 1964).

5. *See* Murg & Scharman, *Employment at Will: Do Exceptions Overwhelm the Rule?*, 23 B.C.L. Rev. 329 (1982); Note, *Defining Public Policy Torts in At-Will Dismissal*, 34 Stan. L. Rev. 153 (1981).

6. *See, e.g., Fortune v. National Cash Register Co.*, 373 Mass. 96, 364 N.E.2d 1251 (1977); *Pine River State Bank v. Mettille*, 333 N.W.2d 622 (Minn. 1983); *Monge v. Beebe Rubber Co.*, 114 N.H. 130, 316 A.2d 549 (1974).

7. *See, e.g., Nees v. Hocks*, 272 Or. 210, 536 P.2d 512 (1975); *Harless v. First Nat'l Bank*, 246 S.E.2d 270 (W. Va. 1978).

8. A minority of courts have used the theory that wrongful discharge amounts to the intentional infliction of emotional distress. *See, e.g., Alcorn v. Anbro Eng'r, Inc.*, 2 Cal. 3d 493, 468 P.2d 216, 86 Cal. Rptr. 88, 2 FEP Cases 712 (1970); *Agis v. Howard Johnson Co.*, 371 Mass. 140, 355 N.E.2d 315 (1976).

9. *Frampton v. Central Ind. Gas Co.*, 260 Ind. 249, 297 N.E.2d 425 (1973); *Sventko v. Kroger Co.*, 69 Mich. App. 644, 245 N.W.2d 151 (1976); *Brown v. Transcon Lines*, 284 Or. 597, 588 P.2d 1087 (1978).

10. *Reuther v. Fowler & Williams, Inc.*, 255 Pa. Super. 28, 386 A.2d 119 (1978).

11. *Petermann v. Teamsters, Local 396*, 174 Cal. App. 2d 184, 344 P.2d 25, 44 LRRM 2968 (1959).

12. *Trombetta v. Detroit, T. & I. R.R.*, 81 Mich. App. 489, 265 N.W.2d 385 (1978).

13. *Harless v. First Nat'l Bank*, 246 S.E.2d 270 (W. Va. 1978).

14. *Monge v. Beebe Rubber Co.*, 114 N.H. 130, 316 A.2d 549 (1974).

15. *Pierce v. Ortho Pharmaceutical Corp.*, 166 N.J. Super. 335, 399 A.2d 1023 (App. Div. 1979).

16. *Cloutier v. Great Atl. & Pac. Tea Co.*, 121 N.H. 915, 436 A.2d 1140 (1981).

17. *Walsh v. Consolidated Freightways, Inc.*, 278 Or. 347, 563 P.2d 1205 (1977).

18. *Perks v. Firestone Tire & Rubber Co.*, 611 F.2d 1363, 1366 (3d Cir. 1979). *But see Bruffett v. Warner Communs., Inc.*, 692 F.2d 910 (3d Cir. 1982) (no cause of action for wrongful discharge based on handicap).

19. In 1980, of a total labor force of 106,500,000, there were 21,784,000 union members and 15,971,000 public employees. U.S. Bureau of the Census, De-

partment of Commerce, Statistical Abstract of the United States: 1980, at 318 (table 520) (government employment), 394 (table 652) (total labor force), and 429 (table 714) (union membership).

20. *See Pearson v. Youngstown Sheet & Tube Co.*, 332 F.2d 439 (7th Cir. 1964); *Munhallon v. Pennsylvania R.R.*, 180 F. Supp. 669, 45 LRRM 2619 (N.D. Ohio 1960); *Citizens Home Ins. Co. v. Glisson*, 191 Va. 582, 61 S.E.2d 859 (1950).

21. *Cameron v. J. C. Lawrence Leather Co.*, 342 S.W.2d 65 (Tenn. App. 1960).

22. 1979 Indus. Rel. Law Rep. 89.

23. W. Prosser, Law of Torts 256 (4th ed. 1971).

24. *Woodward Iron Co. v. Craig*, 256 Ala. 37, 53 So. 2d 586 (1951); *Ransom v. Haner*, 362 P.2d 282 (Alaska 1961); *Robles v. Preciado*, 52 Ariz. 113, 79 P.2d 504 (1938); *Norris v. Daves*, 251 Ark. 101, 470 S.W.2d 937 (1971); *Alber v. Owens*, 66 Cal. 2d 790, 427 P.2d 781, 59 Cal. Rptr. 117 (1967); *Williams v. Sleepy Hollow Mining Co.*, 37 Colo. 62, 86 P. 337 (1906); *Rescigno v. Rosner*, 124 Conn. 253, 198 A. 751 (1938); *Binsau v. Garstin*, 54 Del. 423, 177 A.2d 636 (1962); *Decatur v. Chas. H. Thompkins Co.*, 25 F.2d 526 (D.C. Cir. 1928); *Hicks v. Kemp*, 79 So. 2d 696 (Fla. 1955); *Holland v. McRae Oil & Fertilizer Co.*, 134 Ga. 678, 68 S.E. 555 (1910); *Michel v. Valdastri, Ltd.*, 59 Hawaii 53, 575 P.2d 1299 (1978); *Deshazer v. Tompkins*, 89 Idaho 347, 404 P.2d 604 (1965); *Mueller v. Elm Park Hotel Co.*, 398 Ill. 60, 75 N.E.2d 314 (1947); *U.S. Cement Co. v. Cooper*, 172 Ind. 599, 88 N.E. 69 (1909); *Davis v. Crook*, 261 N.W.2d 500 (Iowa 1978); *Uhlrig v. Shortt*, 194 Kan. 68, 397 P.2d 321 (1964); *Burdette v. Thompson*, 420 S.W.2d 548 (Ky. 1967); *Cambre v. White Castle Lumber Co.*, 144 La. 699, 81 So. 256 (1919); *Erickson v. Monson Consol. Slate Co.*, 100 Me. 107, 60 A. 708 (1905); *Harrison v. Harrison*, 264 Md. 184, 285 A.2d 590 (1972); *Reidy v. Crompton & Knowles Loom Works*, 318 Mass. 135, 60 N.E.2d 589 (1945); *Dehtiar v. Mietkowski*, 372 Mich. 527, 127 N.W.2d 388 (1964); *Baumgartner v. Holslin*, 236 Minn. 325, 52 N.W.2d 763 (1952); *Long v. Woollard*, 249 Miss. 722, 163 So. 2d 698 (1964); *Hightower v. Edwards*, 445 S.W.2d 273 (Mo. 1969); *Pollard v. Todd*, 148 Mont. 171, 418 P.2d 869 (1966); *Lownes v. Furman*, 161 Neb. 57, 71 N.W.2d 661 (1955); *Pershing Quicksilver Co. v. Thiers*, 62 Nev. 382, 152 P.2d 432 (1944); *Moore v. Morse & Malloy Shoe Co.*, 89 N.H. 332, 197 A. 707 (1938); *Clayton v. Ainsworth*, 122 N.J.L. 160, 4 A.2d 274 (1939); *Padilla v. Winsor*, 67 N.M. 267, 354 P.2d 740 (1960); *Maleeny v. Standard Shipbuilding Corp.*, 237 N.Y. 250, 142 N.E. 602 (1923); *Jones v. Douglas Aircraft Co.*, 251 N.C. 832, 112 S.E.2d 257 (1960); *Abelstad v. Johnson*, 41 N.D. 399, 170 N.W. 619 (1919); *Giovinale v. Republic Steel Corp.*, 151 Ohio St. 161, 84 N.E.2d 904 (1949); *McClendon v. McCall*, 489 P.2d 756 (Okla. 1971); *Concannon v. Oregon Portland Cement Co.*, 252 Or. 1, 447 P.2d 290 (1968); *Jerdon v. Sirulnik*, 400 Pa. 423, 162 A.2d 202 (1960); *Faltinali v. Great Atl. & Pac. Tea Co.*, 55 R.I. 438, 182 A. 605 (1936); *Morgan v. Roper*, 250 S.C. 280, 157 S.E.2d 572 (1967); *Smith v. Community Co-Op Ass'n*, 87 S.D. 440, 209 N.W.2d 891 (1973); *Virginia Iron, Coal & Coke Co. v. Hamilton*, 107 Tenn. 705, 65 S.W. 401 (1901); *Farley v. MM Cattle Co.*, 529 S.W.2d 751 (Tex. 1975); *Speight v. Rocky Mountain Bell Tel. Co.*, 36 Utah 483, 107 P. 742 (1910); *Landing v. Town of Fairlee*, 112 Vt. 127, 22 A.2d 179 (1941); *Colonna Shipyard v. Bland*, 150 Va. 349, 143 S.E. 729 (1928); *Guy v. Northwest Bible Coll.*, 64 Wash. 2d 116, 390 P.2d 708 (1964); *Bates v. Sirk*, 230 S.E.2d 738 (W. Va. 1976); *Gordon v. Schultz Savo Stores, Inc.*, 54 Wis. 2d 692, 196 N.W.2d 633 (1972); *Mellor v. Ten Sleep Cattle Co.*, 550 P.2d 500 (Wyo. 1976).

25. Prosser, *supra* note 23, at 526–30.

26. *Id.*

27. For a detailed discussion of workers' compensation, *see* Chapter 12.

28. 145 N.J. Super. 516, 368 A.2d 408 (Ch. Div. 1976).

29. *Smith v. Western Elec. Co.*, 643 S.W.2d 10, 10 OSHC 2001 (Mo. Ct. App. 1982).

30. *Federal Employees for Non-Smokers' Rights v. United States*, 446 F. Supp. 181, 6 OSHC 1407 (D.D.C. 1978), *aff'd*, 598 F.2d 310, 7 OSHC 1634 (D.C. Cir.), *cert. denied*, 444 U.S. 926 (1979).

31. 462 A.2d 10 (D.C. 1983).

32. *Id.* at 15.

33. 545 S.W.2d 45 (Tex. Civ. App. 1977).

34. *Id.* at 47.

35. 639 S.W.2d 192 (Mo. App. 1982).

36. 41 N.J. 555, 197 A.2d 857 (1964).

37. *See Shelton v. Tucker*, 364 U.S. 479 (1960) (school teachers need not disclose organizations to which they belong); *Shuman v. Philadelphia*, 470 F. Supp. 449, 461 (E.D. Pa. 1979) (inquiry into police officer's private sexual activities violated right of privacy); *Government Employees AFGE, Local 421 v. Schlesinger*, 443 F. Supp. 431 (D.D.C. 1978) (employees need not disclose associations of themselves and members of their family). *See also* Memorandum of Alan K. Campbell, Director of Office of Personnel Management (May 12, 1980) (advising federal agencies not to inquire about conduct of applicants and employees that is unrelated to the job, based on Civil Service Reform Act of 1978, 5 U.S.C. §2302(b)(10) (Supp. II 1978)).

38. 385 Mass. 300, 431 N.E.2d 908 (1982).

39. 385 Mass. at ____, 431 N.E.2d at 910.

40. 385 Mass. at ____, 431 N.E.2d at 914.

41. *Spencer v. General Tel. Co.*, 551 F. Supp. 896 (M.D. Pa. 1982).

42. *Ohio Brass Co.*, 261 NLRB No. 18, 110 LRRM 1009 (1982).

43. 117 Ariz. 507, 573 P.2d 907 (Ct. App. 1977).

44. 188 Conn. 44, 448 A.2d 801 (1982).

45. Md. Ann. Code art. 100, §95A (1979).

46. W. Va. Code §21-3-17 (1981).

47. 525 F. Supp. 795 (N.D.N.Y. 1981).

48. *Id.* at 797.

49. *Williams Pipe Line Co.*, 78 LA 617 (Moore, 1982).

50. *Welshhons v. Sivyer Steel Corp.*, 674 F.2d 748, 110 LRRM 2311 (8th Cir. 1982).

51. 29 C.F.R. §1910.1029(j)(l)(iii) (1983).

52. *See* section 11.6.

53. Vinyl chloride, 29 C.F.R. §1910.1017(k)(4) (1983); inorganic arsenic, 29 C.F.R. §1910.1018(n)(6)(D) (1983); inorganic lead, 29 C.F.R. §1910.1025 (j)(3)(v) (1983); coke oven emissions, 29 C.F.R. §1910.1029(j)(5)(iii) (1983); cotton dust, 29 C.F.R. §1910.1043(h)(5)(i) (1983); DBCP, 29 C.F.R. §1910.1044(m)(5)(i) (1983); acrylonitrile, 29 C.F.R. §1910.1045(n)(6)(iii) (1983).

54. OSHA Access to Employee Exposure and Medical Records Standard, 45 Fed. Reg. 35,225 (1980).

55. A. Freedman, Industry Response to Health Risk 17–21 (1981) (citing study by Linowes).

56. *See* section 12.5.

57. Mass. Ann. Laws ch. 149, §19A (1976).

58. *See* Note, *Occupational Health Risks and the Worker's Right to Know*, 90 Yale L.J. 1792 (1981).

59. 48 Fed. Reg. 53,280 (1983), *to be codified at* 29 C.F.R. §1910.1200.

60. By November 25, 1985, chemical manufacturers must complete labeling of containers and provide material safety data sheets to manufacturers. By May 27, 1986, all employers must be in compliance with all provisions of the standard.

61. 1983 Alaska Sess. Laws ch. 93; Cal. Lab. Code §6408 (Deering 1976); Conn. Gen. Stat. Ann. §31-40c (West Supp. 1983-1984); 1983 Ill. Legis. Serv. 1577 (West); Me. Rev. Stat. Ann. tit. 26, §§1701 to 1707 (West Supp. 1982-1983); Mass. Ann. Laws ch. 149, §§142A to 142G (Michie/Law. Co-op. 1976 & Supp. 1983); Mich. Stat. Ann. §17.50(11) (Callaghan 1982); 1983 Minn. Laws 2312 (West); 1983 N.H. Laws ch. 466; 1983 N.J. Sess. Law Serv. 1694 (West); N.Y. Lab. Law, §§875 to 883 (McKinney Supp. 1982-83); Or. Gen. Occup. Health Regs. 22-015 (1981); R.I. Gen. Laws §§28-21-1 to -21-22 (Michie Supp. 1983); Wash. Rev. Code Ann. §49.17.220(3) (Supp. 1983-1984); W. Va. Code §21-3-18 (1981); Wis. Stat. Ann. §101.58 to .599 (West Supp. 1982-1983). In Louisiana, there is a right of access to exposure records only. La. Rev. Stat. Ann. §23:1126 (West Supp. 1983).

62. *See generally* R. Druley & G. Ordway, The Toxic Substances Control Act, Ch. 7 (Rev. ed. 1981).

63. 40 C.F.R. Part 717 (1983); 48 Fed. Reg. 38,178 (1983).

64. Warshaw, *Confidentiality Versus the Need to Know*, 18 J. Occup. Med. 534, 535 (1976).

65. OSHA Access to Exposure and Medical Records Standard, Preamble, 45 Fed. Reg. 35,223-25 (1980).

66. A. Freedman, *supra* note 55, at 17; Roberts, *Mandatory vs. Voluntary Medical Examinations in Industry*, 30 Archives Envtl. Health 205, 207 (1975).

67. 45 Fed. Reg. 35,212 (1980), *codified at* 29 C.F.R. §1910.20 (1983).

68. 45 Fed. Reg. at 35,219-22 (1980).

69. Conn. Gen. Stat. Ann. §31-128c (West Supp. 1983-1984); Me. Rev. Stat. Ann. tit. 26, §631 (Supp. 1982-1983); Mass. Ann. Laws ch. 149, §19A (1976); Ohio Rev. Code Ann. §4113.23 (Page 1980); Wis. Stat. Ann. §103.13 (West Supp. 1982-1983).

70. American Occupational Medical Association Code of Ethical Conduct, Principle 7 (1976).

71. OSHA Access to Employee Exposure and Medical Records Standard, 45 Fed. Reg. at 35,242-43. *See generally The Privacy Commission Recommendations on Employee Access*, Individual Rights in the Corporation (A. Westin ed. 1980); Annas, *Legal Aspects of Confidentiality in the Occupational Setting*, 18 J. Occup. Med. 537 (1976); Reinert, *Federal Protection of Employment Record Privacy*, 18 Harv. J. on Legis. 207 (1981); *Controversy in Medicine: Access to Employee Health Records*, 242 J.A.M.A. 777 (1979).

72. *See* Note, *Privacy in Personal Medical Information: A Diagnosis*, 33 U. Fla. L. Rev. 394, 395 n.7 (1981). *See also* Boyer, *Computerized Medical Records and the Right to Privacy*, 25 Buffalo L. Rev. 37 (1975); Mironi, *The Confidentiality of Personnel Records: A Legal and Ethical View*, 25 Lab. L.J. 270 (1974).

73. Report of the Privacy Protection Study Commission, App. III, at 99 (1977).

74. *See* Subcommittee on Labor–Management Relations, House Committee on Education and Labor, 96th Cong., 2d Sess., Pressures in Today's Workplace 6 (Comm. Print 1980); Henigson, *The Oil Drilling Blacklists*, Dallas Times Herald, Nov. 30, 1981.

75. *Drake v. Covington County Bd. of Educ.*, 371 F. Supp. 974 (M.D. Ala. 1974).

76. *Hammonds v. Aetna Cas. & Surety Co.*, 243 F. Supp. 793 (N.D. Ohio 1965).

77. *See* Note, *Privacy in Personal Medical Information: A Diagnosis*, 33 U. Fla. L. Rev. 394 (1981).

78. *Doe v. Roe*, 93 Misc. 2d 201, 400 N.Y.S.2d 668 (Sup. Ct. 1977).

79. Cal. Civ. Code Ann. §§56 to 56.37 (Deering Supp. 1983).

80. *Id.* §56.20(a), (c).

81. *General Motors Corp. v. Director of NIOSH*, 636 F.2d 163, 9 OSHC 1139 (6th Cir. 1980), *cert. denied*, 454 U.S. 877, 10 OSHC 1032 (1981); *United States v. Westinghouse Elec. Corp.*, 638 F.2d 570, 8 OSHC 2131 (3d Cir. 1980).

82. *West Point Pepperell, Inc.*, 9 OSHC 1784 (1981).

Chapter 8

1. S. Rep. 91-1282, 91st Cong., 2d Sess. at 10-11 (1970).

2. 599 F.2d 622, 7 OSHC 1507 (5th Cir. 1979).

3. 581 F.2d 493, 6 OSHC 1959 (5th Cir. 1978), *aff'd sub nom. Industrial Union Department v. American Petrol. Inst.*, 448 U.S. 607, 8 OSHC 1581 (1980).

4. 599 F.2d at 625, 7 OSHC at 1509.

5. 647 F.2d 1189, 8 OSHC 1810 (D.C. Cir. 1980), *cert. denied sub nom. Lead Indus. Ass'n, Inc. v. Donovan*, 453 U.S. 913 (1981).

6. *See* section 1.1.

7. 29 C.F.R. §1910.1003 to .1016 (1983).

8. *Id.* §1910.1003(g)(1)(i).

9. OSHA Instruction STD 1-23.4(1980), 1 OSHR Ref. File 21:8212.

10. *See* section 1.1.

11. 29 C.F.R. Part 1977 (1983).

12. *See, e.g., Whirlpool Corp. v. Marshall*, 445 U.S. 1, 8 OSHC 1001 (1980).

13. *Taylor v. Brighton Corp.*, 616 F.2d 256, 8 OSHC 1010 (6th Cir. 1980).

14. 29 C.F.R. §1977.22 (1983).

15. *Id.* §1977.5(b).

16. 29 C.F.R. §1910.1017(k)(5) (1983).

17. *Id.* §1910.1001(d)(2)(iv)(c).

18. *Id.* §1910.1025(k).

19. 647 F.2d 1189 (D.C. Cir. 1980), *cert. denied sub nom. Lead Indus. Ass'n, Inc. v. Donovan*, 453 U.S. 913, 11 OSHC 1264 (1981).

20. 647 F.2d at 1236, 8 OSHC at 1840 (emphasis in original).

21. 452 U.S. 490, 9 OSHC 1913 (1981).

22. *Id.* at 540, 9 OSHC at 1932.

23. 30 U.S.C. §843 (b) (1976); 30 C.F.R. §90.3 (1983). *Cf. Matala v. Consolidation Coal Co.*, 647 F.2d 427, 2 MSHC 1265 (4th Cir. 1981) (transferred miner not entitled to receive pay increases given to employees in his pretransfer classification subsequent to his transfer).

24. *See* section 11.4.

25. *See* Note, *Occupationally-Induced Cancer Susceptibility: Regulating the Risk*, 96 Harv. L. Rev. 697 (1983).

26. *Researcher Sees Litigation as Impediment to Monitoring*, 12 OSHR 959 (1983).

27. *See* section 12.5.

28. For a further discussion of OSHA rulemaking, *see* M. Rothstein, Occupational Safety and Health Law ch. 4 (2d ed. 1983).

29. American Conference of Governmental Industrial Hygienists, Threshold Limit Values for Chemical Substances in the Work Environment 2 (1983).

30. 448 U.S. 607, 8 OSHC 1586 (1980).

31. 452 U.S. 490, 9 OSHC 1913 (1981).

31a. 40 Fed. Reg. 32,270 (1975).

32. 448 U.S. at 658, 8 OSHC at 1604.

33. 647 F.2d 1189, 1256–59, 8 OSHC 1810, 1856–58 (D.C. Cir. 1980), *cert. denied sub nom. Lead Indus. Ass'n, Inc. v. Donovan*, 453 U.S. 913, 11 OSHC 1264 (1981).

34. *See* M. Rothstein, *supra* note 28, §145.

35. 489 F.2d 1257, 1265, 1267, 10 OSHC 1422, 1426, 1428 (D.C. Cir. 1973).

36. *Usery v. Marquette Cement Mfg. Co.*, 568 F.2d 902, 905 n.5, 5 OSHC 1793, 1794 n.5 (2d Cir. 1977).

37. 9 OSHC 1596, 1599, 1605 (1981), *petition for review filed*, No. 81-1687 (D.C. Cir. June 22, 1981).

38. 45 Fed. Reg. 35,212 (1980), *codified at* 29 C.F.R. §1910.20 (1983).

39. 657 F.2d 777 (5th Cir. 1981).

40. *Louisiana Chem. Ass'n v. Bingham*, 550 F. Supp. 1136, 10 OSHC 2113 (W.D. La. 1982).

41. *Id.* at 1139, 10 OSHC at 2115.

42. 47 Fed. Reg. 30,420 (1982).

Chapter 9

1. Ala. Code §§21-7-1, 21-7-8 (1975) (state employees only); Alaska Stat. §18.80.220(a)(1) (1981); Cal. Gov't Code §§1413(h), 1420(a), 1432.5 (Deering Supp. 1981); Colo. Rev. Stat. §24-34-801 (1982); Conn. Gen. Stat. §§1-1f, 46a -60 (1981); D.C. Code Ann. §6-1705 (1981); Fla. Const. art. I, §2; Fla. Stat. Ann. §413.08(3) (1979); Ga. Code Ann. §§66-501 to -506 (Supp. 1982); Hawaii Rev. Stat. §§378-1(7), -2, -9 (1976 & Supp. 1980); Idaho Code §§56-701, -707 (1976) (state employees only); Ill. Ann. Stat. ch. 68, §§1-102(A), -103(I), 2-102 (Smith-Hurd Supp. 1981); Ind. Code §§22-9-11 to -13 (1980); Iowa Code Ann. §§601A.2(11), .6(1) (1975); Kan. Stat. §§44-1002(j), -1009(a)(1) (1981); Ky. Rev. Stat. §§207.130(2), .150(1) (1982); La. Rev. Stat. Ann. §§2251 to 2256 (West 1982); Me. Rev. Stat. Ann. tit. 5, §§4553.7-A, 4572 (West 1979); Md. Ann. Code art. 49B, §§49B-15(g), -16 (1957 & 1979); Mass. Ann. Laws ch. 149, §24K (Michie/Law Co-op 1976); Mich. Comp. Laws §§37.1103, .1202 (1979); Minn. Stat. §§363.01(25), .03(2) (1980); Miss. Code Ann. §43-6-15 (1981) (state employees only); Mo. Code State Regs. tit. 4, div. 180, ch. 3; Mont. Code Ann. §§49-1-102, -2-101(13) and (16), -2-303 (1981); Neb. Rev. Stat. §§48-1102(8), -1104, -1108(1) (1978); Nev. Rev. Stat. §§613.330, .350(1) and (2) (1979); N.D. Cent. Code §14-02.4-01 to -21 (1983); N.H. Rev. Stat. Ann. §§354-A:3(13), -A:8 (Supp.

1981); N.J. Stat. Ann. §§10:5-4.1, -5(q) (West Supp. 1981); N.M. Stat. Ann. §§28-10-9 to -12 (1978); N.Y. Exec. Law §§292(21), 296(1) (McKinney 1982); N.C. Gen. Stat. §128-15.3 (1981); Ohio Rev. Code Ann. §§4112.01(13), .02(A) (1980); Okla. Stat. tit. 25, §§1301 to -10 (1981); Or. Rev. Stat. §§659.400(2), .425 (1981); Pa. Stat. Ann. tit. 43, §§954(p), 955 (Purdon Supp. 1981); R.I. Gen. Laws §§28-5-6(H), 28-5-7 (1979); 1983 S.C. Acts _____; S.D. Codified Laws Ann. §3-6A-15 (1980); Tenn. Code Ann. §8-50-103 (1980); Tex. Hum. Res. Code Ann. §121.003 (Vernon 1980); Utah Code Ann. §34.35-6 (Allen Smith Supp. 1981); Va. Code §40.1-28.7 (1981); Vt. Stat. Ann. tit 21, §495 (Supp. 1982); Wash. Rev. Code §49.60.180 (1981); W. Va. Code §5-11-2 (Michie Supp. 1982); Wis. Stat. §§111.32(5)(a), (f) (1979–80).

2. *Uncertainty in the Figures*, N.Y. Times, Feb. 13, 1977, §4 at 8, col. 1, *cited in* Wolff, *Protecting the Disabled Minority: Rights and Remedies under Sections 503 and 504 of the Rehabilitation Act of 1973*, 22 St. Louis U.L.J. 25, 30 (1978).

3. *E.g.*, *OFCCP v. E.E. Black, Ltd.*, 19 FEP Cases 1624 (U.S. Dep't of Labor 1979).

4. *Davis v. United Airlines, Inc.*, 662 F.2d 120, 26 FEP Cases 1527 (2d Cir. 1981), *cert. denied*, 456 U.S. 965, 28 FEP Cases 1200 (1982); *Beam v. Sun Shipbuilding & Drydock Co.*, 679 F.2d 1077 (3d Cir. 1982); *Rogers v. Frito-Lay, Inc.*, 611 F.2d 1074, 22 FEP Cases 16 (5th Cir. 1979), *cert. denied sub nom. Moon v. Roadway Express, Inc.*, 449 U.S. 889, 23 FEP Cases 1668 (1980); *Hoopes v. Equifax, Inc.*, 611 F.2d 134, 22 FEP Cases 957 (6th Cir. 1979); *Simpson v. Reynolds Metals Co.*, 629 F.2d 1226, 23 FEP Cases 868 (7th Cir. 1980); *Simon v. St. Louis County*, 656 F.2d 316, 26 FEP Cases 1003 (8th Cir. 1981); *Fisher v. City of Tucson*, 663 F.2d 861, 27 FEP Cases 892 (9th Cir. 1981); *Coleman v. Darden*, 595 F.2d 533, 19 FEP Cases 137 (10th Cir.), *cert. denied*, 444 U.S. 927, 21 FEP Cases 96 (1979).

5. *"Hire the Handicapped": Now More Than Just A Slogan*, St. Louis Post-Dispatch, May 15, 1977, at B6, *cited in* Wolff, *supra* note 2, at 26 n.9.

6. 45 C.F.R. §85.5 (1983).

7. *See University of Texas v. Camenisch*, 450 U.S. 390 (1981); *Southeastern Commun. College v. Davis*, 442 U.S. 397 (1980).

8. *Leary v. Crapsey*, 566 F.2d 863 (2d Cir. 1977); *Kampmeier v. Nyquist*, 553 F.2d 296 (2d Cir. 1977); *NAACP v. Medical Center, Inc.*, 599 F.2d 1247 (3d Cir. 1979); *Doe v. Colautti*, 592 F.2d 704 (3d Cir. 1978); *Davis v. Southeastern Commun. College*, 574 F.2d 1158 (4th Cir. 1978), *rev'd on other grounds*, 442 U.S. 397 (1979); *Camenisch v. University of Texas*, 616 F.2d 127 (5th Cir. 1980), *vacated and remanded as moot*, 451 U.S. 390 (1981); *Rogers v. Frito-Lay, Inc.*, 611 F.2d 1074, 22 FEP Cases 16 (5th Cir.), *cert. denied sub nom. Moon v. Roadway Express, Inc.*, 449 U.S. 889, 23 FEP Cases 1668 (1980); *Lloyd v. Regional Transp. Auth.*, 548 F.2d 1277 (7th Cir. 1977); *United Handicapped Fed'n v. Andre*, 558 F.2d 413 (8th Cir. 1977); *Kling v. County of Los Angeles*, 633 F.2d 876 (9th Cir. 1980); *Pushkin v. Regents of University of Colorado*, 658 F.2d 1372 (10th Cir. 1981).

9. *See Pushkin v. Regents of University of Colorado*, 658 F.2d 1372 (10th Cir. 1981); *Swan v. Stoneman*, 635 F.2d 97 (2d Cir. 1980); *Kling v. County of Los Angeles*, 633 F.2d 876 (9th Cir. 1980).

10. *Scanlon v. Atascacero State Hosp.*, 677 F.2d 1271, 28 FEP Cases 1695 (9th Cir. 1982); *Doyle v. University of Alabama in Birmingham*, 680 F.2d 1323, 29 FEP Cases 777 (11th Cir. 1982); *United States v. Cabrini Med. Center*, 639 F.2d 908,

24 FEP Cases 1688 (2d Cir. 1981); *Brown v. Sibley*, 650 F.2d 760, 26 FEP Cases 1008 (5th Cir. 1981); *Simpson v. Reynolds Metals Co.*, 629 F.2d 1226, 23 FEP Cases 868 (7th Cir. 1980); *Carmi v. Metropolitan St. Louis Sewer Dist.*, 620 F.2d 672, 22 FEP Cases 1107 (8th Cir.), *cert. denied*, 449 U.S. 892, 23 FEP Cases 1668 (1980); *Trageser v. Libbie Rehab. Center*, 590 F.2d 87, 18 FEP Cases 1141 (4th Cir. 1978), *cert. denied*, 442 U.S. 947, 19 FEP Cases 1680 (1979).

11. *See LeStrange v. Consolidated Rail Corp.*, 687 F.2d 767, 29 FEP Cases 1150 (3d Cir. 1982), *cert. granted sub nom. Consolidated Rail Corp. v. Darrone*, 103 S. Ct. 1181 (1983).

12. 442 U.S. 397 (1979).

13. *Id. at* 410.

14. 45 C.F.R. §§84.14, 85.55 (1983).

15. 41 C.F.R. §60-741.6 (1983).

16. 444 F.2d 791, 3 FEP Cases 653 (4th Cir.), *cert. dismissed under Rule 60*, 404 U.S. 1006 (1971).

17. 444 F.2d at 798 (footnote omitted).

18. N.J. Stat. Ann. §10:5-5(y) (West Supp. 1982).

19. Fla. Stat. Ann. tit. 30, §448.075 (West 1981); La. Rev. Stat. Ann. §§23:1001 to :1004 (West Supp. 1983); N.C. Gen. Stat. §95-28.1 (Michie 1981).

20. 19 FEP Cases 1624 (U.S. Dep't of Labor 1979).

21. *Id.* at 1631 (footnote omitted).

22. *E.E. Black, Ltd. v. Donovan*, 497 F. Supp. 1088, 23 FEP Cases 1253 (D. Hawaii 1980).

23. *E.E. Black, Ltd. v. Donovan*, 26 FEP Cases 1183 (D. Hawaii 1981).

24. 549 F. Supp. 85, 29 FEP Cases 1197 (W.D. Wash. 1982).

25. *Id.* at 87.

26. *Id.*

27. La. Rev. Stat. Ann. tit. 46, §2253(2) (West 1981).

28. *American Nat'l Ins. Co. v. Fair Empl. & Housing Comm'n*, 32 Cal. 3d 603, 651 P.2d 1151, 186 Cal. Rptr. 345 (1982).

29. *Shelby Township Fire Dep't v. Shields*, 115 Mich. App. 98, 320 N.W.2d 306 (1982).

30. *Goldsmith v. New York Psychoanalytic Inst.*, 73 A.D.2d 16, 425 N.Y.S.2d 561 (1980).

31. *Burgess v. Joseph Schlitz Brewing Co.*, 298 N.C. 520, 259 S.E.2d 248, 21 FEP Cases 379 (Ct. App. 1979).

32. *Pennsylvania State Police v. Pennsylvania Hum. Rels. Comm'n*, 72 Pa. Commw. 520, 456 A.2d 584 (1983).

33. *Holland v. Boeing Co.*, 18 FEP Cases 37 (Wash. 1978).

34. *Dairy Equip. Co. v. Department of Indus., Lab. & Hum. Rels.*, 95 Wis. 2d 319, 290 N.W.2d 330 (1980).

35. *Connecticut Gen'l Life Ins. Co. v. Department of Indus., Lab. & Hum. Rels.*, 13 FEP Cases 1811 (Wis. Cir. Ct. 1976).

36. *Journal Co. v. Department of Indus., Lab. & Hum. Rels.*, 13 FEP Cases 1655 (Wis. Cir. Ct. 1976).

37. *J. C. Penney Co. v. Department of Indus., Lab. & Hum. Rels.*, 12 FEP Cases 1109 (Wis. Cir. Ct. 1976).

38. *Lyons v. Heritage House Restaurants, Inc.*, 89 Ill. 2d 163, 432 N.E.2d 270 (1982).

39. *Advocates for Handicapped v. Sears, Roebuck & Co.*, 67 Ill. App. 3d 512, 385 N.E.2d 39, 21 FEP Cases 506 (1978), *cert. denied*, 444 U.S. 981, 21 FEP Cases 604 (1979).

40. *Philadelphia Elec. Co. v. Commonwealth*, 70 Pa. Commw. 343, 448 A.2d 701 (1982).

41. *Providence Journal Co. v. Mason*, 116 R.I. 614, 359 A.2d 682, 13 FEP Cases 385 (1976).

42. *Greene v. Union Pac. R.R.*, 548 F. Supp. 3 (W.D. Wash. 1981).

43. *American Motors Corp. v. Labor & Indus. Rev. Comm'n*, 338 N.W.2d 518 (Wis. Cir. Ct. 1983).

44. S. Rep. No. 318, 93d Cong., 1st Sess., *reprinted in* 1973 U.S. Code Cong. & Ad. News 2078, 2092.

45. *Cf. Barnes v. Washington Natural Gas Co.*, 22 Wash. App. 576, 591 P.2d 461 (1979) (individual discharged because of erroneous belief he had epilepsy *is* a handicapped person under the state law). *See also Kirby v. Illinois Cent. Gulf R.R.*, ____ Ill. App. 3d ____, 454 N.E.2d 816 (1983).

46. 497 F. Supp. at 1104.

47. *Id.*

48. 422 U.S. 405, 10 FEP Cases 1181 (1975).

49. *Id.* at 432, *quoting* 29 C.F.R. §1607.4(c).

50. *Treadwell v. Alexander*, 27 FEP Cases 543 (S.D. Ga. 1981), *aff'd*, 707 F.2d 473, 32 FEP Cases 62 (11th Cir. 1983).

51. *Clark v. Milwaukee Road*, 87 Wash. 2d 802, 557 P.2d 307 (1976).

52. *High v. Power Flame Div., Inc.*, 29 EPD ¶ 32,866 (Kan. Dist. Ct. 1982).

53. *Boynton Cab Co. v. Department of Indus., Lab. & Hum. Rels.*, 18 FEP Cases 841 (Wis. Cir. Ct. 1978) (employer's defense rejected).

54. *National R.R. Passenger Corp. (AMTRAK) v. Commonwealth*, 70 Pa. Commw. 62, 452 A.2d 301 (1982). *Cf. Norcross v. Sneed*, 573 F. Supp. 533 (W.D. Ark. 1983) (legally blind applicant rejected for job as librarian).

55. 21 FEP Cases 1733 (Wis. Cir. Ct. 1977).

56. 185 N.J. Super. 109, 447 A.2d 589 (App. Div. 1982).

57. 694 F.2d 619, 30 FEP Cases 875 (9th Cir. 1982).

58. *Id.* at 622 (citation omitted) (ellipses in original).

59. *Id.* at 623 n.3.

60. *Chicago, M., St. P. & Pac. R.R. v. Department of Indus., Lab. & Hum. Rels.*, 62 Wis. 2d 392, 215 N.W.2d 443, 8 FEP Cases 938 (1974).

61. *Id. But see Lewis v. Remmele Eng'g, Inc.*, 314 N.W.2d 1, 29 FEP Cases 576 (Minn. 1981) (safety concerns justified employer's refusal to hire an epileptic machinist).

62. *Bucyrus-Erie Co. v. Department of Indus., Lab. & Hum. Rels.*, 90 Wis. 2d 408, 280 N.W.2d 142, 22 FEP Cases 563 (1979).

63. *Chrysler Outboard Corp. v. Department of Indus., Lab. & Hum. Rels.*, 14 FEP Cases 344 (Wis. Cir. Ct. 1976).

64. *Chicago, M., St. P. & Pac. R.R. v. Dep't of Indus., Lab. & Hum. Rels.*, 8 FEP Cases 937 (Wis. Cir. Ct. 1971), *aff'd as modified*, 62 Wis. 2d 392, 215 N.W.2d 443, 8 FEP Cases 938 (1974).

65. *In re Montgomery Ward & Co.*, 280 Or. 163, 570 P.2d 76, 16 FEP Cases 80 (1977).

66. *Accord, Pacific Motor Trucking Co. v. Bureau of Labor & Indus.*, 64 Or. App. 361, 668 P.2d 446 (1983) (back x-ray of truck driver revealed spondylolisthesis).

67. 121 Cal. App. 3d 791, 175 Cal. Rptr. 548, 28 FEP Cases 1351 (1981).

68. *Id.* at 800, 175 Cal. Rptr. at 552.

69. *Westinghouse Elec. Corp. v. State Div. of Hum. Rts.*, 63 A.D.2d 170, 406 N.Y.S.2d 912, 30 FEP Cases 411 (1978).

70. *See Dauten v. County of Muskegon,* _____ Mich. App. _____, 340 N.W.2d 117 (1983) (plaintiff denied job of lifeguard because of back condition which might result in back spasms when confronted with a life-saving situation). *See generally* McGarity & Schroeder, *Risk-Oriented Employment Screening,* 59 Tex. L. Rev. 999, 1038–49 (1981).

71. *See, e.g., Usery v. Tamiami Trail Tours, Inc.,* 531 F.2d 224, 12 FEP Cases 1233 (5th Cir. 1976); *Lewis v. Metropolitan Transit Comm'n,* 320 N.W.2d 426, 29 FEP Cases 578 (Minn. 1982).

72. *Los Angeles Dep't of Water & Power v. Manhart,* 435 U.S. 702, 710, 17 FEP Cases 395 (1978).

73. 89 N.J. 483, 446 A.2d 486 (1982).

74. *Silverstein v. Sisters of Charity,* 43 Colo. App. 446, 614 P.2d 891, 21 FEP Cases 1077 (1979).

75. *Connecticut Inst. for Blind v. Connecticut Comm'n on Human Rts. & Opportunities,* 176 Conn. 88, 405 A.2d 618, 18 FEP Cases 42 (1978).

76. *Chambers v. Illinois Fair Empl. Prac. Comm'n,* 96 Ill. App. 3d 884, 422 N.E.2d 130 (1981).

77. *Frito-Lay, Inc. v. Wisconsin Labor & Indus. Review Comm'n,* 95 Wis. 2d 395, 290 N.W.2d 551, 30 FEP Cases 406 (Ct. App. 1979), *aff'd by an equally divided court,* 101 Wis. 2d 169, 303 N.W.2d 668, 30 FEP Cases 410, *cert. denied,* 454 U.S. 885 (1981). *But see Ranger Div., Ryder Truck Lines, Inc. v. Bayne,* 333 N.W.2d 891 (Neb. 1983) (federal regulation prohibiting employment of truck drivers with impairment of hand justified employer's refusal to hire an individual who lacked a thumb and fingers on his right hand even though he had worked as a truck driver for 25 years).

78. *Maine Hum. Rts. Comm'n v. Canadian Pac., Ltd.,* 458 A.2d 1225, 31 FEP Cases 1028 (Me. 1983).

79. 510 F. Supp. 301, 26 FEP Cases 351 (W.D. Ky. 1980).

80. 30 FEP Cases 1301 (E.D. Mo. 1982), *rev'd,* 720 F.2d 539, 33 FEP Cases 292 (8th Cir. 1983).

81. 442 U.S. 397, 412–13 (1979).

82. *Prewitt v. United States Postal Serv.,* 662 F.2d 292, 307 & n.21, 27 FEP Cases 1043 (5th Cir. 1981).

83. *See, e.g., Wardlow v. Great Lakes Express Co.,* _____ Mich. App. _____, 339 N.W.2d 670 (1983).

84. 662 F.2d 292, 27 FEP Cases 1043 (5th Cir. 1981).

85. *Id.* at 308.

Chapter 10

1. *Teamsters v. United States,* 431 U.S. 324, 335 n.15, 14 FEP Cases 1514 (1977).

2. 401 U.S. 424, 3 FEP Cases 175 (1971).

3. *Id.* at 432.

4. 422 U.S. 405, 10 FEP Cases 1181 (1975).

5. *Id.* at 425.

6. *Id., quoting Griggs v. Duke Power Co.,* 401 U.S. 424, 432, 3 FEP Cases 175 (1971).

7. 422 U.S. at 426.

8. 430 U.S. 482, 496–97 n.17 (1977).

9. *See, e.g., New York City Transit Auth. v. Beazer*, 440 U.S. 568, 19 FEP Cases 149 (1979); *Dothard v. Rawlinson*, 433 U.S. 321, 15 FEP Cases 10 (1977); *Craig v. County of Los Angeles*, 626 F.2d 659, 24 FEP Cases 1105 (9th Cir. 1980); *Chance v. Board of Examiners*, 458 F.2d 1167, 4 FEP Cases 596 (2d Cir. 1972).

10. 29 C.F.R. §1607.4 (1983).

11. *See Guardians Ass'n v. Civil Serv. Comm'n*, 630 F.2d 79, 91, 23 FEP Cases 909 (2d Cir. 1980). *See generally* D. Baldus & J. Cole, Statistical Proof of Discrimination 330–42 (1980); Furnish, *A Path Through the Maze: Disparate Impact and Disparate Treatment Under Title VII of the Civil Rights Act of 1964 After Beazer and Burdine*, 23 B.C.L. Rev. 419 (1982).

12. 457 U.S. 440, 29 FEP Cases 1 (1982).

13. *Id.* at 455–56, *quoting Griggs v. Duke Power Co.*, 401 U.S. 424, 431, 3 FEP Cases 175 (1971) (emphasis in original).

14. Butler, *Sister-chromatid Exchange in Four Human Races*, 91 Mutation Res. 377 (1981).

15. EEOC Dec. No. 82-1, 28 FEP Cases 1840 (1982).

16. *Kisco Co. v. Missouri Comm'n on Hum. Rts.*, 634 S.W.2d 497 (Mo. Ct. App. 1982).

17. 401 U.S. at 431.

18. *Green v. Missouri Pac. R.R.*, 523 F.2d 1290, 10 FEP Cases 1409 (8th Cir. 1975).

19. *Wallace v. Delron Corp.*, 494 F.2d 674, 7 FEP Cases 595 (8th Cir. 1974).

20. *Teamsters v. United States*, 431 U.S. 324, 14 FEP Cases 1514 (1977).

21. *Griggs v. Duke Power Co.*, 401 U.S. 424, 3 FEP Cases 175 (1971).

22. *Dothard v. Rawlinson*, 433 U.S. 321, 15 FEP Cases 10 (1977).

23. *Washington v. Davis*, 426 U.S. 229, 12 FEP Cases 1415 (1976).

24. *Robinson v. Lorillard Corp.*, 444 F.2d 791, 798, 3 FEP Cases 653 (4th Cir.), *cert. dismissed*, 404 U.S. 1006 (1971).

25. *Woods v. Safeway Stores, Inc.*, 420 F. Supp. 35, 13 FEP Cases 114 (E.D. Va. 1979).

26. *See Spurlock v. United Airlines, Inc.*, 475 F.2d 216, 219, 5 FEP Cases 17 (10th Cir. 1972).

27. 555 F.2d 1283, 15 FEP Cases 290 (5th Cir. 1977).

28. EEOC Dec. No. 81-8, 27 FEP Cases 1781 (1980).

29. 530 F. Supp. 54, 27 FEP Cases 801 (D. Colo. 1981).

30. *Accord, Shelby Township Fire Dep't v. Shields*, 98 Mich. App. 115, 320 N.W.2d 306 (1982) ("no beard" rule, as applied to plaintiff with pseudofolliculitis barbae, violates state handicap discrimination law). *But see EEOC v. Greyhound Lines, Inc.*, 635 F.2d 188, 24 FEP Cases 7 (3d Cir. 1980); *Smith v. Delta Air Lines, Inc.*, 486 F.2d 512, 6 FEP Cases 1009 (5th Cir. 1973); *EEOC v. Sambo's of Ga., Inc.*, 530 F. Supp. 86, 27 FEP Cases 1210 (N.D. Ga. 1981).

31. 422 U.S. 405, 10 FEP Cases 1181 (1975).

32. *Id.* at 432, *quoting* 29 C.F.R. §1607.4(c).

33. *See generally* Note, *Business Necessity Under Title VII of the Civil Rights Act of 1964: A No-Alternative Approach*, 84 Yale L.J. 98 (1974).

34. *Cf.* Z. Harsanyi & R. Hutton, Genetic Prophecy: Beyond the Double Helix 16 (1981) (women with blood type A who take oral contraceptives are five times more susceptible to blood clots).

35. 444 F.2d 1219, 3 FEP Cases 604 (9th Cir. 1971).

36. *Id.* at 1225 (citations omitted).

37. 188 Conn. 44, 448 A.2d 801 (1982).

38. 435 U.S. 702 (1978).

39. *Id.* at 708. *Accord, Arizona Governing Comm. v. Norris*, 103 S.Ct. 3492, 32 FEP Cases 233 (1983).

40. *Cf.* Root & Daley, *Are Women Safer Workers? A New Look at the Data*, Monthly Lab. Rev., Sept. 1980, at 3.

41. B. Schlei & P. Grossman, Employment Discrimination Law 403 (2d ed. 1983).

42. 400 U.S. 542, 3 FEP Cases 40 (1971).

43. *See, e.g., Sprogis v. United Air Lines, Inc.*, 444 F.2d 1194, 3 FEP Cases 621 (7th Cir.), *cert. denied*, 404 U.S. 991, 4 FEP Cases 37 (1971); *Vuyanich v. Republic Nat'l Bank*, 409 F. Supp. 1083, 13 FEP Cases 48 (N.D. Tex. 1976). *Cf. Jacobs v. Martin Sweets Co.*, 550 F.2d 364, 14 FEP Cases 687 (6th Cir. 1977) (constructive discharge of unwed pregnant woman where unwed father would not have been discharged held to violate Title VII).

44. *Allen v. Lovejoy*, 553 F.2d 522, 14 FEP Cases 1194 (6th Cir. 1977).

45. *Dothard v. Rawlinson*, 433 U.S. 321, 15 FEP Cases 10 (1977).

46. *Yuhas v. Libby Owens-Ford Co.*, 562 F.2d 496, 16 FEP Cases 891 (7th Cir. 1977), *cert. denied*, 435 U.S. 434, 17 FEP Cases 87 (1978).

47. 29 C.F.R. §1604.2 (1983).

48. *Dothard v. Rawlinson*, 433 U.S. 321, 15 FEP Cases 10 (1977).

49. *Weeks v. Southern Bell Tel. & Tel. Co.*, 408 F.2d 228, 235, 1 FEP Cases 656 (5th Cir. 1969). *See Phillips v. Martin Marietta Corp.*, 400 U.S. 542, 3 FEP Cases 40 (1971). *See generally* Sirota, *Sex Discrimination: Title VII and the Bona Fide Occupational Qualification*, 55 Tex. L. Rev. 1025 (1977).

50. *See, e.g., Dothard v. Rawlinson*, 433 U.S. 321, 15 FEP Cases 10 (1977) (potential disruption of prison security justified exclusion of female guards from ''contact'' positions in maximum security prisons).´

51. *See, e.g., Brooks v. ACF Indus., Inc.*, 537 F. Supp. 1122, 28 FEP Cases 1373 (S.D. W. Va. 1982) (upholding exclusion of women from job of male bathhouse janitor); *Fesel v. Masonic Home of Del., Inc.*, 447 F. Supp. 1346, 17 FEP Cases 330 (D. Del. 1978) (upholding exclusion of male nurse from small nursing home with female patients whose privacy would be infringed).

52. *See, e.g., Button v. Rockefeller*, 76 Misc. 2d 701, 351 N.Y.S.2d 488 (1973) (authenticity requirement justified hiring of only women for position of undercover policewoman). EEOC's example of authenticity is actor or actress. *See* 29 C.F.R. §1604.2(a)(2) (1983).

53. Williams, *Firing the Woman to Protect the Fetus: The Reconciliation of Fetal Protection with Employment Opportunity Goals Under Title VII*, 69 Geo. L.J. 641, 681 & n.230 (1981).

54. 661 F.2d 369, 29 FEP Cases 448 (5th Cir. 1981).

55. 649 F.2d 670, 24 FEP Cases 947 (9th Cir. 1980).

56. 429 U.S. 125, 13 FEP Cases 1657 (1976).

57. *Maclennan v. American Airlines, Inc.*, 440 F. Supp. 466, 472, 15 FEP Cases 1684 (E.D. Va. 1977).

58. 692 F.2d 986, 30 FEP Cases 650 (5th Cir. 1982).

59. *Id.* at 992.

60. 546 F. Supp. 259, 29 FEP Cases 1173 (N.D. Ala. 1982).

61. *Id.* at 264.

62. *Id.*

63. *Id.* (footnote omitted).

64. 64 LA 511 (Brown, 1975).

65. 549 F. Supp. 1324 (E.D. Ark. 1982).

66. *See generally* Crowell & Copus, *Safety and Equality at Odds: OSHA and Title VII Clash Over Health Hazards in the Workplace*, 2 Indus. Rel. L.J. 567 (1978); Finneran, *Title VII and Restrictions on Employment of Fertile Women*, 31 Lab. L.J. 223 (1980); Furnish, *Prenatal Exposure to Fetally Toxic Work Environments: The Dilemma of the 1978 Pregnancy Amendment to Title VII of the Civil Rights Act of 1964*, 66 Iowa L. Rev. 63 (1980); Howard, *Hazardous Substances in the Workplace: Implications for the Employment Rights of Women*, 129 U. Pa. L. Rev. 798 (1981); Williams, *supra* note 53; Note, *Employment Rights of Women in the Toxic Workplace*, 65 Calif. L. Rev. 1113 (1977); Note, *Exclusionary Employment Practices in Hazardous Industries: Protection or Discrimination?*, 5 Colum. J. Envtl. L. 97 (1978); Note, *Birth Defects Caused by Parental Exposure to Workplace Hazards: The Interface of Title VII with OSHA and Tort Law*, 12 U. Mich. J.L. Ref. 237 (1979).

67. 45 Fed. Reg. 7514 (1980).

68. 46 Fed. Reg. 3916 (1981).

69. 697 F.2d 1172, 30 FEP Cases 889 (4th Cir. 1982).

70. *Id.* at 1182.

71. *Id.* at 1184.

72. *Id.* at 1185 & n.20.

73. *Id.* at 1189–90 (footnote omitted).

74. Conn. Gen. Stat. Ann. §§46a-60(a)(7) to -60(a)(10) (West Supp. 1983–1984).

75. *See* Note, *The Cost of Growing Old: Business Necessity and the Age Discrimination in Employment Act*, 88 Yale L.J. 565 (1979).

76. 27 FEP Cases 127 (N.D. Tex. 1981).

77. 635 F.2d 1027, 24 FEP Cases 920 (2d Cir. 1980), *cert. denied*, 451 U.S. 945, 25 FEP Cases 847 (1981).

78. 401 U.S. 424, 3 FEP Cases 175 (1970).

79. 635 F.2d at 1032.

80. *See Leftwich v. Harris-Stowe State College*, 702 F.2d 686, 31 FEP Cases 376 (8th Cir. 1983). *Cf. Kelly v. American Standard Co.*, 640 F.2d 974, 980 n.9, 25 FEP Cases 94 (9th Cir. 1981); *Syvock v. Milwaukee Boiler Mfg. Co.*, 665 F.2d 149, 157, 27 FEP Cases 610 (7th Cir. 1981); *Goodman v. Heublein, Inc.*, 645 F.2d 127, 131 n.6, 25 FEP Cases 645 (2d Cir. 1981) (dictum) (recognizing disparate impact theory). *See generally* Harper, *Statistics as Evidence of Age Discrimination*, 32 Hastings L.J. 1347 (1981).

81. 451 U.S. at 947, 25 FEP Cases 847. *See* Note, *Age Discrimination and the Disparate Impact Doctrine*, 34 Stan. L. Rev. 837 (1982).

82. *Smallwood v. United Air Lines, Inc.*, 661 F.2d 303, 308, 26 FEP Cases 1655 (4th Cir. 1981).

83. *Usery v. Tamiami Trail Tours, Inc.*, 531 F.2d 224, 238, 12 FEP Cases 1233 (5th Cir. 1976).

84. *Compare Murnane v. American Airlines, Inc.*, 667 F.2d 99, 26 FEP Cases 1537 (D.C. Cir. 1981) (pilot; defense sustained) *with Houghton v. McDonnell Douglas Corp.*, 553 F.2d 561, 14 FEP Cases 1594 (8th Cir. 1977), *cert. denied*, 434 U.S. 966, 16 FEP Cases 146 (1978) (pilot; defense rejected).

85. *See Smallwood v. United Air Lines, Inc.*, 661 F.2d 303, 308–09, 26 FEP Cases 1655 (4th Cir. 1981).

86. *See, e.g., Pettway v. American Cast Iron Pipe Co.*, 411 F.2d 998, 1 FEP Cases 752 (5th Cir. 1969).

87. *Armstrong v. Index Journal Co.*, 647 F.2d 441, 25 FEP Cases 1081 (4th Cir. 1981).
88. *Tidwell v. American Oil Co.*, 332 F. Supp. 424, 3 FEP Cases 1007 (D. Utah 1971).
89. See *Hochstadt v. Worcester Fdn. for Experimental Biology, Inc.*, 545 F.2d 222, 13 FEP Cases 804 (5th Cir. 1976).
90. *Munoz v. Stage Employees*, 563 F.2d 205, 16 FEP Cases 307 (5th Cir. 1977) (written examination).
91. *See, e.g., Payne v. McLemore's Wholesale & Retail Stores*, 654 F.2d 1130, 26 FEP Cases 1500 (5th Cir. 1981), *cert. denied*, 455 U.S. 1000, 28 FEP Cases 288 (1982); *Moneiro v. Poole Silver Co.*, 615 F.2d 4 (1st Cir. 1980).

Chapter 11

1. 388 F.2d 495, 67 LRRM 2083 (2d Cir. 1967).
2. *Id.* at 500.
3. 221 NLRB 999, 91 LRRM 1131 (1975).
4. 268 NLRB No. 73, 115 LRRM 1025 (1984).
5. *Jim Causley Pontiac v. NLRB*, 620 F.2d 122, 104 LRRM 2190 (6th Cir. 1980).
6. *NLRB v. Bighorn Beverage*, 614 F.2d 1238, 103 LRRM 3008 (9th Cir. 1980).
7. *City Disposal Systems, Inc. v. NLRB*, 683 F.2d 1005, 110 LRRM 3225 (6th Cir. 1982), *petition for cert. granted*, 103 S. Ct. 1496 (1983).
8. *Pioneer Finishing Corp. v. NLRB*, 667 F.2d 199, 109 LRRM 2112 (1st Cir. 1981).
9. *Empire Steel Mfg. Co.*, 234 NLRB 530, 97 LRRM 1304 (1978).
10. *Welco Indus., Inc.*, 237 NLRB 294, 98 LRRM 1576 (1978).
11. See *Stauffer Chem. Co.*, 262 NLRB No. 179, 111 LRRM 1020 (1982).
12. *Michigan Metal Processing Corp.*, 262 NLRB No. 25, 110 LRRM 1280 (1982).
13. *NLRB v. Modern Carpet Indus.*, 611 F.2d 811, 103 LRRM 2167 (10th Cir. 1979).
14. *NLRB v. Wooster Div. of Borg-Warner Corp.*, 356 U.S. 342, 42 LRRM 2034 (1958).
15. *NLRB v. Gulf Power Co.*, 348 F.2d 822, 66 LRRM 2501 (5th Cir. 1967); *San Isabel Elec. Servs., Inc.*, 225 NLRB 1073, 93 LRRM 1055 (1976).
16. *J.P. Stevens & Co.*, 239 NLRB 738, 100 LRRM 1052 (1978), *enf'd in part, mod'd in part*, 623 F.2d 322, 104 LRRM 2573 (4th Cir. 1980).
17. *Electriflex Co.*, 238 NLRB No. 97, 99 LRRM 1510 (1978).
18. 621 F.2d 756, 104 LRRM 2985 (5th Cir. 1980).
19. *Id.* at 759–60.
20. *NLRB v. Truitt Mfg. Co.*, 351 U.S. 149, 38 LRRM 2042 (1956).
21. *NLRB v. Acme Indus. Co.*, 385 U.S. 432, 64 LRRM 2069 (1967).
22. 252 NLRB 368, 105 LRRM 1379 (1980).
23. 261 NLRB No. 2, 109 LRRM 1345 (1982). See Comment, *Unions' Right to Information About Occupational Health Hazards Under the National Labor Relations Act*, 5 Indus. Rel. L.J. 247 (1983).
24. *Colgate-Palmolive Co.*, 261 NLRB No. 7, 109 LRRM 1352 (1982); *Borden Chemical*, 261 NLRB No. 6, 109 LRRM 1358 (1982). *Accord, Kelly-Springfield Tire Co.*, 266 NLRB No. 102, 112 LRRM 1401 (1983); *Goodyear Atomic Corp.*, 266 NLRB No. 160, 113 LRRM 1057 (1983).

25. 109 LRRM at 1348.
26. *OCAW v. NLRB*, 711 F.2d 348, 113 LRRM 3163 (D.C. Cir. 1983).
27. *Id.* at 361.
28. 47 Fed. Reg. 30,420 (1982). *See* section 8.5.
29. 257 NLRB No. 101, 107 LRRM 1605 (1978).
30. The Bureau of National Affairs, Inc., Basic Patterns in Union Contracts 108 (10th ed. 1983).
31. Cohen, *The Occupational Safety and Health Act: A Labor Lawyer's Overview*, 33 Ohio St. L.J. 788, 789 (1972).
32. The Bureau of National Affairs, Inc., OSHA and the Unions: Bargaining on Job Safety and Health, A BNA Special Report 9, 14, 15 (1973).
33. L. Bacow, Bargaining for Job Safety and Health 101 (1980).
34. The Bureau of National Affairs, Inc., *supra* note 30, at 108–11.
35. Labor Occupational Health Program, Workplace Health and Safety: A Guide to Collective Bargaining 26 (1980) [hereinafter cited as Guide to Collective Bargaining].
36. *Id.* at 24–26.
37. H. Northrup, R. Rowan, & C. Perry, The Impact of OSHA 247 (1978).
38. *See NLRB v. Washington Aluminum Co.*, 370 U.S. 9, 50 LRRM 3225 (1962).
39. *See, e.g., Daniel Constr. Co.*, 264 NLRB No. 104, 111 LRRM 1321 (1982); *Borden, Inc.*, 257 NLRB No. 128, 108 LRRM 1013 (1981). *See also* section 7.3.
40. *NLRB v. Mackay Radio & Tel. Co.*, 304 U.S. 333, 2 LRRM 610 (1938).
41. Guide to Collective Bargaining, *supra* note 35, at 25.
42. *Phelps Dodge Corp. v. NLRB*, 313 U.S. 177, 8 LRRM 439 (1941); *NLRB v. Mount Desert Island Hosp.*, 695 F.2d 634, 638, 112 LRRM 2118 (1st Cir. 1982).
43. 83-1 ARB ¶8079 (Lilly, 1983).
44. *See* 29 C.F.R. §785.43 (1983).
45. 83-2 ARB ¶8402 (Williamson, 1983). *See United States Steel Corp.*, 83-2 ARB ¶8555 (Dybeck, 1983) (return to work could not be conditioned on employee's release of hospital records after his physician released him for work).
46. 73 LA 291 (Knudson, 1979).
47. *Id.* at 295.
48. *See, e.g., North Am. Rayon Corp.*, 83-2 ARB ¶8602 (Williams, 1983). *See generally* F. Elkouri & E. Elkouri, How Arbitration Works 669 (3d ed. 1973).
49. 64 LA 1061 (Conant, 1977).
50. 81-1 ARB ¶8169 (Abernathy, 1981).
51. 71 LA 879 (Dash, 1978).
52. 81-1 ARB ¶8097 (Witt, 1980).
53. 83-1 ARB ¶8206 (Killion, 1983).
54. 79-2 ARB ¶8398 (Rock, 1978).
55. 83-1 ARB ¶8616 (Daly, 1982).
56. 77 LA 1085 (Katz, 1981). *But see Texas Util. Generating Co.*, 84-1 ARB ¶8025 (Edes, 1984) (off-duty employee improperly discharged for refusing to take a marijuana test).
57. *Hollywood Turf Club*, 79-2 ARB ¶8407 (Gentile, 1979).
58. *Fred Pagels Storage Co.*, 78-2 ARB ¶8309 (Chapman, 1978).
59. *Pennsylvania Tire & Rubber Co.*, 59 LA 1078 (Simon, 1972).
60. *Cominco Am., Inc.*, 52 LA 1152 (Belcher, 1969).
61. *Nalco Chem. Co.*, 77-1 ARB ¶8183 (Milentz, 1977).
62. 70 LA 596 (Dyke, 1978).

63. 50 LA 1171 (Seinsheimer, 1967).
64. 80-1 ARB ¶8034 (Seinsheimer, 1979).
65. *Id.* at 3144.
66. 73 LA 729 (Porter, 1979).
67. 73 LA 1269 (Abrams, 1980).
68. 78 LA 1276 (Bailey, 1982).
69. 64 LA 293 (Traynor, 1975).
70. 64 LA 447 (Reel, 1975). *See Mead Corp.*, 83-2 ARB ¶8601 (Heinsz, 1983) (long-time employee who was discharged after five diabetic seizures on the job was ordered reinstated after the medical causes of his diabetic attacks had been eliminated).
71. 83-1 ARB ¶8052 (Light, 1983).
72. 386 U.S. 171, 64 LRRM 2369 (1967).
73. *Id.* at 190.
74. 345 U.S. 330, 31 LRRM 2548 (1953).
75. *Id.* at 338.
76. Freed, Polsby, & Spitzer, *Unions, Fairness, and the Conundrums of Collective Choice,* 56 So. Cal. L. Rev. 461, 463 n.2 (1983).
77. *Phelps Dodge Corp. v. NLRB,* 313 U.S. 177, 8 LRRM 439 (1941).
78. *See* R. Gorman, Labor Law—Basic Text 698 (1976).
79. 416 F.2d 313, 72 LRRM 2383 (6th Cir. 1969).
80. *Houston Maritime Ass'n,* 168 NLRB 615, 617 n.14, 66 LRRM 1337 (1967).
81. *Bryant v. United Mine Workers,* 467 F.2d 1, 81 LRRM 2401 (6th Cir. 1972), *cert. denied,* 410 U.S. 930, 82 LRRM 2597 (1973); *Brough v. United Steelworkers of America,* 437 F.2d 748, 76 LRRM 2430 (1st Cir. 1971).
82. *Dente v. International Organ. of Masters, Mates, & Pilots,* 492 F.2d 10, 84 LRRM 2982 (9th Cir. 1973), *cert. denied,* 417 U.S. 910, 86 LRRM 2428 (1974); *Hoffman v. Lonza, Inc.,* 658 F.2d 519, 108 LRRM 2311 (7th Cir. 1981).
83. 564 S.W.2d 313, 98 LRRM 2905 (Mo. Ct. App.), *cert. denied,* 439 U.S. 959, 99 LRRM 3033 (1978).
84. *Brooks v. New Jersey Mfrs. Ins. Co.,* 170 N.J. Super. 20, 405 A.2d 466, 103 LRRM 2136 (App. Div. 1979).
85. *Wentz v. International Bhd. of Elec. Workers,* 578 F.2d 1271, 98 LRRM 2962 (8th Cir.), *cert. denied,* 439 U.S. 983, 99 LRRM 3330 (1978).
86. 683 F.2d 590, 110 LRRM 3244 (1st Cir. 1982).
87. *Id.* at 595. *See House v. Mine Safety Appliances Co.,* 417 F. Supp. 939, 92 LRRM 3688 (D. Idaho 1976); *Carollo v. Forty-Eight Insulation, Inc.,* 252 Pa. Super. 422, 381 A.2d 990 (1977).
88. Hawaii Rev. Stat. §386-8.5 (Supp. 1982).
89. Mich. Stat. Ann. §17.237(827)(8) (Callaghan Supp. 1983–1984).

Chapter 12

1. W. Prosser, Law of Torts 526–30 (4th ed. 1971).
2. *Id.*
3. U.S. Chamber of Commerce, Analysis of Workers' Compensation Laws 1983, at vii (1983).
4. *See* Note, *Compensating Victims of Occupational Disease,* 93 Harv. L. Rev. 916 (1980).

5. *See* F. Baron, Handling Occupational Disease Cases 3 (1981).

6. Shor, An Analysis of the 1978 Survey of Disability and Work 53 (1981) (report prepared for U.S. Department of Labor).

7. P. Barth & H. Hunt, Workers' Compensation and Work-Related Illnesses and Diseases 178–81 (1980).

8. 88 S.D. 27, 215 N.W.2d 830 (1974).

9. 589 P.2d 835 (Wyo. 1979).

10. This provision of the Wyoming Workers' Compensation Act, Wyo. Stat. §27-12-503(b), was finally amended in 1983 to require that a claim be filed within one year of diagnosis or three years from last exposure, whichever comes *last*.

11. 74 A.D.2d 681, 424 N.Y.S.2d 784 (App. Div. 1980). *See also McKinney v. Feldspar Corp.*, 612 S.W.2d 157 (Tenn. 1981); *Garrison v. Prince William Bd. of Supervisors*, 220 Va. 913, 265 S.E.2d 687 (1980). *See generally* 3 A. Larson, Workmen's Compensation Law §§78.41 and 42 (1983).

12. Analysis of Workers' Compensation Laws, *supra* note 3, at 15–16.

13. *Id.* at 18.

14. A. Larson, Workmen's Compensation Law, vol. 1B §§41.62, 41.63 (1980 & Supp. 1982), and cases cited therein.

15. *Id.*, vol. 1, §12.20, at 3-275.

16. *See, e.g., Thompson v. State Accident Ins. Fund Corp.*, 51 Or. App. 395, 625 P.2d 1348 (1980).

17. A. Larson, *supra* note 14, §41.61.

18. *See State Dep't of Indus. Rel. v. Clark*, 369 So. 2d 561 (Ala. App.), *cert. denied*, 369 So. 2d 562 (Ala. 1979) (dermatitis); *Alexander v. Unemployment Ins. Appeals Bd.*, 104 Cal. App. 3d 97, 163 Cal. Rptr. 411 (1980) (cigarette smoke); *Anderson v. Industrial Comm'n*, 447 P.2d 221 (Colo. 1968) (swollen ankles); *Smallwood v. Florida Dep't of Commerce*, 350 So. 2d 121 (Fla. 1977) (cataracts); *Ellis v. Iowa Dep't of Job Service*, 285 N.W.2d 153 (Iowa 1979) (pollen allergy); *McComber v. Iowa Employment Security Comm'n*, 254 Iowa 957, 119 N.W.2d 792 (1963) (dermatitis); *Deliss v. Unemployment Comp. Bd. of Review*, 475 Pa. 547, 381 A.2d 132 (1977) (anxiety). *But see Brooks v. District of Columbia Dep't of Empl. Servs.*, 453 A.2d 812 (D.C. 1982) (pregnant woman quit because equipment she was required to wear pressed on her stomach and made her sick); *Wells v. Lockwood*, 371 So. 2d 1192 (La. 1979) (diabetes and enlarged esophagus vein not job-related); *Ruckstuhl v. Commonwealth*, 57 Pa. Commw. 302, 426 A.2d 719 (1981) (cigarette smoke).

19. *See, e.g., Kellogg v. Workers' Comp. Appeals Bd.*, 26 Cal. 3d 450, 605 P.2d 422, 161 Cal. Rptr. 783 (1980); *McAllister v. Workmen's Comp. Appeals Bd.*, 69 Cal. 2d 708, 445 P.2d 313, 71 Cal. Rptr. 697 (1968).

20. *See, e.g., Burlington Indus. v. Morrison*, 282 S.E.2d 458 (N.C. 1981) (smoking and cotton dust). *But see Rutledge v. Tultex Corp./Kings Yarn*, 301 S.E.2d 359 (N.C. 1983).

21. *Marion v. American Smelting & Refining Co.*, 192 Neb. 457, 222 N.W.2d 366 (1974) (gout and hypertension caused by alcohol consumption rather than lead exposure); *Clark v. Burlington Indus.*, 271 S.E.2d 101 (N.C. App. 1980) (respiratory illness caused by smoking rather than byssinosis).

22. 681 F.2d 37 (1st Cir. 1982).

23. *Id.* at 40. *See generally* McElveen & Postol, *Compensating Occupational Disease Victims Under the Longshoremen's and Harbor Workers' Compensation Act*, 32 Am. U.L. Rev. 717 (1983).

24. Larson, Analysis of Current Laws Reflecting Worker Benefits for Occupational Diseases 47–48 (1979) (report prepared for Assistant Secretary for Policy, Evaluation, and Research (ASPER), U.S. Department of Labor).

25. Conn. Gen. Stat. Ann. §31-325 (West Supp. 1982).

26. Mass. Ann. Laws ch. 152, §46 (Law. Co-op. 1976).

27. A. Larson, *supra* note 11, vol. 2, §59.10.

28. *Id.*, §59.00.

29. *Id.*, §59.31(a).

30. *Id.*, §59.20.

31. *Id.*

32. *Id.*, §59.22.

33. *See, e.g., Brammer v. Workers' Comp. Appeals Bd.*, 108 Cal. App. 3d 265, 166 Cal. Rptr. 769 (1980); *Dade County School Bd. v. Walker*, 379 So. 2d 1026 (Fla. 1980); *Bolton v. Catalytic Constr. Co.*, 309 So. 2d 167 (Miss. 1975).

34. A. Larson, *supra* note 11, vol. 2, §59.31(a).

35. *Id.* §59.33(b).

36. California Workers' Compensation Institute, Cumulative Injury in California: A Report to the Industry 1 (1977), *cited in* La Dou, Mulryan, & McCarthy, *Cumulative Injury or Disease Claims: An Attempt to Define Employers' Liability for Workers' Compensation*, 6 Am. J.L. & Med. 1, 8 (1980).

37. California Workers' Compensation Institute, Cumulative Injury in California: The Continuing Dilemma 8 (1978), *cited in* La Dou et al., *supra* note 36.

38. *Id.* at 9.

39. *See* 20 C.F.R. Part 725 (1983). *See generally* Lopatto, *The Federal Black Lung Program: A 1983 Primer*, 88 W. Va. L. Rev. 67 (1983).

40. U.S. Chamber of Commerce, Analysis of Workers' Compensation Laws 1983, at 2 (1983).

41. *See* 20 C.F.R. Part 718 (1983).

42. 20 C.F.R. §718. 302 (1983).

43. *Id.* §718.304.

44. *Id.* §718.101.

45. *See, e.g., Jones v. Bouza*, 7 Mich. App. 561, 152 N.W.2d 393 (1967), *aff'd*, 381 Mich. 299, 160 N.W.2d 881 (1968); *Proctor v. Ford Motor Co.*, 36 Ohio St. 2d 3, 302 N.E.2d 580 (1973). *Cf. McDaniel v. Sage*, 419 N.E.2d 1322 (Ind. App. 1981) (action against company nurse for negligent injection not barred by workers' compensation).

46. *See, e.g., Grantham v. Denke*, 359 So. 2d 785 (Ala. 1978); *Halenar v. Superior Court*, 109 Ariz. 27, 504 P.2d 928 (1972).

47. A. Larson, Workmen's Compensation Law, vol. 2A, §72.81, at 14-229 (1982). *See* Annot., 23 ALR 4th 1151 (1983).

48. 39 Cal. 2d 781, 249 P.2d 8 (1952). In 1982 the California legislature amended the workers' compensation act to preclude actions based on dual capacity. Cal. Lab. Code §3602(a) (Deering Supp. 1983).

49. *See, e.g., Wright v. United States*, 717 F.2d 254 (6th Cir. 1983) (Federal Tort Claims Act); *Guy v. Arthur H. Thomas Co.*, 55 Ohio St. 2d 183, 378 N.E.2d 488 (1978); *Tatrai v. Presbyterian University Hosp.*, 497 Pa. 247, 439 A.2d 1162 (1982).

50. *See, e.g., Boyle v. Breme*, 187 N.J. Super. 129, 453 A.2d 1335 (App. Div. 1982); *McAllister v. Methodist Hosp.*, 550 S.W.2d 240 (Tenn. 1977).

51. *See, e.g., McCormick v. Caterpillar Tractor Co.*, 85 Ill. 2d 352, 423 N.E.2d 876 (1981); *Jenkins v. Sabournin*, 104 Wis. 2d 309, 311 N.W.2d 600 (1981).

52. 428 So. 2d 33 (Ala. 1983).
53. 661 P.2d 1167 (Colo. 1983).
54. *Id.* at 1169. *See Ross v. Shubert*, 388 N.E.2d 623 (Ind. App. 1979) (company physician held to be independent contractor).
55. 88 Mich. App. 482, 276 N.W.2d 624 (1979). *Accord, Hoover v. Williamson*, 203 A.2d 861 (Md. 1964) (silicosis).
56. *See, e.g., Betesh v. United States*, 400 F. Supp. 238 (D.D.C. 1974) (Hodgkins disease); *In re Allen*, 78 A.D.2d 917, 433 N.Y.S.2d 512 (App. Div. 1980); *Wojcik v. Aluminum Co. of America*, 18 Misc. 2d 740, 183 N.Y.S.2d 351 (1959) (tuberculosis).
57. *See Brown v. Scullin Steel Co.*, 364 Mo. 225, 260 S.W.2d 513 (1953); *Riste v. General Elec. Co.*, 47 Wash. 2d 680, 289 P.2d 338 (1955).
58. 65 Mich. App. 644, 237 N.W.2d 595 (1975). *Accord, Keene v. Wiggins*, 69 Cal. App. 3d 308, 138 Cal. Rptr. 3 (1977).
59. *But see Sambula v. Central Gulf Steamship Co.*, 268 F. Supp. 1 (S.D. Tex. 1967).
60. *See, e.g., Betesh v. United States*, 400 F. Supp. 239 (D.D.C. 1974); *Mrachek v. Sunshine Biscuit, Inc.*, 308 N.Y. 116, 123 N.E.2d 801 (1954).
61. *See, e.g., James v. United States*, 483 F. Supp. 581 (N.D. Cal. 1980); *Coffee v. McDonnell-Douglas Corp.*, 8 Cal. 3d 551, 503 P.2d 1366, 105 Cal. Rptr. 358 (1972). *See generally* Blum, *Corporate Liability for In-house Medical Malpractice*, 22 St. Louis U.L.J. 433 (1978).
62. *See* 9 OSHR 163 (1979).
63. 6 Ohio St.3d 447, 453 N.E.2d 693 (1983).
64. 648 S.W.2d 167 (Mo. App. 1983).
65. *Id.* at 168.
66. *Cf. Rodriguez v. Industrial Comm'n*, 95 Ill. 2d 166, 447 N.E.2d 186 (1982) (injuries sustained by employee when co-employee hit him over the head with a two-by-four held compensable).
67. 246 S.E.2d 907 (W. Va. 1978).
68. *Id.* at 914. In 1983 the West Virginia legislature amended the workers' compensation statute to preclude the award of punitive damages in these kinds of cases. W. Va. Code §23-4-2 (1983).
69. *See, e.g., Houston v. Bechtel Assoc. Prof. Corp.*, 522 F. Supp. 1094 (D.D.C. 1981); *Sanford v. Presto Mfg. Co.*, 92 N.M. 746, 594 P.2d 1202 (1979).
70. *Blankenship v. Cincinnati Milacron Chem., Inc.*, 69 Ohio St. 2d 608, 433 N.E.2d 572, *cert. denied*, 103 S. Ct. 127 (1982).
71. 64 Ohio App. 2d 159, 411 N.E.2d 814 (1978).
72. 27 Cal. 3d 465, 612 P.2d 948, 165 Cal. Rptr. 858 (1980). *See In re Johns-Manville Asbestosis Cases*, 511 F. Supp. 1229 (N.D. Ill. 1981).
73. *See* M. Rothstein, Occupational Safety and Health Law §506 (2d ed. 1983).
74. 631 F.2d 989 (D.C. Cir. 1980).
75. 532 F. Supp. 1348 (D. Md. 1982).
76. *See* M. Rothstein, *supra* note 73, at §§508, 510.
77. 493 F.2d 1076 (5th Cir. 1973), *cert. denied*, 419 U.S. 869 (1974).
78. 493 F.2d at 1103.
79. 641 F.2d 1128 (5th Cir. 1981).
80. *E.g., Bell v. Industrial Vangas, Inc.*, 30 Cal. 3d 268, 637 P.2d 266, 179 Cal. Rptr. 30 (1981); *Mercer v. Uniroyal, Inc.*, 49 Ohio App. 2d 279, 361 N.E.2d 492 (1977). *See* Note, *Dual Capacity Doctrine: Third Party Liability of Employer-Manufacturer in Products Liability Litigation*, 12 Ind. L. Rev. 553 (1979).
81. *E.g., Lowe v. Chemical Sealing Corp.*, 535 F. Supp. 1280 (N.D. Ga. 1982); *Billy*

      v. Consolidated Machine Tool Corp., 51 N.Y.2d 152, 412 N.E.2d 934, 432
N.Y.S.2d 879 (1980).

82. *Dietrich v. Inhabitants of Northampton*, 138 Mass. 14 (1884) (Holmes, J.). *See
generally* Gordon, *The Unborn Plaintiff*, 63 Mich. L. Rev. 579 (1963); Note,
The Impact of Medical Knowledge on the Law Relating to Prenatal Injuries, 110 U.
Pa. L. Rev. 554 (1962).

83. *See Bonbrest v. Kotz*, 65 F. Supp. 138 (D.D.C. 1946).

84. W. Prosser, *supra* note 1, at 335–37. This is sometimes referred to as the "live
birth rule."

85. *Eich v. Gulf Shores*, 293 Ala. 95, 300 So. 2d 354 (1974); *Hatala v. Markiewicz*,
26 Conn. Supp. 358, 224 A.2d 406 (1966); *Worgan v. Greggo & Ferrara, Inc.*,
50 Del. 258, 128 A.2d 557 (1956); *Simmons v. Howard Univ.*, 323 F. Supp. 529
(D.D.C. 1971); *Porter v. Lassiter*, 91 Ga. App. 712, 87 S.E.2d 100 (1955);
Green v. Smith, 71 Ill. 2d 501, 377 N.E.2d 37 (1978); *Britt v. Sears*, 150 Ind.
App. 487, 277 N.E.2d 20 (1971); *Hale v. Manion*, 189 Kan. 143, 368 P.2d 1
(1962); *Rice v. Rizk*, 453 S.W.2d 732 (Ky. 1970); *Wascom v. American Indem.
Corp.*, 383 So. 2d 1037 (La. App.), *cert. granted*, 385 So. 2d 256 (La. 1980);
State ex rel. Oldham v. Sherman, 234 Md. 179, 198 A.2d 71 (1964); *Mone v.
Greyhound Lines*, 368 Mass. 354, 331 N.E.2d 916 (1975); *O'Neill v. Morse*, 385
Mich. 130, 188 N.W.2d 785 (1971); *Pehrson v. Kistner*, 301 Minn. 299, 222
N.W.2d 334 (1974); *Rainey v. Horn*, 221 Miss. 269, 72 So. 2d 434 (1954);
O'Grady v. Brown, 654 S.W.2d 904 (Mo. 1983); *White v. Yup*, 85 Nev. 527,
458 P.2d 617 (1969); *Poliquin v. MacDonald*, 101 N.H. 104, 135 A.2d 249
(1957); *Stidam v. Ashmore*, 109 Ohio App. 431, 167 N.E.2d 106 (1959); *Evans
v. Olson*, 550 P.2d 924 (Okla. 1976); *Libbee v. Permanente Clinic*, 268 Or. 258,
518 P.2d 636 (1974); *Presley v. Newport Hosp.*, 117 R.I. 177, 365 A.2d 748
(R.I. 1976); *Fowler v. Woodward*, 244 S.C. 608, 138 S.E.2d 42 (1964); *Moen v.
Hanson*, 85 Wash. 2d 597, 537 P.2d 266 (1975); *Baldwin v. Butcher*, 155 W.
Va. 431, 184 S.E.2d 428 (1971); *Kwaterski v. State Farm Mut. Auto Ins. Co.*, 34
Wis. 2d 14, 148 N.W.2d 107 (1967).

86. *Mace v. Jung*, 210 F. Supp. 706 (D. Alaska 1962); *Kilmer v. Hicks*, 22 Ariz.
App. 552, 529 P.2d 706 (1974); *Justus v. Atchison*, 19 Cal. 3d 564, 565 P.2d
122, 139 Cal. Rptr. 97 (1977); *Duncan v. Flynn*, 358 So. 2d 178 (Fla. 1978);
McKillup v. Zimmerman, 191 N.W.2d 706 (Iowa 1971); *Drabbels v. Skelly Oil
Co.*, 155 Neb. 17, 50 N.W.2d 229 (1951); *Graf v. Taggert*, 43 N.J. 303, 204
A.2d 140 (1964); *Endresz v. Friedberg*, 24 N.Y.2d 478, 248 N.E.2d 901, 301
N.Y.S.2d 65 (1969); *Gay v. Thompson*, 266 N.C. 394, 146 S.E.2d 425 (1966);
Marko v. Philadelphia Transp. Co., 420 Pa. 124, 216 A.2d 502 (1966); *West v.
McCoy*, 233 S.C. 369, 105 S.E.2d 88 (1958); *Durrett v. Owens*, 212 Tenn. 614,
371 S.W.2d 433 (1963); *Laurence v. Craven Tire Co.*, 210 Va. 138, 169 S.E.2d
440 (1969).

87. *See Porter v. Lassiter*, 91 Ga. App. 712, 87 S.E.2d 100 (1955) ("quick" child,
even if nonviable); *Presley v. Newport Hosp.*, 365 A.2d 748 (R.I. 1976) (viability irrelevant). All of the other jurisdictions permitting recovery require viability. *See generally* Marketos, *Tort Liability for Preconception Injuries*, 1978 Ann.
Surv. Am. L. 69; Morrison, *Torts Involving the Unborn—A Limited Cosmology*,
31 Baylor L. Rev. 131 (1979); Robertson, *Toward Rational Boundaries of Tort
Liability for Injury to the Unborn: Prenatal Injuries, Preconception Injuries and Wrongful Life*, 1978 Duke L.J. 1401; Note, *Torts—Expanding the Right of Recovery for
Preconception Torts*, 52 Tul. L. Rev. 893 (1978).

88. This position was originally expressed in *Allaire v. St. Luke's Hosp.*, 184 Ill. 359, 56 N.E. 638 (1900) (Boggs, J., dissenting). The concept of "viability" has been relied upon by the Supreme Court in ruling on the constitutionality of abortion. *See Roe v. Wade*, 410 U.S. 113, 160-65 (1973).

89. *See Sylvia v. Gobeille*, 101 R.I. 76, 220 A.2d 222 (R.I. 1976), and cases cited therein. There is, however, some authority to the contrary. *See Evans v. Olson*, 550 P.2d 924, 926 n.1 (Okla. 1976).

90. 67 Ill. 2d 348, 367 N.E.2d 1250 (1977).

91. *Bergstresser v. Mitchell*, 577 F.2d 22 (8th Cir. 1978).

92. *Jorgensen v. Meade Johnson Labs., Inc.*, 483 F.2d 237 (10th Cir. 1973).

93. 35 Mich. App. 603, 192 N.W.2d 661 (1971).

94. Whorton, *Dibromochloropropane Health Effects*, in Environmental and Occupational Medicine 573 (W. Rom ed. 1983).

95. *See generally* Comment, *Birth Defects Caused by Parental Exposure to Workplace Hazards: The Interface of Title VII with OSHA and Tort Law*, 12 U. Mich. J.L. Ref. 237, 253-58 (1979).

96. *See* W. Prosser, *supra* note 1, at 490.

97. *Id.* at 447. *See also* Note, *Recovery for Prenatal Injuries: The Right of a Child Against Its Mother*, 10 Suffolk L. Rev. 582 (1976).

98. *See Cowden v. Bear Country, Inc.*, 382 F. Supp. 1321, 1327 (D.S.D. 1974). This argument, however, will not succeed where the intervening cause was foreseeable. Restatement (Second) of Torts §447 (1965).

99. Restatement (Second) of Torts §452(2) Comment f (1965).

100. 701 F.2d 1112 (5th Cir. 1983).

101. 689 F.2d 147 (8th Cir. 1982).

102. Genetic Screening and the Handling of High-Risk Groups in the Workplace, Hearing Before the Subcommittee on Investigations and Oversight, House Committee on Science and Technology, 97th Cong., 1st Sess. (Oct. 14, 1981), at 113.

103. 296 Md. 656, 464 A.2d 1020 (1983).

Chapter 13

1. Further accounts of these events are contained in editions of the Richmond News Leader and Richmond Times-Dispatch, May 11–13, 1983, front sections.

2. Jacobs & Chovil, *Economic Evaluation of Corporate Medical Programs*, 25 J. Occup. Med. 273 (1983).

3. *See, e.g.*, Boor, *Relationships Between Unemployment Rates and Suicide Rates in Eight Countries, 1962-1976*, 47 Psychological Reps. 1095 (1980); *New Health Hazard: Being Out of Work*, 92 U.S. News & World Rep., June 14, 1982, at 81.

4. *See, e.g.*, Rodgers, *Benefits, Costs, and Risks: Oversight of Health and Environmental Decisionmaking*, 4 Harv. Envtl. L. Rev. 191 (1980).

5. *See generally* J. Mendeloff, Regulating Safety: An Economic and Political Analysis of Occupational Safety and Health Policy (1979); A. Ferguson & E. LeVeen, eds., The Benefits of Health and Safety Regulation (1981).

6. Subcommittee on Labor, Senate Committee on Labor and Public Welfare, 92d Cong., 1st Sess., Legislative History of the Occupational Safety and Health Act of 1970, at 510 (Comm. Print 1971).

7. *See* Office of Technology Assessment, United States Congress, The Role of Genetic Testing in the Prevention of Occupational Disease 141–50 (1983); President's Commission for the Study of Ethical Problems in Medicine and Biomedical and Behavioral Research, Screening and Counseling for Genetic Conditions 41–86 (1983); Lappé, *Ethical Issues in Testing for Differential Sensitivity to Occupational Hazards*, 25 J. Occup. Med. 797 (1983); Murray, *Warning: Screening Workers for Genetic Risk*, Hastings Center Rep., Feb. 1983, at 5–8; Schneiderman, *Standard Setting: Implications of Sensitivity, and a Search for an Ethical Base*, 3 Annals Am. Conf. Govtl. Indus. Hygienists 133 (1982).

8. Schneiderman, *supra* note 7, at 136.

9. *Jacobellis v. Ohio*, 378 U.S. 184, 197 (1964) (Stewart, J., concurring) ("I shall not today attempt further to define the kinds of material I understand to be embraced within that shorthand description; and perhaps I could never succeed in intelligently doing so. But I know it when I see it. . . .).

10. Underwood, *Law and the Crystal Ball: Predicting Behavior with Statistical Inference and Individualized Judgment*, 88 Yale L.J. 1408, 1442 (1979).

11. *Frontiero v. Richardson*, 411 U.S. 677, 686 (1973) (Brennan, J.).

12. Subcommittee on Investigations and Oversight, House Committee on Science and Technology, 97th Cong., 1st Sess., Genetic Screening and the Handling of High-Risk Groups in the Workplace, at 115 (1981).

13. Murray, *supra* note 7, at 8.

14. One of the prerequisites for being employable is a relatively good state of health. The more physically demanding the job the higher the health requirements. Those who are not fit will not be hired, and those already employed will not remain so once their health deteriorates below a certain level. This selective process, enforced by pre-employment examinations, periodic check-ups and other activities of occupational health services, results in lower death rates than in the general population for occupationally active groups—provided that no life-shortening hazards occur in the work environment. It has become commonplace to call this phenomenon the "healthy worker effect." Hernberg, *Epidemiology in Occupational Health*, Developments in Occupational Medicine 34 (C. Zenz ed. 1980).

15. Z. Harsanyi & R. Hutton, Genetic Prophecy: Beyond the Double Helix 117–18 (1981).

16. Bayer, *Reproductive Hazards in the Workplace: Bearing the Burden of Fetal Risk*, 82 Milbank Memorial Fund Q. 633, 651–52 (1982).

17. Abraham, *Underdiagnosis of Pulmonary Asbestosis*, 302 New Eng. J. Med. 464 (1980).

18. Walsh & Marantz, *The Roles of the Corporate Medical Director*, in Industry and Health Care, vol. I., Corporate Medical Departments: A Changing Agenda? 79 (R. Egdahl & D. Walsh eds. 1983).

19. Derbyshire, *How Effective is Medical Self-Regulation?*, 7 L. & Human Behavior 193, 202 (1983).

20. *See* Fisher et al., *An Experiment to Test the Feasibility of Integrating Occupational Health Services in an HMO*, 2 J. Pub. Health Pol'y 261 (1981).

21. *See* Orris, Kennedy, Guerriero, Hessl, Hryhorczuk, & Hoffman, *Activities of an Employer Independent Occupational Medicine Clinic, Cook County Hospital, 1979–1981*, 72 Am. J. Pub. Health 1165 (1982).

22. Richards, *Arsenic: A Dark Cloud Over "Big Sky Country,"* Washington Post, Feb. 3, 1976, at A1. *See also City on the Spot: Give up Jobs or Risk Health*, 95 U.S. News & World Rep., Nov. 14, 1983, at 71.

23.   12 OSHR 978 (1983).

24.   Settergren, Wilbur, Hartwell, & Rassweiler, *Comparison of Respondents and Nonrespondents to a Worksite Health Screen*, 25 J. Occup. Med. 475 (1983).

25.   Taylor & Raffle, *Preliminary, Periodic and Other Routine Medical Examinations*, in Occupational Health Practice 182 (R. Schilling ed. 1981).

26.   12 OSHR 1065 (1983).

27.   Alaska Stat. §23.10.037 (1981); Cal. Lab. Code §432.2 (Deering Supp. 1983); Conn. Gen. Stat. Ann. §§31 to 51g (West Supp. 1983–1984); Del. Code Ann. tit. 19, §704 (1979); D.C. Code Ann. §§36-801 to -803 (1981); Hawaii Rev. Stat. §§378-21, -22 (1976); Idaho Code §§44-903, -904 (1977); 1983 Iowa Legis. Serv. 274 (West); Me. Rev. Stat. Ann. tit. 32, §7166 (West Supp. 1982–83); Md. Code Ann. art. 100, §95 (Michie 1979); Mass. Ann. Laws ch. 149, §19B (Michie/Law. Co-op. 1976); Mich. Stat Ann. §17.65(3) (Callaghan Supp. 1983–1984); Minn. Stat. §181.75 (West Supp. 1983); Mont. Code Ann. §39-2-304 (1981); N.J. Stat. Ann. §2C:40A-1 (West 1982); N.Y. Consol. Laws Ann. art. 20B, §§733 to 739 (McKinney Supp. 1983–84); Or. Rev. Stat. §§659.225 to .227 (1981); 18 Pa. Cons. Stat. Ann. §7321 (Purdon 1973); R.I. Gen. Laws §§28-6.1-1 to -2 (1979); Wash. Rev. Code Ann. §§49.44.120, .130 (Supp. 1983–1984); W. Va. Code §§21- §§21-5-5a to -5d (Michie Supp. 1983).

28.   Proposals to amend Title VII to protect handicapped individuals have been introduced in Congress, the most recent attempt being in 1983. H. R. Rep. No. 1200, 98th Cong., 1st Sess., 129 Cong. Rec. H289–90 (daily ed. Feb. 2, 1983). *Compare* Peck, *Employment Problems of the Handicapped: Would Title VII Remedies Be Appropriate and Effective?*, 16 U. Mich. J.L. Ref. 343 (1983) (arguing against such an amendment) *with* Note, *The Need to Amend Title VII to Protect the Disabled*, Loyola (Chi.) L.J. 814 (1977) (arguing for such an amendment).

GLOSSARY OF MEDICAL AND SCIENTIFIC TERMS

acatalasemia—the absence of the enzyme catalase from the blood, a condition that may be associated with extensive ulceration and gangrene of the oral tissues.

acetylation—a metabolic pathway in the liver; the speed of acetylation is genetically determined by a single gene and is implicated in differential susceptibility to certain potential carcinogens.

aflatoxins—toxic fungi which have produced disease in animals eating contaminated peanut meal and other feed.

allergic rhinitis—swelling of nasal mucosa associated with sneezing and watery discharge, attributable to hypersensitivity to foreign substances.

alpha₁ antitrypsin deficiency—see serum alpha₁ antitrypsin deficiency.

anaphylactoid—an extreme allergic reaction or hypersensitive response to an antigen.

angina pectoris—a severe constricting pain in the chest.

angiosarcoma—a rare liver cancer related to vinyl chloride exposure.

ankylosing spondylitis—a disease that causes spinal immobility; associated with the HLA antigen B27.

anthropometric—dealing with the comparative measurements of the human body and its several parts.

aryl hydrocarbon hydroxylase—enzyme known to catalyze the first step in the metabolism of polycyclic aromatic hydrocarbons; correlated with lung cancer.

asphyxia—impaired exchange of oxygen and carbon dioxide usually on a ventilatory, not circulatory, basis.

assay—any technique that measures a biological response.

benzidine—chemical agent found in many industrial dyes; a potent carcinogen.

bilirubin—a red bile pigment found as sodium bilirubinate.

blastocyst—the modified blastula stage of mammalian embryos where the cells of the embryo form a hollow sphere.

byssinosis—occupational respiratory disease of cotton, flax, and hemp workers.

257

carbon oxidation—a genetic trait; the differential ability of individuals to oxidize various compounds may explain differential susceptibility to compounds requiring oxidation to become activated as a carcinogen.

carcinogenicity—the state of being cancer-producing.

cerebral palsy—defect of motor power and coordination related to damage of the brain.

chelation—the use of one or more drugs to reduce the levels of lead in the body.

cholinesterase—enzyme that maintains the proper levels of acetylcholine essential to the transfer of energy along the nerves.

chronic obstructive pulmonary disease—chronic conditions in which there is increased resistance to the flow of air; includes chronic bronchitis and chronic obstructive emphysema.

cirrhosis—progressive disease of the liver.

clastogens—chromosome-damaging agents.

COPD—see chronic obstructive pulmonary disease.

cruciferous—plants of the mustard family, including the mustards, cabbages, cresses, etc., with flowers having four parts that form a cross.

cyanosis—a dark bluish or purplish coloration of the skin and mucous membrane due to deficient oxygenation of the blood.

cystic fibrosis—congenital disease characterized by an abnormal increase in the amount of connective tissue in an organ, malfunctioning of the pancreas, and frequent respiratory infections.

cytogenetic—the branch of genetics concerned with the structure and function of the cell, especially the chromosomes, the structures in the cell nucleus that store and transmit genetic information.

cytology—the anatomy, physiology, pathology, and chemistry of the cell.

cytotoxic—destructive to cells.

deviated septum—abnormality of the wall dividing the nasal cavity into halves.

eco-genetics—the study of the relationship between environmental and host factors.

edema—an accumulation of an excessive amount of fluid in cells, tissues, or serous cavities.

embryofetotoxins—chemicals which manifest an effect upon the conceptus during any of the stages of gestation, from fertilization until birth.

enzyme—a protein secreted by cells that acts as a catalyst to induce chemical changes in other substances.

epichlorohydrin—a colorless liquid used in the manufacture of many glyceral derivatives and epoxy resins, and as an intermediate in preparation of paints, varnishes, etc.

epidemiology—the study of the prevalence and spread of disease in a community, especially infectious and epidemic diseases.

epithelia—the purely cellular, avascular (without blood or lymphatic vessels) layers covering all the free surfaces, cutaneous (skin), mucous membrane, and serous (serum producing), including the glands.

etiology—the study of the cause of disease.

farmer's lung—fungus infection from grain dust.

gametotoxin—agent that causes sterility or infertility.

genetics—the branch of science that deals with heredity.

germ cell—egg or sperm.

germinal epithelium—layer of cells covering the gonadial ridges.

glaucoma—a disease of the eye, characterized by increased tension within, and hardening of, the eyeball.

glucose-6-phosphate dehydrogenase deficiency—a genetic red blood cell condition characterized by an enzyme deficiency which can result in anemia.

G-6-PD—see glucose-6-phosphate dehydrogenase deficiency.

hematologic—having to do with blood and blood-forming tissues.

heterozygote—an individual possessing a variant gene and a normal gene at the identical site.

hilar shadow—abnormality on chest x-ray that could imply enlarged lymph nodes.

histocompatibility—state of immunologic similarity or identity of tissues sufficient to permit successful transplantation; implies identity of histocompatibility genes in donor and recipient with respect to the particular tissue.

HLA—see human leukocyte antigen.

Hodgkins disease—type of lymphoma (neoplastic disease of lymphoid tissues) marked by chronic enlargement of the lymph nodes, together with enlargement of the spleen and often the liver.

homozygote—individual possessing an identical pair of alleles (pair of genes), either both normal or both variant, at identical site.

human leukocyte antigen—array of cellular surface proteins of the leukocyte which is unique to each individual; a biochemical ''fingerprint.''

hypersensitivity—special condition of certain persons whose bodies react (often with an exaggerated response) to relatively low levels of a foreign agent.

hypersensitivity pneumonitis—lung inflammation triggered by inhalation of antigen (allergen) dust.

hypersusceptibility—biological predisposition to the harmful effects of an infective, chemical, or other agent.

hypocatalasemia—deficiency of the enzyme catalase in the red blood cells.

incidence—the frequency of a condition's occurring within a stated period of time.

in vitro—in the test tube; often refers to laboratory studies.

in vivo—in the living body; referring to chemical processes occurring within cells; often refers to animal studies.

ketoacidosis—diabetic acidosis, or imbalance between acids and alkalines in the body fluids.

laminectomy—excision of a vertebral lamina, a thin plate or flat layer.

Leber's optic atrophy—hereditary disease resulting in the degeneration of the optic nerve.

leukocyte—any one of the white blood cells.

melanoma—a type of skin cancer.

mesothelioma—asbestos-caused cancer, developing from the cells of the pleura (membrane enveloping the lungs), peritoneum (serous sac lining abdominal cavity), or pericardium (membrane around the heart).

methemoglobin—hemoglobin containing oxygen in firm union with Perric iron; found in sanguineous effusions and in the circulating blood after poisoning.

morbidity—the ratio of sick to well persons in a community.

mortality—death rate.

mutagenicity—character or state of being able to produce mutations or changes in the genetic material of living cells.

myocardial infarction—local arrest or sudden insufficiency of the blood supply in an area of the heart.

NADH dehydrogenase deficiency—deficiency of the enzyme NADH (nicotinamide-adenosine dinucleotide) dehydrogenase which is utilized in the reduction of hemoglobin (respiratory protein of red blood cells) from an oxidized state.

necrosis—the pathological death of one or more cells, or of a portion of tissue or organ resulting from irreversible damage.

neoplasm—a cellular outgrowth which is characterized by rapid cell multiplication; it may be benign or malignant.

neuritis—inflammation of a nerve.

neuropathy—a disease involving cranial or spinal nerves.

nitrosamines—reactive class of organic nitrogen compounds widely used in synthetic chemical reactions; a potent carcinogen.

organogenesis—formation of organs during prenatal development.

ototoxic—having a toxic action upon the ear.

PEL—see permissible exposure limit.

peritoneal—relating to the serous sac that lines the abdominal cavity.

permissible exposure limit—an employee's permitted exposure to any material listed in Table Z-1, Z-2, or Z-3 of the OSHA standard for air contaminants.

physiology—the science that deals with the normal vital processes of animal and vegetable organisms.

pneumoconiosis—the accumulation of dust in the lungs and the tissue reaction to its presence.

polycyclic aromatic hydrocarbons—compounds containing only hydrogen and carbon; capable of inducing cancer.

polymorphism—occurrence in several forms; the existence in the same species or other natural group of several morphologic (structural) types.

porphyria—disorder of porphyrin (blood pigment) metabolism; may be heritable disease, of which four types have been described, or may be acquired, as from the effects of certain chemical agents.

predictive value (positive)—value of a positive test result in predicting the presence of the tested-for condition in the person tested.

prevalence—percentage of the entire population with a condition.

protease—descriptive term for enzymes affecting the decomposition of proteins.

proteolytic—relating to or affecting the decomposition of protein.

pseudofolliculitis barbae—condition caused by ingrown beard stubble; aggravated by shaving.

Raynaud's disease—disease of the nerves in which the digits (fingers and toes) become cold, pale, and painful as a result of arterial and arteriolar contraction brought on by cold or vibration.

renal—relating to the kidney or kidneys.

SAT—see serum alpha$_1$ antitrypsin deficiency.

scoliosis—lateral curvature of the spine.

sensitivity—measure of a test's accuracy in correctly identifying persons with the tested-for condition.

serum alpha$_1$ antitrypsin deficiency—lack of the serum protein that protects the lung from proteolytic (protein decomposing) enzymes; genetic trait correlated with susceptibility to emphysema.

silicosis—a form of pneumoconiosis caused by the inhalation of stone dust or quartz.

sister chromatid exchange—exchanges of apparently equivalent sections of the sister chromatids (strands of duplicated chromosome) of the same chromosome.

somatic—all cells of the body other than germ cells.

specificity—measure of a test's accuracy in correctly identifying persons free of the tested-for condition.

steroids—a large family of chemical substances, comprising many hormones, vitamins, body constituents, and drugs.

synergistic—having a greater total effect through the coordinated or correlated operation of two or more agencies than the sum of their individual effects.

TDI—see toluene diisocyanate.

TLV—see threshold limit value.

teratogen—a drug or other agent that causes abnormal development of the fetus.

thalassemia—any of a group of inherited disorders of hemoglobin metabolism with varying clinical conditions.

thorax—the chest; the upper part of the trunk between the neck and abdomen.

threshold limit value—the maximum time-weighted average concentration to which a healthy worker may be exposed for a normal 40-hour week, up to eight hours a day, over a working lifetime (40–50 years) without becoming ill.

toluene diisocyanate—chemical utilized in the production of foam rubber.

toxicity—a state of being poisonous.

toxicology—the science of poisons, their sources, chemical compositions, actions, tests, and antidotes.

transplacental carcinogens—substances capable of crossing the placenta and causing cancer in the fetus.

trauma—an injury caused by rough contact with a physical object; accidental or inflicted wound.

tyrosinemia—a heritable disorder characterized by elevated blood concentrations of the amino acid tyrosine.

Wilson's disease—hepatolenticular (liver-lens) degenerative disease characterized by cirrhosis and high levels of copper in the liver, brain, kidneys, and lenticular (lens of the eye) nucleus.

GLOSSARY OF LEGAL TERMS

action—legal action or lawsuit.

ADEA—Age Discrimination in Employment Act.

agency—relation where one person acts for another, such as employee-employer.

assumption of risk—a defense to a negligence or other tort action; where the plaintiff knowingly assumes the risk of potential injury through the fault of no one or of someone else.

"at-will" doctrine—common law doctrine giving the employer the right to fire employees for any or no reason.

BFOQ—bona fide occupational qualification; statutory defense to Title VII case permitting employers to differentiate on the basis of religion, sex, or national origin when necessary to the normal operation of the business.

business necessity—a defense to an employment discrimination case; a legitimate business purpose so compelling as to override any adverse impact resulting from such practice.

certiorari—a discretionary writ giving a superior court the jurisdiction to review the decision of an inferior court; an appeal.

charge—a complaint filed with an administrative agency.

civil—as distinguished from criminal; relating to the private rights of individuals and to legal actions involving these rights.

common law—body of rules and principles established over time by usage and custom, or from the judgments or decrees of the courts.

compensatory damages—money judgment to replace the loss suffered by the plaintiff.

constructive discharge—employer practices in making working conditions so intolerable that the employee is forced to quit the job.

contributory negligence—a defense to a negligence or other tort action; act or omission on the part of the complaining party which amounts to lack of ordinary care.

covenant—agreement, convention, or promise; may be expressed or implied by law.

263

decedent—the deceased, or dead person.

dictum—a statement in a judicial opinion concerning some point of law not essential to the case at hand and therefore lacking the force of an adjudication.

dual capacity doctrine—tort doctrine permitting employee to recover from employer when the employer has acted in a second capacity, such as the provider of medical services.

EEOC—Equal Employment Opportunity Commission; federal agency charged with administering Title VII of the Civil Rights Act of 1964 and the Age Discrimination in Employment Act.

Federal Rules of Civil Procedure—rules regulating the conduct of civil trials in federal courts.

fellow servant rule—the common law rule that the employer is not liable for injuries to an employee caused by the negligence of a fellow employee.

injunction—a writ or order issued by a court requiring a party to do or refrain from doing a particular thing.

intentional tort—wrongful act performed with desire to injure or with substantial certainty that harm will result.

job-relatedness—defense to Title VII cases; use of selection criteria significantly correlated with essential elements of the job.

loss of companionship—damages awarded to compensate for the loss of affection of a close relative.

malpractice—professional negligence.

medical removal protection (MRP)—an employee showing symptoms of adverse effects of exposure to a toxic substance is removed from further exposure until it is medically advisable to return.

negligence—an act which a reasonably prudent person would not perform, or an omission of what a reasonably prudent person would do.

NIOSH—National Institute for Occupational Safety and Health; part of U.S. Department of Health and Human Services responsible for research on job safety and health matters.

NLRA—National Labor Relations Act.

NLRB—National Labor Relations Board; independent agency charged with enforcement and adjudication under the NLRA.

OFCCP—Office of Federal Contract Compliance Programs; part of U.S. Department of Labor charged with enforcing legal obligations of government contractors, including section 503 of the Rehabilitation Act.

prima facie case—the essential elements of the plaintiff's case which are established by sufficient evidence, and can be rebutted only be contradicting and overcoming the evidence.

punitive damages—exemplary damages; increased damages awarded for extreme actions by the defendant to punish the wrongdoer and to deter future misconduct.

rate retention (RR)—maintenance of wage and benefit levels during a period of medical removal.

respondeat superior—principle that master is liable for acts of a servant performed within scope of employment.

rulemaking—legal process by which administrative rules are promulgated.

statute of limitations—statute declaring that no suit shall be maintained on the specified cause of action unless brought within a specified time after the right accrued.

strict liability—tort liability not based on negligence or fault; legal theory permitting injured party to recover from responsible party for personal injury and property damage caused by wild animals, ultrahazardous activities (*e.g.*, blasting), and defective products based on the fair and efficient allocation of risks and other policies.

subpoena—a legal process (or paper) issued by a court or other authorized body requiring a witness to appear and give testimony, or to produce certain documents.

summary judgment—motion granted when movant can demonstrate that there is no genuine issue (dispute) of material fact and that movant is entitled to prevail as a matter of law.

Title VII—part of the Civil Rights Act of 1964 prohibiting discrimination in employment based on race, color, religion, sex, or national origin.

tort—a private or civil wrong, independent of a contract, arising from a violation of a duty.

wrongful death—statutory action permitting beneficiaries (*i.e.*, spouse, children) to recover for the death of their decedent.

TABLE OF KEY CASES

INDEX

*See also Glossary of Medical and Scientific Terms and
Glossary of Legal Terms*

A

absolute risk 125, 198
accommodation to handicaps 129, 197, 198
ACGIH (American Conference of Governmental Industrial Hygienists) 104–05
acrylonitrile 21
ADEA (Age Discrimination in Employment Act) 144–47
Administrative Procedure Act 111
age 27, 144–47
AIDS (acquired immune deficiency syndrome) 72–73
Alcoa 8, 70
alcohol 2, 35, 120
Allied Chemical 77
American Board of Preventive Medicine 1, 3
American Cyanamid 77
AOMA (American Occupational Medical Association) 1–2, 4–6, 8, 41, 50
amputation 128
angina 126
applicants 158–60, 166, 206
arbitration 141, 151, 159–64
Army, U.S. 70
arsenic 20, 204
asbestos 4, 10, 20, 23, 33, 43, 100, 151, 161–62, 166, 172, 176, 182–83, 187–90, 198, 202, 205
asthma 126, 164
"at-will" doctrine 81–83, 204
audiometric tests 18, 19
autonomy 195, 200–01

B

Bacow, Lawrence S. 156
bankruptcy 187
Barth, Peter S. 169
Bayer, Ronald 200
beards 37, 133–35, 161
behavioral factors 198
Belk, Dean 8
bentonite 170
benzene 43, 105, 187, 200–01
benzidine 30
B. F. Goodrich 77
BFOQ (bona fide occupational qualification) 138, 140–41, 146–47
Bingham, Eula 68, 97
birth defects 78–79, 184–90
black lung 175
blindness 163, 197
blood tests 18, 151, 191, 197
Boeing Co. 45
Borden Chemical Co. 152
business necessity 117–18, 122, 133–35, 138, 140–42
byssinosis 34

C

cancer 27–36, 38, 43, 120–21, 169, 178, 190, 204
carcinogens 20, 26, 68, 98, 102, 104–05
Centers for Disease Control 113
cerebral palsy 120
chelation 3, 4, 205

271

ABOUT THE AUTHOR

Mark A. Rothstein is a Professor of Law at West Virginia University College of Law. He received his B.A. from the University of Pittsburgh in 1970 and his J.D. from Georgetown University in 1973. From 1973 to 1975 he was attorney-adviser to a member of the Occupational Safety and Health Review Commission. He left the Commission in 1975 to teach law.

Since 1980 Professor Rothstein has been at West Virginia University, where he teaches courses on OSHA, labor law, and torts. In addition, he is Legal Director of the West Virginia University Occupational Health Law and Medicine Clinic, an outpatient clinic providing medical treatment and legal counseling to individuals suffering from occupational illness. He is also an Adjunct Professor of Public Health at the Graduate School of Public Health of the University of Pittsburgh.

Professor Rothstein has written widely in the field of occupational safety and health. His first book, *Occupational Safety and Health Law* (West Publishing Co. 1978, 2d ed. 1983), is a standard reference book for lawyers. He has also written several articles in leading law journals, including the *Michigan Law Review*, *Vanderbilt Law Review*, and *Duke Law Journal*. A frequent lecturer on occupational health issues, Professor Rothstein has appeared before both legal organizations and groups of health professionals such as the American Industrial Hygiene Association, American Medical Association, American Society of Law and Medicine, and the Hastings Center Institute.

Professor Rothstein was a major contributor to the last two reports on occupational safety and health of the Office of Technology Assessment of the United States Congress. He was the principal legal contractor for the report on genetic testing of workers and a member of the advisory panel for the report on control technology in the workplace.